The SuperProject Expert

The SuperProject Expert

by

Andrew C Johnson

I/O Press

First Published 1992
©I/O Press
Cover Design: Jane M Patience
ISBN 1 871962 23-4

British Library Cataloguing in Publication Data
A catalogue record for this book is available from the British Library

All Rights Reserved. No part of this publication may be reproduced, stored in a retrieval system, or transmitted in any form or by any means, electronic, mechanical, photocopying, recording or otherwise, without prior written permission.

Products mentioned within this text may be protected by trade marks, in which case full acknowledgement is hereby given.

Although every effort has been made to ensure the correctness of the information contained herein neither the publisher nor the author accept liability for any omissions or errors that may remain.

Typeset by I/O Press

Printed and bound in Great Britain by Cromwell Press Limited,
Broughton Gifford, Wiltshire

Preface

Project management is an exercise in complexity control. Small projects can be managed without the aid of a computer and perhaps even without the need of pencil and paper! However, the limitations of the human brain quickly become apparent when the number of tasks, resources or indeed the number of individual projects increases to even modest proportions.

The solution is to use a computer to record and manage the project details. In an ideal world it might be possible to enter all of the details of a project and then allow the machine to get on with the job of scheduling and managing the project without the help or interference of a human. Unfortunately, the current state of the art is somewhat different, and you still need a human to manage the subtleties of real world project management. The project database is best regarded as a model of the project and the theoretical ideal is to have the model match the characteristics of the real world with complete accuracy. In practice the model is never 100% accurate, partly because of the difficulties encountered in creating such a model, but also because the cost of creation is too high. So at the moment project management packages such as CA-SuperProject are aids rather than replacements for the skills of a human project manager.

This means that to make effective use of SuperProject you have to understand the way it works. You have to know its preferences and idiosyncrasies so that you are confident in what it does, and feel able to modify what it produces. In this book I have tried to convey as accurately as I can exactly how SuperProject treats the project data that you enter, both in the planning and control phases of running a project. I have also explicitly adopted the attitude that the project data, and the way that SuperProject processes it, constitute an imperfect model of reality. The conclusions from this have to be interpreted, and perhaps modified, in the knowledge of real world factors that are not present in the model.

CA-SuperProject is perhaps the most sophisticated and comprehensive of all project management packages and as such it is a very powerful but also highly complex piece of software. It contains so many aspects that it is unlikely that any one project manager will ever need to make use of all of it - so don't feel that you have to read and fully understand every chapter and section of this book. It often helps to want to make use of a facility before you attempt to understand its precise workings. My advice therefore, about reading this book, is to concentrate first on the ideas that interest you particularly at the moment. Skim read the rest and don't worry about understanding it all. Try to get a feel for the facilities that are on offer and return to the relevant sections when you encounter a need for them.

One of the major difficulties in managing any project is the total volume of data that has to be understood. For the purposes of illustration I have used small examples with their emphasis on showing exactly how SuperProject works. I have also opted to leave the default task and resource labels, since giving objects meaningful names would add nothing to the exposition of the underlying ideas.

My thanks are due to I/O Press who have given me the help and encouragement required to produce a book that I now hope will help every other user of SuperProject. I would also like to thank Computer Associates for their very practical assistance.

Andrew Johnson   Edinburgh
                                                   November 1992

Contents

Chapter 1   The Project Model   1

What you need to know, Versions of CA-SuperProject, Using a mouse, First contact, Entering tasks, Entering durations, Task dependencies, Adding links, The value of a model, Saving project models, Help, The Project Manager's Assistant, Beginner and Expert modes

Chapter 2   Resources   21

Tasks and resources, Assigning a resource, Resource scheduling, Partial allocation, Group resources, Task scheduling, Efficiency factors, Resource conflicts, Resource Outline view, The paint project

Chapter 3   Calendars   35

The project calendar, Viewing the calendars, Weekends and holidays, A standard calendar, Tasks without resources, Resource calendars, Resources and holidays, Calc, Workday override - the general case, How long is a standard day?, The standard work pattern, More than one resource, Painting a room, Resource assignment, Quick ways with dates

Chapter 4   Complexity Control   61

Hierarchies, Top down, SuperProject's hierarchy, Scheduling the hierarchy, A painting hierarchy, Viewing hierarchies, Editing task position, Cut and Paste, Milestones, Resource assignment

Chapter 5   Views and Outlines   77

The Views menu, The Layout menu, Making a layout the default, Controlling Task Outline view, View options, Resource Outline, Date Outline view, Column widths, Advanced layout and reporting

Chapter 6   PERT and WBS Charts   91

The PERT chart, SuperProject's PERT view, Editing, Layouts, Work Breakdown Structure Chart, Using the WBS

Chapter 7   Advanced Tasks   103
Link types, A link example, PERT links, Lag, Task schedule type, Just in time, Must dates, The project start and finish date, The Civic Xmas tree

Chapter 8   Resource and Task Types   123
Modelling, Scheduled duration, Task options, Resource driven, Workday driven, Effort driven, Elapsed, Span, Partial allocation, Effort driven partial allocation, Estimating resource time, The pop-up editor

Chapter 9   Large Models   143
Stage 1 - Roughing out the hierarchy, Stage 2 - Refining the hierarchy, Stage 3 - Task definitions, Defining tasks, Stage 4 - Phase 1 details, Stage 5 - Production, Stage 6 - Assigning resources, Model validity, Estimating task durations, Working with large models, Column layout, Selection filters, Checking dependencies, Task descriptions

Chapter 10   Advanced Scheduling   165
Levelling, Controlling levelling, Task order and priority, Assigning priorities, Levelling by float, Splitting assignments, Staggering assignments, Assignment status, Early and late dates, Smoothing, Partial allocation, Setting overtime, Using overtime, Living with conflict, Levelling a real project, Assignment delay, Probability fields

Chapter 11   Tracking   205
Today, Tracking the paint project, The baseline model, Actuals, Just another baseline?, Ignoring actuals, Current date feedback, Done and to-be-done, Percentage complete, Auto Actuals, Editing actuals, Actuals and resources, Task status, Tracking the paint project

Chapter 12   Costing   227
The cost fields, Scheduled costs, Costing the paint project, Viewing costs, Resource Details view, Painting with overtime, Account outline view, Custom account codes, Entering the account mask, WBS codes, Tracking costs - actuals, The cost of painting, Earned value analysis, Schedule performance, Budget performance, A combined measure, Predicting the final costs, Accrual methods, Reporting earned value

Chapter 13 Material Resources and User Fields 259

Resource type, Material fields, Material allocation, Inventory and costs, Levelling, Building blocks - an exercise in material scheduling, User-defined fields

Chapter 14 Presentation 275

WYSIWYG, Layouts, Outline layout, Totals, Crosstabs, Customising the Gantt chart, Adding histograms, Other views, PERT and WBS layout, Fonts and colours, Printing reports, A report example

Chapter 15 SuperProject Systems 301

Subprojects, Linked projects, Updating subprojects, Retrospective subprojects, Links to tasks - Version 3 only, Templates, Network sharing, Import/Export, DDE, DDE commands and Realizer

Update Service

Like many computer applications, CA-SuperProject is an evolving program. During the writing of this book both a DOS upgrade (Version 2.1) and a new Windows version (Version 3.0) became available and an OS/2 version, which will be similar in its scope and operation to the Windows Version 3.0, was announced. To cater for any future changes that would significantly affect this book, I/O Press offers its Update Service and will issue booklets to bring revisions to the attention of our readers. If you would like to take advantage of this service just send a self-addressed envelope large enough to take an A5 booklet and stamped with sufficient postage for 100gms. This will be kept on file until an update booklet is printed and will ensure that you will automatically receive any future documentation.

Send your update request to:

> I/O Press (SuperProject Update Service)
> Oak Tree House
> Leyburn
> North Yorkshire
> DL8 5SE

There is no need to include any letter or proof of purchase.

Chapter 1
The Project Model

Most people have a clear intuitive grasp of what is meant by 'a project' but providing an accurate definition of something so varied and subtle can be very difficult. As far as it is possible this book takes a very down-to-earth approach to the activity of project management and only occasionally strays into areas of what might be called the philosophy of the subject. Of course there is a more technical theoretical side to be discussed but in the main none of these theories are in the least bit difficult as long as they are explained in terms of the practicalities of managing a project.

A project manager program such as SuperProject takes much of the hard work out of planning a project and it also makes it possible to go much further than with traditional planning tools. However, this richness of possibility often confuses and bewilders the newcomer. Yes, you can make use of very complex project management procedures, but it is better to learn to walk before attempting to run. You will find that the material in this book is organised so that it becomes increasingly advanced and more specialised as you work through it. This means that you might want to skip the first few chapters or some of the later chapters, depending on your prior knowledge and current needs. In either case it is advisable to read the first few paragraphs and the key points at the end of any chapter that you are considering skipping.

What you need to know

To avoid spending too much time explaining the very basic ideas of using a computer it is assumed that:

» CA-SuperProject for MS-DOS or for Windows has already been installed on your computer

» you can start SuperProject and know a little of how to use the keyboard or mouse

» you are familiar with the general behaviour of your machine and know how to use diskettes, files and directories either via MS-DOS or Windows

In short it is assumed that you are not a complete beginner at using a computer, MS-DOS or Windows. This book is about using SuperProject and to do justice to its main subject it cannot devote much space to general computer topics. However, any keypresses and commands or behaviour in any way out of the ordinary or special to SuperProject will be described in detail.

Versions of CA-SuperProject

All the examples and discussion in this book apply equally to SuperProject running under MS-DOS or under Windows. The version of SuperProject used for all examples and screen illustrations is Version 3 for Windows. Any differences between this version and the MS-DOS version or the earlier Windows versions will be noted in the text. In nearly all cases the differences between the MS-DOS and Windows version are minor and cosmetic. The change from Version 2 to Version 3 is characterised by additions and minor reorganisation of some parts of the menu structure. The MS-DOS Version 2.1 includes many of the improvements to the PERT and Gantt charts found in Version 3.

If you have a choice of which version to use then SuperProject for Windows is easier to use and more powerful, especially so in its Version 3 form. The Windows version has better access to memory and so is capable of dealing with larger projects without fuss and its multi-window views make it much easier to work with multiple projects. If you are planning to upgrade your machine to run the Windows version then it is worth saying that you should buy at least a 386SX with 4MBytes of RAM, SVGA graphics and 100MByte hard disk - but of course if you can better any of these specifications do so. It is also worth saying that the cost of upgrading an MS-DOS-only machine to have more memory is almost a comparable expense to starting again with a brand new Windows capable machine! If you need more advice on a suitable machine then see *The 386/486: A Power User's Guide* by Harry Fairhead.

Using a mouse

Although it is possible to use SuperProject without a mouse it is so much easier with one that it is a false economy not to have one. A mouse can be added to most systems for as little as £20 and will quickly repay its cost in terms of time saved. For this reason the use of SuperProject via a mouse is described in this book although equivalent keypresses, especially when they are time saving, are also given.

First contact

When you first see SuperProject on the screen it can look intimidatingly complicated. The most important piece of advice that I can give you is not to worry about features that you currently don't need. Follow the step-by-step approach to using more and more of the facilities that SuperProject provides and you will find it all very easy. It is surprising how much more obvious it all is once you know why you need something.

4 *The Project Model* Chapter 1

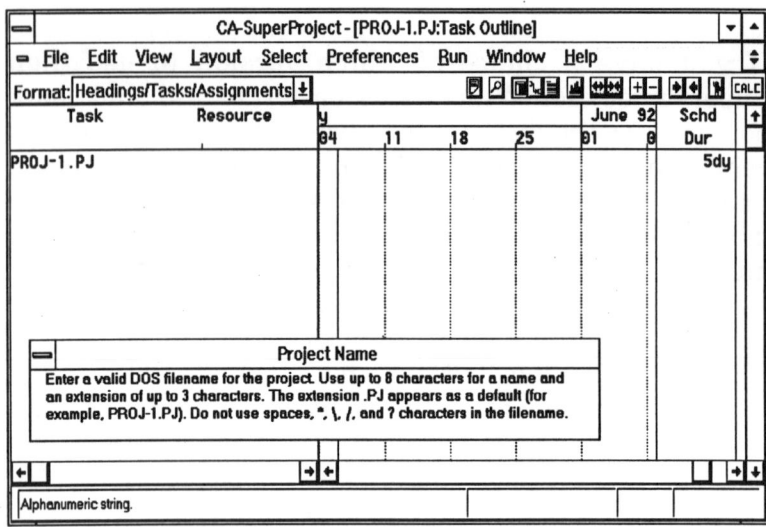

Figure 1.1
SuperProject for Windows default display

If you haven't already done so, load SuperProject now and look at its default display - Figure 1.1 shows the Windows version and Figure 1.2 the MS-DOS version. Although there are many details that could distract you the important feature is the list of tasks at the far left. All projects can be thought of as a collection of 'tasks' - roughly speaking individual components of the project that have to be

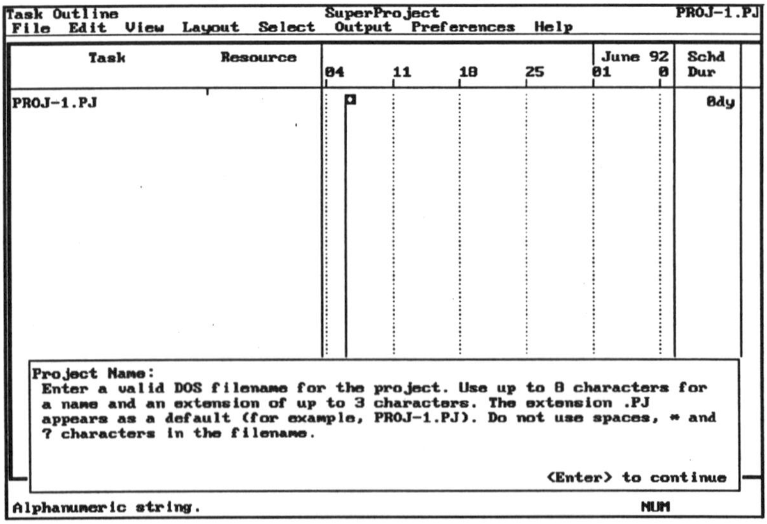

Figure 1.2
SuperProject for MS-DOS default display

completed for the entire project to be completed. Providing an accurate and complete definition of a task is difficult and for the moment the intuitive notion of 'something to be done' will serve our purpose.

As you might imagine, the first step in using SuperProject to plan a project is to enter the names of the individual tasks that make up the project. For example, if the project is to paint a room, something that most people will know a little about, then the tasks might be:

>Clear room
>Strip walls
>Paint ceiling
>Paint woodwork
>Let paint dry
>Paper walls
>Refurnish room

To start our first practical example all that is necessary is to type in this list of tasks into the column headed Tasks.

Entering tasks

Starting from the default display as shown in Figures 1.1 or 1.2, place the cursor in the first column and in the blank position just under the default project name, PROJ1.PJ. To move the cursor simply click on the location using the mouse or use the cursor keys. Type in the name of the first task:

>Clear room

and press the down arrow key. This enters the task name and moves the cursor on to the next line ready for you to enter the next task name. If you press Enter, or one of the other arrow keys, the only difference is that the cursor will move to some other location and you will have to use the mouse or the arrow keys to move it back to the Task column. If you enter the full list of task names you should see a display something like that in Figure 1.3.

6 *The Project Model*   *Chapter 1*

```
┌──────────────────────────────────────────────────────────────────────┐
│ ▭           CA-SuperProject - [PROJ1.PJ:Task Outline]         ▼ ▲   │
│  ▭ File  Edit  View  Layout  Select  Preferences  Run  Window  Help │
│  Format: Headings/Tasks/Assignments ↕                                │
│   Task           Resource    4                  Schd    Task        │
│                             04   11   18    2   Dur     ID          │
│  PROJ1.PJ                   ▬▬▬▬                5dy     P1          │
│  Clear room                 ▬▬▬▬                5dy     001         │
│  Strip walls                ▬▬▬▬                5dy     002         │
│  Paint ceiling              ▬▬▬▬                5dy     003         │
│  Paint woodwork             ▬▬▬▬                5dy     004         │
│  Let paint dry              ▬▬▬▬                5dy     005         │
│  Paper walls                ▬▬▬▬                5dy     006         │
│  Refurnish room             ▬▬▬▬                5dy     007         │
│                                                                      │
│  Alphanumeric string.                                                │
└──────────────────────────────────────────────────────────────────────┘
```

Figure 1.3
The painting a room task list

Now that you have a list of task names you have taken the first step in creating a model of the project using SuperProject. If you look at the display to the immediate right of the list of task names you will see a graphical display of how long each task is estimated to take. This is a Gantt chart named after Henry L Gantt who first used it during the World War I. The same information is listed in the next column headed Schd Dur - standing for Scheduled Duration. Notice that each task is given a default duration of 5 days and in this case this is clearly not reasonable.

If you want to delete a task from the list all you have to do is place the cursor over it and press F5. In a similar way, to insert a new task at a location that already contains a task simply press F3.

Entering durations

The next step in modelling the project is to enter an estimate of how long each task will take. For the moment we will ignore any practical difficulties in estimating how long a task will take and assume that it is possible to provide reasonable estimates simply by examining the nature of the

Entering durations 7

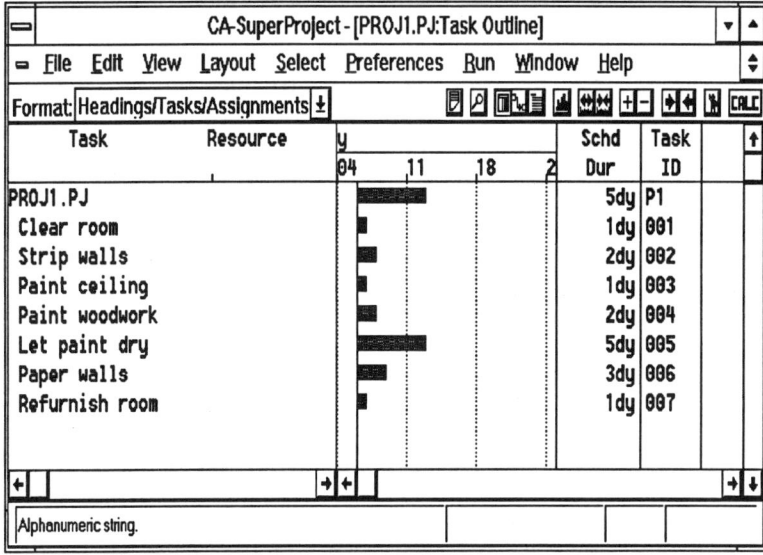

Figure 1.4
The task list plus estimated task durations

task. Later on in this book we will look at the interaction between tasks and the resources needed to complete them but for the moment task duration is the fundamental quantity of interest.

In this example, therefore, the estimates are:

Clear room	1 day
Strip walls	2 days
Paint ceiling	1 day
Paint woodwork	2 days
Let paint dry	5 days
Paper walls	3 days
Refurnish room	1 day

You can enter these estimates in the same way that you entered the task names - place the cursor in the first location in which you want to enter a task duration, type the number and press the down arrow key. Notice that you don't have to type the units used for the duration as days is the default unit of time. You can enter durations using other units by using hr to mean hours, mn for minutes, wk for weeks, mo for months and yr for years. For example, 1wk is a duration of one week. You can also actually type dy for days just to be certain of the units in use. Notice that the Gantt chart has been automatically updated so that it shows bars next to each task that correspond to the estimated duration. Also notice that task start and finish dates take into account weekends, which are not counted as working days. Later you will discover how to enter additional holidays and part working days.

Task dependencies

So far the model of the painting project isn't very satisfactory as it really only amounts to a list of tasks and estimated durations. In reality tasks have an interdependence that our model doesn't capture. For example, it is obvious that the **Clear room** task should be completed before any other tasks are started and yet this, and other similar dependencies, are not built into the model. Indeed, if you look at Figure 1.4 you will see from the Gantt chart that all of the tasks are assumed to start at the same time! In this model of the project the tasks run in parallel and the time to complete the project is just the longest estimated task duration. If you look more carefully at the Gantt chart on a colour screen then you will see that the bar corresponding to **Let paint dry** is red and the rest are blue (assuming a default colour assignment). The red bar shows which task determines the overall length of the project and in this sense is the most critical or important for scheduling. If you also look at the bar opposite the label PROJ-1.PJ you will notice that it too is red and gives the overall time for the project.

All of this is very reasonable but the Gantt chart is actually of little use because the task dependencies are not built into it. The tasks do not all start at the same time and run in parallel. There is a wide range of possible constraints that can apply to tasks but the most common is where one task cannot start before another has ended. This is the so called Finish-Start dependency link.

Adding links

To build some structure into the project model we have to specify how the starting of each task depends on the finishing of other tasks. For example it seems obvious that you cannot **Refurnish room** until **Let paint dry** is completed.

You can create a Finish-Start dependency link between these two tasks by simply clicking on the **Let paint dry** bar and then moving the mouse, while holding the left button down, to the **Refurnish room** bar. Moving the mouse with the left button held down is called 'dragging' so another way of describing how to link tasks is to say that you drag from the first bar to the second. While you are dragging between the two bars you will see a line from the first bar to the current mouse position. This line becomes the stylised symbol showing the dependency between the two tasks as soon as you let go of the mouse button. For example, see Figure 1.5 which shows the Gantt chart after the Finish-Start dependency between the tasks has been entered.

You may be surprised at this point to discover that while the tasks are linked the **Refurnish room** task hasn't moved

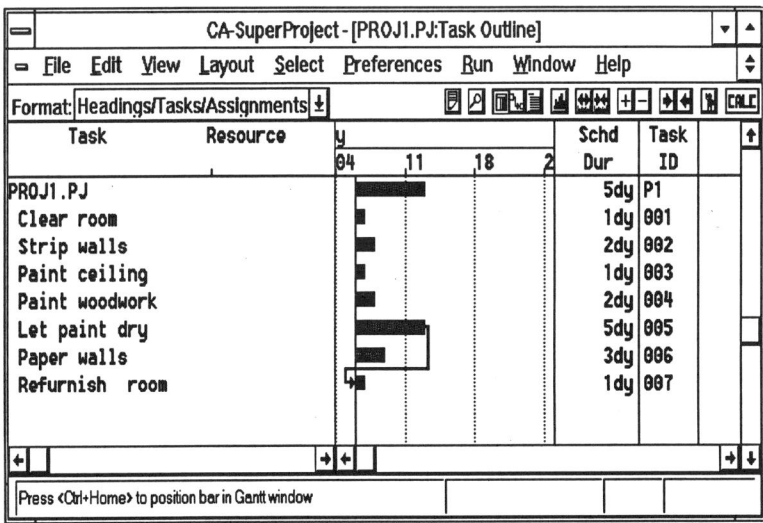

Figure 1.5
A Finish-Start dependency between Let paint dry and Refurnish room

10 *The Project Model*   *Chapter 1*

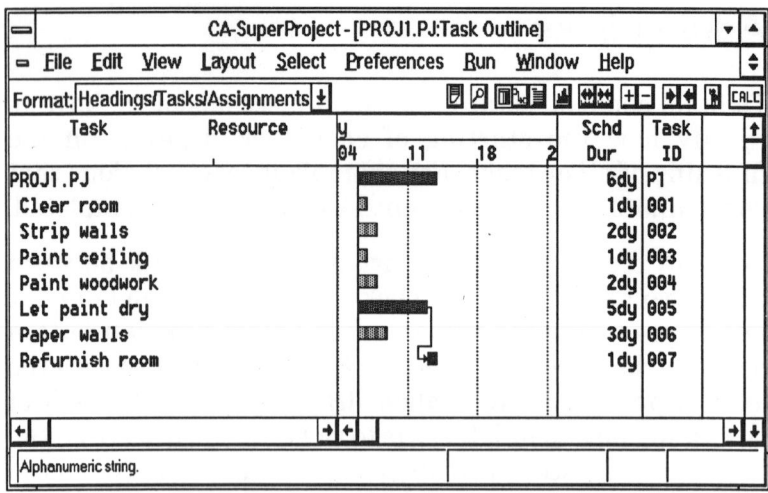

Figure 1.6
A Finish-Start dependency after recalculation

to start after the **Let paint dry** task has finished. The reason for this is that SuperProject hasn't recalculated the schedule taking the link into account. You can set up SuperProject so that it automatically recalculates after every change to the project data and if you or someone else has done this you may not see this intermediate stage. In most cases, however, it is better to keep control of when the project is recalculated. To recalculate the project schedule simply press F9 or click on the Calc icon. After recalculation the project schedule should look like Figure 1.6.

Notice that now that the tasks are linked the **Refurnish room** task is moved on the Gantt chart so that it starts only when the **Let paint dry** task has finished. Also notice that now the total length of the project is increased to 6 days because the pair of tasks can now no longer run concurrently.

You can also link tasks using the keyboard. If you press F4, or select Link Tasks from the Edit menu, a Link dialog box or on-screen form appears which you can fill in instead of clicking and dragging. You can type the name of the task or its Task ID number which is listed in the column next to

Adding links 11

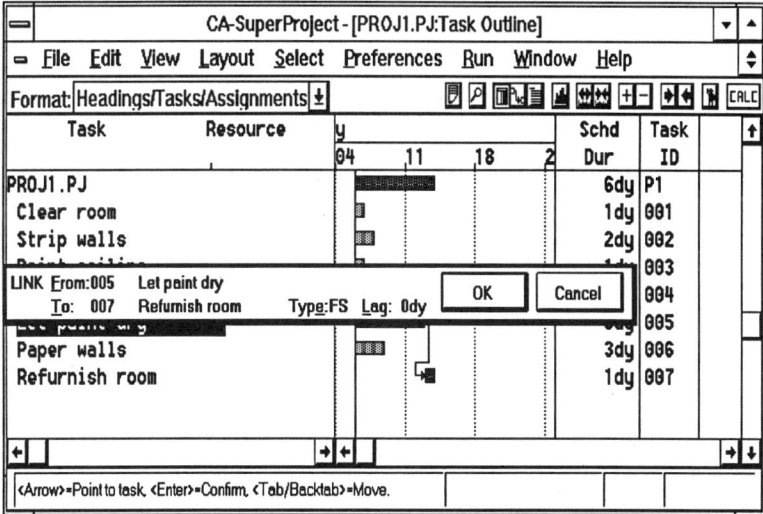

Figure 1.7
The Link dialog box - press F4

Schd Dur. Notice that every task is automatically assigned a unique identity number as it is entered. There are also times when you need to use the Link dialog box even if the mouse is your preferred way of working, so it is worth remembering F4 as the key to press to link tasks. Also notice that you can fill in the Link dialog box by clicking on the task name or the id number of the Gantt chart bar that you want to link.

When linking a number of tasks it is almost impossible not to make mistakes. You can edit an existing link by clicking on, or placing the cursor on, the task that starts the link and then pressing F4. This produces the Link dialog box in the usual way and allows you to edit the tasks that are linked. If you want to delete a link select the task at the start of the link and then press F2 or select Unlink from the Edit menu.

Now that you know how to make, edit and delete links it is time to order the tasks that make up the project. You should make Finish-Start links between the following pairs of tasks:

12 *The Project Model*   *Chapter 1*

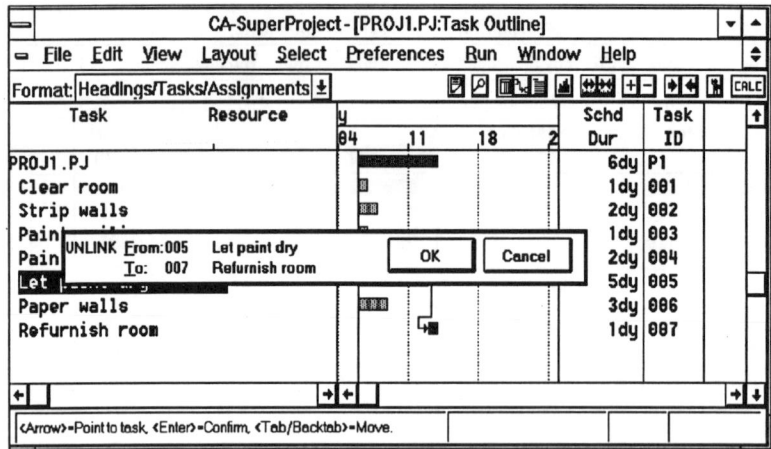

Figure 1.8
Unlink dialog box - press F2

       Clear room -> Strip walls
       Strip walls -> Paint ceiling
       Strip walls -> Paint woodwork
       Paint ceiling -> Let paint dry
       Paint woodwork -> Let paint dry
       Paint ceiling -> Paper walls
       Paint woodwork -> Paper walls
       Let paint dry -> Refurnish room
       Paper walls -> Refurnish room

When you have finished the Gantt chart should look like Figure 1.9. Notice now that the estimated duration of the entire project is 11 days. If you look at the Gantt chart on a colour screen you will also see the critical path shown in red (darker bars in Figure 1.9). The critical path is simply the sequence of tasks that determines the total duration of the project; that is, it is the path with the longest total duration.

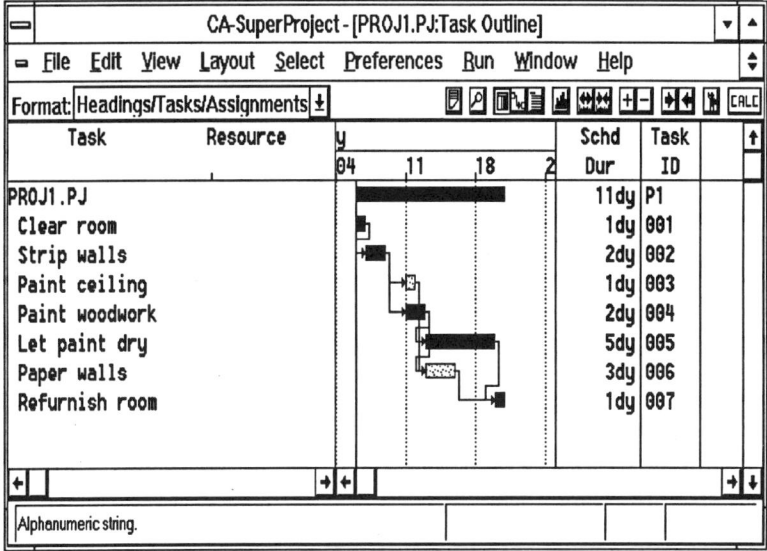

Figure 1.9
The finished project model

The value of a model

Even at this very simple stage in learning to use SuperProject you can begin to see the advantages of creating a model of the project. At the start of the process you only had a list of tasks and durations. At the end you have an estimate of how long the whole project will take and have identified the critical tasks. You can use the Gantt chart to see the effect of any changes to the duration of a task. For example, it is obvious that extending the time to paint the ceiling by a day would have no effect at all but reducing the time to paint the woodwork by a day would reduce the whole project duration by a day. Of course, in the case of a project with so few tasks you can achieve the same results and insights simply by thinking about the nature of the tasks and their relationships. In the case of a larger project, however, you would obtain real benefits from the application of even this simple level of modelling.

The modelling procedure as described still leaves much to be desired. In a larger project making a straightforward but very long list of tasks is clearly undesirable. A much better idea is to organise the tasks into hierarchies of tasks and sub-tasks that make them up. This produces a model that is easier to use and which results in a cleaner looking Gantt chart.

Another shortcoming of the current method is that the only structuring of the tasks is via Finish-Start constraints. In real life the availability of resources needed to complete a task often affects the way tasks have to be scheduled. For example, it is all very well showing the **Paint ceiling** and **Paint woodwork** tasks as running concurrently but what if there is only a single painter available for both tasks? In later chapters the idea of resources is introduced as part of the modelling process. You will discover that it is just as easy to discover the effect of changing the availability of resources on the duration of a project as it is to change task durations. You can even ask SuperProject to optimise the allocation of resources to create a favourable schedule.

Once you have introduced the idea of resources and their allocation there are other questions that you can ask. For example, you can ask how well the resources are utilised and can explore many other questions concerning cost. This inclusion of project accounting data makes the model even more useful.

There are many other aspects of real life projects that can be incorporated into a project model but it is worth bearing in mind that the easiest way to learn how to use SuperProject is a step-by-step approach. There is no doubt that the simple model of painting a room created in this chapter grossly under-uses the power of SuperProject but it does illustrate its most basic features - make sure that you understand them before moving on.

Finally, before leaving this example notice that the actual start date used for the project will be the current date on your machine's clock, i.e. usually today's date. You can set the start date of the project to any value you like by typing a date directly into the column headed Scheduled Start -

but the use of this column and other ways of setting the project start date are described in more detail in later chapters.

Saving project models

Before drawing this example to a close it is worth giving the project that we have created a name and saving it on disk. To give it a name simply click on or move the cursor to the topmost task name, i.e. PROJ-1.PJ, and type PAINT. SuperProject automatically adds the .PJ to the end making the name PAINT.PJ. After this you can save the project data on disk using the command File,Save or by pressing Ctrl-S. The project data is saved on disk in the current directory in a file with the same name as the project, i.e. PAINT.PJ.

If you have used other applications such as a spreadsheet or a word processor you may be a little confused about the way that SuperProject deals with saving and loading. As with other applications, a file that is stored on disk cannot be used until it is loaded into memory. The usual sequence is to load a project file using the File,Open command and then modify it in some way. If you are satisfied with the changes that you have made you can save the file using the File,Save command. At this point you might began a little surprised to discover that SuperProject tells you that the file already exists and asks if you want to overwrite it.

Most applications packages assume that if you load a file and change it then saving it back to disk under the same name is what you will usually want to do. In the case of a project model things are slightly different because just loading a file can cause it to change because of the new current date. When working with SuperProject it is more usual to load an existing file, change it and then save it back to disk under a different name. This approach results in a sequence of project models stored on disk that represent the project at different dates. However, if you are trying to refine or correct an existing project model then it is quite reasonable to save the changes back onto disk using the same name.

What if you have made changes and do not want to save the project model? The solution to this problem is to use the command File,Discard. This really does delete the current project model and there is no way to get it back. However, it is important to realise that File,Discard, despite its name, does not delete any project model files stored on disk.

Help

One of the most useful features of SuperProject is the extensive online help that it offers. When you first start using it you will find Assist mode useful. In Assist mode there is a small window, visible on the screen all of the time, which tells you what type of entry you can make given the current cursor position. After a while this low level help becomes something of an irritation. To turn it off simply use the command Help,Assist Mode. Using the command a second time turns it back on.

You can ask for help about what you are trying to do at any time by pressing F1. This produces a condensed help message that tells you about whatever the cursor is currently on. If you click the OK button in the help window a fuller help screen appears. If you are happy that you understand the abbreviated help then click the Cancel button to return to SuperProject.

For example, if you press F1 while the cursor is in the scheduled duration column the help screen shown in Figure 1.10 appears. If this is sufficient explanation then simply click on the Cancel button.

You can gain access to the fuller help facility using the command Help,Screen Help which produces information about the current screen view and Help,Table of Contents which provides general help. You can also lookup

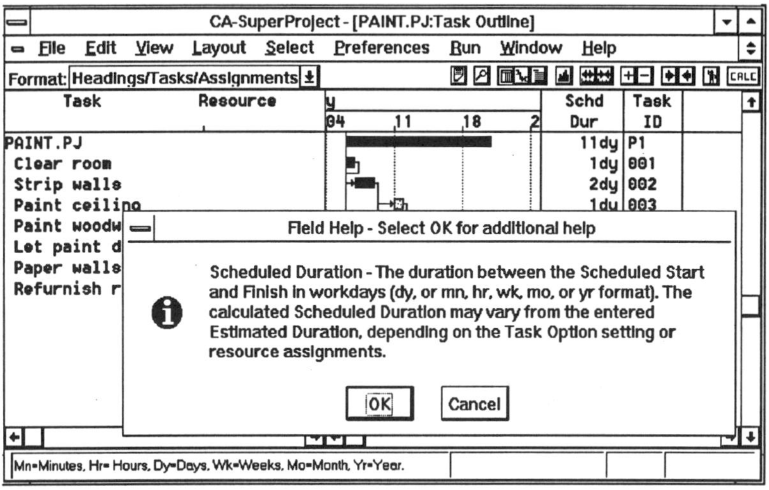

Figure 1.10
Help on the Scheduled duration column

keypresses using Help,Quick Keys or watch a tutorial by using Help,Tutorial.

The Project Manager's Assistant

The Project Manager's Assistant (PMA) is a new facility in Version 3 that helps you learn how to perform operations in SuperProject. It can be started using the command Run PM Assistant. (If this command isn't available your version of SuperProject has been modified from the default settings. See Chapter 15 to discover how to add the PMA to the Run menu.)

The PMA presents you with a menu system that you can use to select the topic in which you are interested. After this it will guide you through data entry, configuration or whatever it is you are trying to achieve. It will prompt you for each item of data and explain what it happening. The PMA is an excellent way of finding out how SuperProject can be and should be used. Although the PMA is so useful it will not be used in the examples in this book because to

```
┌─────────────────────────────────────────────────────────┐
│ −           Project Manager's Assistant          ▼ ▲    │
├─────────────────────────────────────────────────────────┤
│                                                         │
│  Project Manager's Assistant                            │
│         ○ Fast Start                                    │
│         ● Project Foundations              ┌────────┐   │
│         ○ Customizing Preferences          │   OK   │   │
│                                            ├────────┤   │
│         ○ Defining Tasks                   │  Exit  │   │
│         ○ Defining Resources and Costs     └────────┘   │
│         ○ Assigning Resources to Tasks                  │
│         ○ Shortening Project Duration                   │
│         ○ Resolving Resource Conflict                   │
│         ○ Recording Progress and Re-Planning            │
│         ○ Analysis                         ┌────────┐   │
│         ○ Reporting       ○ Run List       │  Help  │   │
│                                            └────────┘   │
│  ┌───────────────────────────────────────────────────┐  │
│  │ Recording project goals and notes, general project│  │
│  │ information, the project start or finish date, the│  │
│  │ project workweek, project variables, and the      │  │
│  │ Project Calendar.                                 │  │
│  └───────────────────────────────────────────────────┘  │
└─────────────────────────────────────────────────────────┘
```

Figure 1.11
The PMA's opening menu

do so would add nothing to the explanations being presented. As far as this book is concerned the PMA is treated as an alternative and additional learning resource. You should try the PMA out with some standard procedures such as entering tasks and then always remember that it is available when you find yourself actually sitting in front of SuperProject. Also notice that the PMA can provide a way of automating some standard tasks and a way of training others to do standard data entry and update.

Beginner and Expert modes

SuperProject has a number of different levels of operation. When you first start using it SuperProject will generally be in Beginner mode. In this mode it displays fewer columns of data and fewer commands in the menu. This makes it less confusing an environment when you are first starting

Beginner and Expert modes 19

to use it but eventually you will have to move on to Expert mode. Expert mode is in fact a set of modes, each one including all of the facilities of the previous one. As you progress through this book you will discover that more and more columns of data are added to the project model along with extra commands in the menu structure. If you cannot find a menu command or data column described in the text then the chances are that you are in Beginner mode or the wrong Expert mode.

To change to Beginner mode simply use the command Preferences,Beginner,Mode. To change to one of the Expert modes use the command Preferences,Expert Mode and select one of the options available. If you do opt to work in one of the expert modes all of the time then you will see additional data columns and commands, so be prepared for displays that are different from those pictured in the early chapters of this book.

Key points

» Tasks are the sub-components of a project.

» The simplest project model consists of tasks with estimated durations plus constraints that determine when one task cannot start until another has finished.

» The basic SuperProject procedures that have been introduced in this chapter are:
　entering task names
　entering estimated task durations
　linking dependent tasks

» The function keys that have been discussed are:
　F2 Unlink tasks
　F3 Create a new task
　F4 Create a link between tasks
　F5 Delete a task

» You can save a project model on disk using the command File,Save. Once saved a project model can be loaded back into memory using the command File,Open.

» If you want to dispose of a project model in memory without saving it to disk use the command File,Discard. This does not delete any files stored on disk.

» SuperProject includes an extensive online help system accessed via the F1 key or the Help menu.

» Version 3 introduces the Project Manager's Assistant as a way of learning how to perform standard procedures.

» SuperProject has a Beginner mode which presents the user with a reduced number of data columns and commands.

Chapter 2
Resources

In Chapter 1 the idea of modelling a project as a set of interrelated tasks was introduced. This is the simplest possible project model but in some situations it is sufficient. However, in most cases the more complex aspects of project management relate to the efficient utilisation of resources needed to complete the tasks. SuperProject can be used to build project models that include details of resource allocation and accounting of surprising sophistication - but we will start at the beginning.

Tasks and resources

A project is composed of tasks that have to be completed as the project proceeds. To complete any given task particular resources will be needed according to the nature of the task. For example, in the case of the **Paint woodwork** task used in the example in Chapter 1 the resources needed to complete the task are a painter complete with tools of the trade and some paint. Later we will look at how different types of resources can be handled within a project model but for the moment we will only deal with resources that have the properties of personnel or labour.

What characterises a resource is how it affects the progress of the task, how it is used up and how it is charged. Labour is available for only so many hours per day but this availability can often be increased by using overtime charged at a higher rate. Initially SuperProject assumes that a Labor resource is available for 8 hours per day but this default can be changed. Indeed many of the characteristics of a labour resource can be changed but for the moment it is more important see how resources and tasks interact.

Assigning a resource

SuperProject maintains a list of named resources that can be allocated to tasks. To create a new resource all you have to do is allocate a resource with a name that hasn't been used before. For example, if you start a new project and enter a single task - Task-1 by default, then you can allocate a resource by pressing F6 while the cursor is positioned on the task. Alternatively you can select Add-Assignment from the Edit menu or click on the Add-Assignment icon, the small man next to the CALC button in the Windows version. This produces the resource dialog box, see Figure 2.1. You can type in the name of a new resource or select one from the list of resources that have already been defined. In Figure 2.1 there are no resources already defined and SuperProject offers its usual default name for a resource, i.e. Rsrc-1. You can type over this default with a more

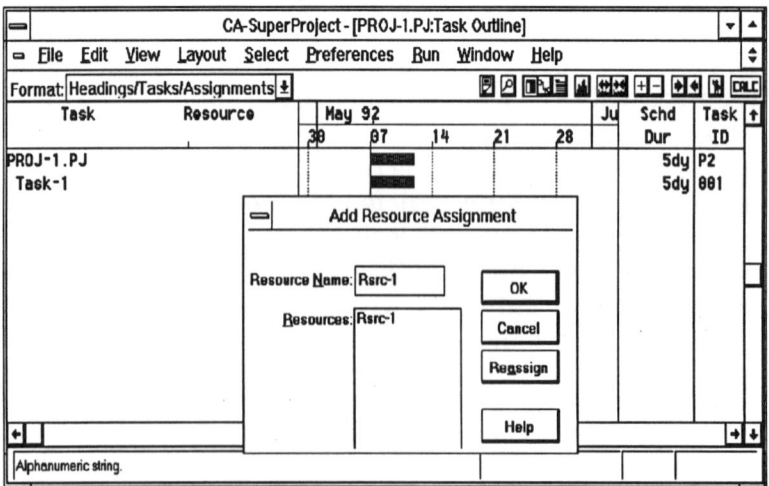

Figure 2.1
Assigning a resource

Assigning a resource **23**

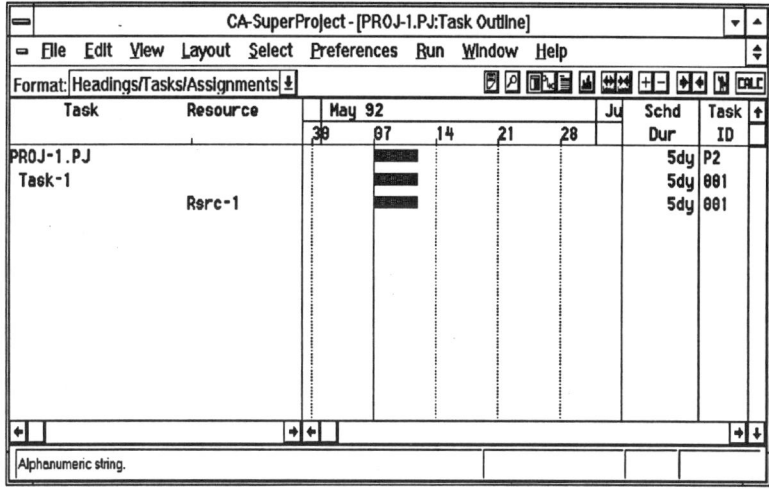

Figure 2.2
Resource Rsrc-1 assigned to Task-1

appropriate name but in order to concentrate on the general behaviour of labour resources simply accept the name Rsrc-1. SuperProject will prompt to discover if you really want to create a new resource as a way of guarding against spelling mistakes. In this case you should answer Yes to the question and so create a new resource - the result can be seen in Figure 2.2. Notice that the resource occupies a new line in the project plan. All of the resources allocated to a particular task are listed below that task in the Resource column. This form of listing allows you to see at a glance the mix and time allocation for resources on a per-task basis. Later you will discover that there are other ways to organise the display of resources.

You can allocate other resources to tasks in the same way. All you have to do is place the cursor on the task, press F6 and then select the resource name from the dialog box that appears. To delete a resource assignment simply select the resource by placing the cursor over it and press F5. Using these techniques you can build up a picture of how available resources are allocated to tasks during the life of the project.

Resource scheduling

When you enter details of a task you specify how long it is expected to take. This estimate is used as a starting point to calculate the number of hours that the resource is needed for that task. For example, if you have estimated a task's duration as 5 days then allocating a resource to it results in the resource being assigned for 40 hours. This allocation is worked out using a value that is stored as part of every resource definition - the resource's standard day. Unless you have changed aspects of SuperProject's working that we have yet to discuss (see Chapter 3), the default standard day for all resources will be 8 hours per day.

The important fact to realise is that SuperProject will calculate the number of hours for which the resource is allocated to the task for using the formula:

hours = task duration x standard day

This is in fact the simplest sort of resource scheduling calculation that SuperProject uses.

If you move the cursor to the right of the screen you will eventually scroll the screen to see additional columns. If you are using the Windows version of SuperProject then you can also scroll the screen by using the small arrow at the bottom right of the screen. The column that is of interest is headed Sched Rsrc Total Hrs. If you look at the example in Figure 2.3 then you can see that Rsrc-1 has indeed been scheduled for 40 hours, i.e. 5 days time at 8 hours per day.

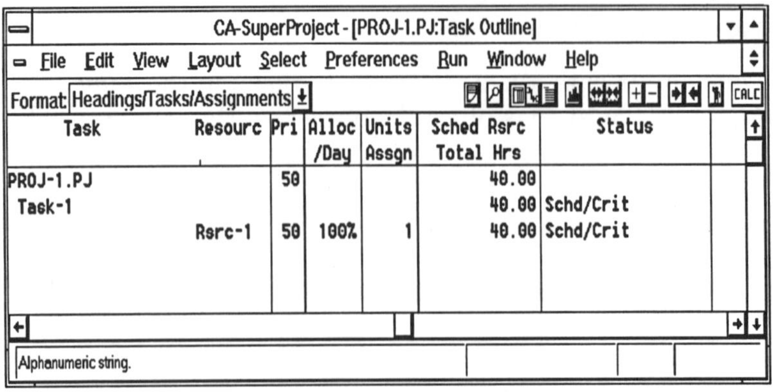

Task	Resourc	Pri	Alloc /Day	Units Assgn	Sched Rsrc Total Hrs	Status
PROJ-1.PJ			50		40.00	
Task-1					40.00	Schd/Crit
	Rsrc-1		50	100%	1	40.00	Schd/Crit

Figure 2.3
Resource scheduling information

Partial allocation

At the moment the only sort of resource allocation that you can make is one that gives the whole of its time to a single given task. However, it might be that the task can be completed in the estimated time using only a part of the resource's available time each day. For example, suppose it was possible to complete the **Paint woodwork** task using only half of a painter's 8 hour day for 5 days. In this case the number of hours that the painter should be allocated to the task is 5 days for 4 hours per day i.e. 20 hours. Presumably the remaining resource hours would be allocated to another task on the same day. If not they would represent under-utilisation of the resource - but sometimes this is unavoidable!

You can adjust the number of hours per day allocated to a task by entering a value into the column headed Alloc/Day. You can specify the value as a percentage of the working day or as a given number of hours per day. If you simply enter a numeric value such as 50 or follow the value by a percentage sign then the resource is assigned for the corresponding percentage of each working day. If you enter a value followed by hr, e.g. 5hr, then it is interpreted to be the number of hours per day that the resource is allocated. In each case the total allocation of the resource is calculated as the number of hours per day times the number of days that the task is estimated to take.

Notice that while using a percentage partial allocation is convenient it can also be dangerous. For example, if there are three tasks that you would like someone to work on in parallel then it is tempting to simply enter 33% as the partial allocation. This would indeed divide the working day into thirds but is only reasonable if each of the tasks can be completed with only 2.64 hours per day for the estimated duration of the task. There is also the added complication that if you try to extend the working day using overtime so as to provide free time for another task the percentage will be recalculated to allocate the additional time to the existing tasks - hence the result isn't extra time that can be allocate to another task but more time spent on the existing tasks.

If you are estimating resource allocations from task durations then it is often better to specify partial allocations in terms of hours per day rather than percentage allocations, but whatever you do you should still check that the resulting total allocations are appropriate for the task.

Partial allocation is one of the more sophisticated, and potentially confusing, concepts in SuperProject. In general you are advised to read through the sections dealing with partial allocation as they arise but don't worry too much about fully understanding what is going on until you have allowed time for all the other ideas to mature. Partial allocations are fully described in Chapter 8.

Group resources

As well as partial allocation you can also assign more than one unit of the resource to the task. All you have to do is place the cursor in the column headed by default Units Assgn. For example, if you wanted to allocate two painters to the **Paint woodwork** task you could simply enter 2 in the Units Assigned column. If you actually try this then you are most likely to see an error message! The reason is that SuperProject stores a value for the maximum number of units that can be allocated for any resource as a sensible check to make sure that you don't allocate more than are available. The default for this value is 1 and so unless you change this, a procedure that is explained in a wider context in Chapter 8, you cannot allocate more than 1 unit of any resource.

However, suppose for a moment that you can and do allocate more than 1 unit to a task, what would be the effect on the task duration? Surely 2 painters will get the job done in less time than 1? This type of argument is perfectly reasonable and SuperProject is quite capable of including this assumption in the model as will be explained in Chapter 8 but for the moment this isn't how things are set up. At the moment we are using SuperProject to calculate the resource allocation using the estimated task duration. What actually happens if you allocate 2 painters to the **Paint woodwork** task is that the calculated resource hours double. For example, if the task duration is 5 days and you allocate 2 painters then the total resource allocation is 5 days times 8 hours per day times 2, i.e. 80 hours.

Task scheduling

When using SuperProject in the way described so far you are estimating the task duration and this is then used to calculate the resource hours needed using the additional information you provide. In Chapter 8 we will discover how to make resource allocations determine the task duration rather than vice versa. At the moment what matters is that you can see that there is a difference and can appreciate that if you estimate task duration all resource allocations are calculated from this. That is, SuperProject assumes that when you allocate resources these are needed for the whole estimated duration of the task to complete it in the given time.

The important fact to keep in mind is that the number of hours for which a resource is scheduled when you assign it to a task is given by:

resource hours = task duration in days x
            resources standard day x
               percentage daily allocation x
                  number of units

or, if you specify the daily allocation in hours, by:

resource hours = task duration in days x
            daily allocation in hours x
               number of units

Also notice that a task is assumed to need all of the allocated resources working for the total of their resource hours. In other words, if you allocate Rsrc-1 and SuperProject calculates that it works for 40 hours you do not reduce or shorten the task duration by allocating a second resource. That is, allocating a second resource, Rsrc-2 say, with a separate allocation of 40 hours simply implies that 80 hours of resource time are necessary to complete the task. Always remember that the default action is to use task duration to estimate resource hours.

In Chapter 8 you will discover that the way that resource allocation affects task duration can be changed from its current default behaviour.

Efficiency factors

The calculations listed above form the basis for all resource assignments and it is important that you understand them. The only additional component is the availability of an efficiency factor for more advanced project modelling. This allows you to estimate the efficiency of each resource and this is used as an extra factor in determining the allocated hours. If you defined a resource as having an efficiency factor of 50% then assigning it to a task results in double the standard resource hours being allocated. In the same way assigning a 200% efficient resource results in only half the allocation and so on. Clearly in general the rule is that resource hours, taking efficiency into account, is given by:

$$\frac{\text{resource hours} \times 100}{\text{efficiency factor}}$$

Efficiency factors are clearly a useful component of advanced models where scheduling is strongly dependent on the skill level of each resource. How to work with efficiency factors is discussed in more detail in Chapter 8. For the moment we will assume that all resources are 100% efficient which is, of course, the SuperProject default.

Resource conflicts

Using partial allocation you can distribute a resource's time between a number of projects. However, there is nothing to stop you from allocating more time than a resource has in a single working day! This is our first example of a resource conflict. SuperProject can alter task durations and starting times so as to resolve resource conflicts but this is an advanced technique described in Chapter 10. For many projects all that is necessary is to detect when a resource conflict occurs and then manual methods can deal with the problem quite adequately.

For example, if you look at Figure 2.4 it is clear that Rsrc-1 has been allocated to two different 5 day tasks which run concurrently. Clearly this is a resource conflict and it is fairly obvious, but imagine if this was just a tiny part of a much larger project. It could easily go undetected until the actual starting date of the task! The solution is to change to Resource Outline view.

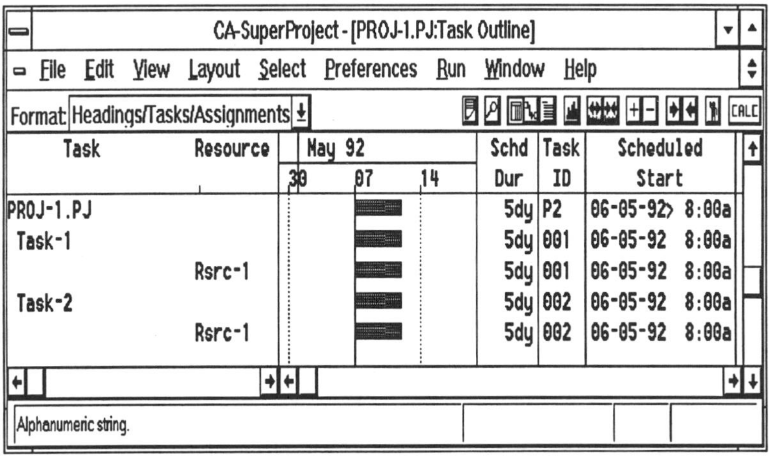

Task	Resource	May 92			Schd Dur	Task ID	Scheduled Start
		30	07	14			
PROJ-1.PJ					5dy	P2	06-05-92 8:00a
Task-1					5dy	001	06-05-92 8:00a
	Rsrc-1				5dy	001	06-05-92 8:00a
Task-2					5dy	002	06-05-92 8:00a
	Rsrc-1				5dy	002	06-05-92 8:00a

Figure 2.4
A simple resource conflict

Resource Outline view

So far we have looked at all of the project models that have been created using a task oriented view. In practice there are many ways of organising the project data to emphasise a particular aspect. SuperProject supports a number of standard views of your project data and these will be introduced as appropriate. In the case of resource management the appropriate view is the Resource Outline view.

To change to Resource Outline view all you have to do is select Resource Outline from the View menu. With this view selected the project data is presented using resources as main headings and the tasks that they have been assigned to as sub-headings. You can almost instantly see if there has been a resource conflict because the tasks to which a resource has been allocated are next to each other in the listing. However, noticing a conflict isn't as easy as noticing that two or more of a resource's bars on the Gantt chart run for the same period. The reason is that if a resource has only been partially allocated to a task the overlap could be reasonable and indeed intentional.

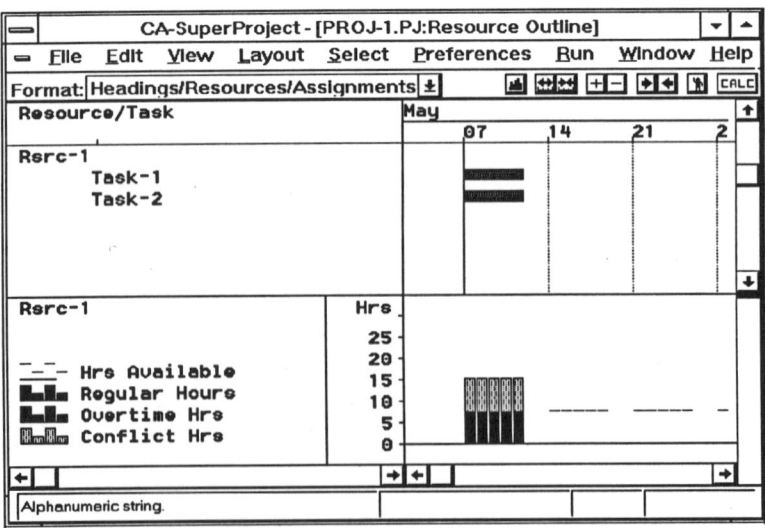

Figure 2.5
A simple resource conflict in Resource Outline view

To make it even easier to understand the work pattern for a resource, and to spot conflicts, there is also a graph showing hours committed for each day. Each day's work assignment is shown broken down into regular hours, overtime hours and conflict hours as different colours within each bar. You can examine a resource's schedule by placing the cursor on each resource in turn, see Figure 2.5.

To resolve the conflict involving the double assignment of Rsrc-1 you can do any of the obvious things that you would do when managing a real project. That is you can:

» delay the start of one of the tasks until the other is complete
» make use of overtime
» assign another resource

or

» lengthen the duration of both tasks

In this case modifying the resource assignments to resolve the conflict is relatively easy because the consequences of each action can be readily seen. In a more complex project model this may not be the case. To help with resource scheduling in complex situations SuperProject can automatically alter task duration and start to resolve conflicts. This is called levelling but it is not a completely foolproof procedure and it isn't a substitute for understanding the project model that you have created.

The paint project

Allocating resources to tasks is a very simple process but it is still worth seeing how it fits in with a development of a real, albeit simple, project model. The painting a room project obviously needs some resources to complete the tasks. Personnel amounts to two painters and decorators - Bill whose expertise is wallpapering and Tom who prefers to paint and hates wallpapering!

32 *Resources*   *Chapter 2*

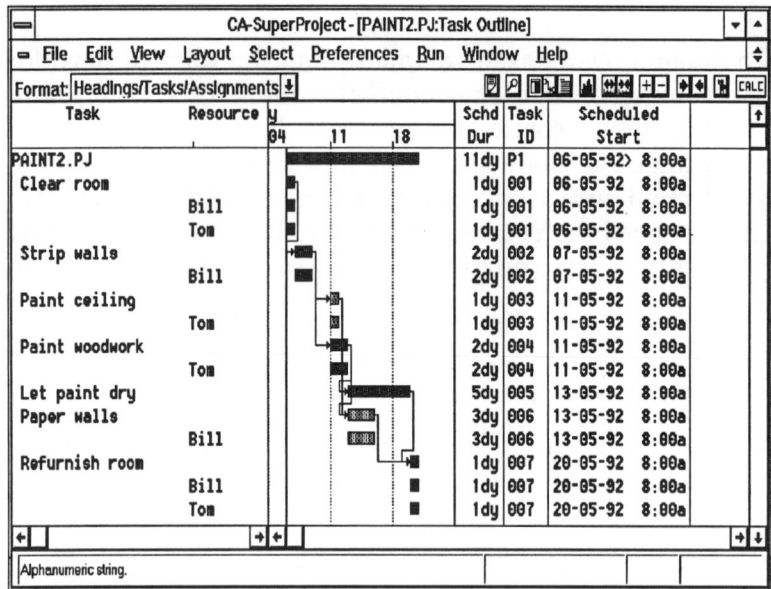

Figure 2.6
Resource allocation

The first step is to reload the previous project model saved under the name PAINT.PJ at the end of Chapter 1. Once you have the familiar Task Outline view on the screen enter the resource assignments as shown in Figure 2.6. Simply place the cursor on each task and press F6. The first time you assign a resource you will have to type in its name to overwrite the default but after that you can simply select it from a list.

If you look at the resulting project plan in Figure 2.6 it looks fine. The Gantt chart now looks a little more complicated but at least you can see the connections between tasks more clearly. Ways of customising the display layout will be discussed later.

The next step is to examine the resource allocation in more detail by selecting the Resource Outline view from the View menu. This produces the display shown in Figure 2.7 for Bill and Figure 2.8 for Tom. Notice that it is immediately clear that Tom is over-scheduled on one particular day. You can also see by examining the bar chart for Bill that he isn't allocated on the day on which Tom is doubly allocated, so

The paint project 33

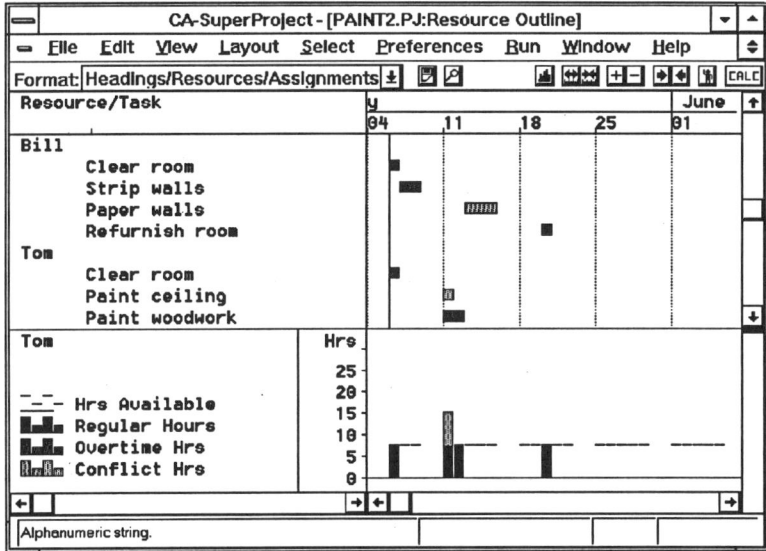

Figure 2.7
Resource allocation for Tom

the simplest solution is to reallocate the **Paint ceiling** task to Bill. Alternatively the **Paint woodwork** task could have been re-scheduled to start after the **Paint ceilings** task but this would increase the total time of the project. Having finished your examination, save this project as PAINT2.PJ.

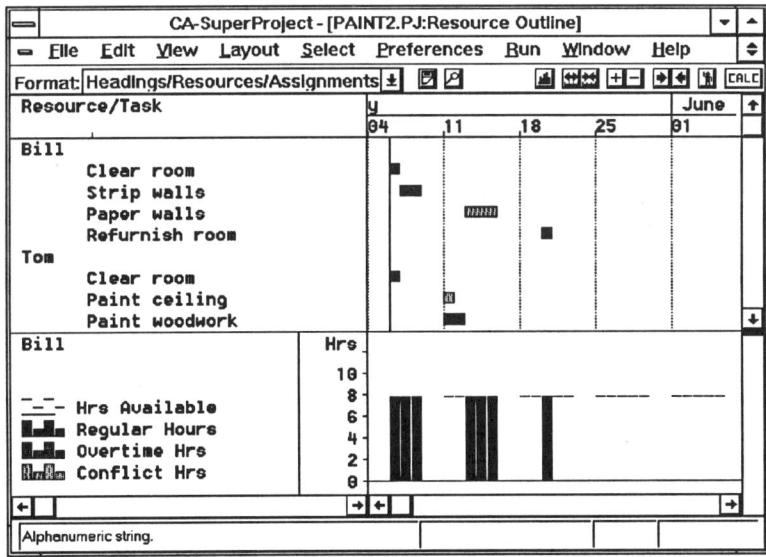

Figure 2.8
Resource allocation for Bill

Key points

» Resources are used in the completion of tasks.

» Resources differ according to the way that they are used up and are charged for.

» The default SuperProject resource is Labor which roughly corresponds to time-charged personnel.

» Resources can be created and assigned to tasks.

» The time that a resource is scheduled for a given task is calculated from the estimated task duration.

» You can allocate part of a resource's working day to a task and multiple units of a resource. In this case the resource is scheduled using the formula:
    duration of task x standard day x
        percentage allocation x number of units
or
    duration of task x hours per day x number of units

» Using Resource Outline view you can examine a resource's schedule in detail and identify conflicts caused by over-scheduling.

» The SuperProject procedures that have been introduced in this chapter include:
    how to create and allocate a labour resource
    the partial and multiple allocation of a resource
    using Resource Outline view

» The keypresses that have been introduced are:
    F6 Assign/create a resource
    F5 Delete a resource

Chapter 3
Calendars

One of the most difficult parts of basic project management is making sure that the effects of non-work days, part time working and available overtime are taken into account. SuperProject automatically schedules tasks taking into account weekends but you can also add details of holidays and working patterns - both for the project as a whole and for each resource.

The project calendar

There is a single calendar of holidays and lengths of workdays which applies to the entire project. It is, however, possible to override many of the settings of the project calendar by altering the individual resource calendars.

For example, while a weekend is a regular project holiday you can override this by entering work hours on a resource's calendar for Saturday or Sunday. The best way to think about the project calendar is as a template used to create each resource's calendar when the resource itself is defined. That is, when you create a resource it inherits a copy of the project calendar as its own 'personal' calendar. Any deviations from the project calendar can then be entered onto the resource's calendar and any subsequent changes to the project calendar will not be passed on to the resource calendars - with one exception.

The one exception to this simple rule is that project holidays - i.e. one-off whole day holidays - entered onto the project calendar are immediately scheduled as non-workdays for all resources.

In other words:

» A project whole day holiday stops all resources working on that day even if they were created before the calendar change.

However, a project holiday can be overridden for a particular resource simply by entering the number of hours that it is scheduled to work.

Viewing the calendars

To see the project, or any, calendar all you have to do is select Calendars from the View menu. This will produce a week-per-row calendar display - see Figure 3.1.

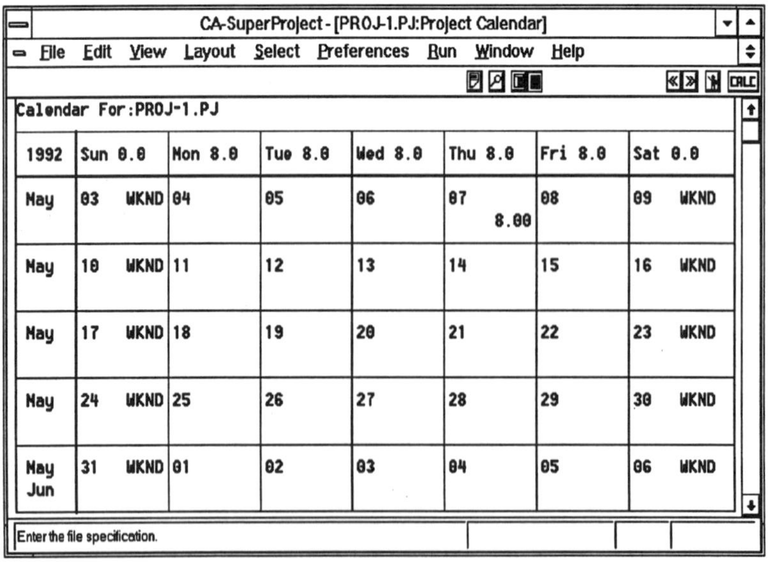
CA-SuperProject - [PROJ-1.PJ:Project Calendar]
File Edit View Layout Select Preferences Run Window Help
Calendar For:PROJ-1.PJ
1992
Sun 0.0
Mon 8.0
Tue 8.0
Wed 8.0
Thu 8.0
Fri 8.0
Sat 0.0
May 03 WKND 04 05 06 07 8.00 08 09 WKND
May 10 WKND 11 12 13 14 15 16 WKND
May 17 WKND 18 19 20 21 22 23 WKND
May 24 WKND 25 26 27 28 29 30 WKND
May Jun 31 WKND 01 02 03 04 05 06 WKND
Enter the file specification.

Figure 3.1
The project calendar

Viewing the calendars **37**

```
┌─────────────────────────────────────────────────────┐
│  ─│        Date Format & International Preferences  │
├─────────────────────────────────────────────────────┤
│                                                      │
│   Date Format: ○ mm/dd/yy   ⦿ dd/mm/yy  ○ dyMon Yr   ┌──────┐
│                ○ DayNumber  ○ yy/mm/dd  ○ yywwd      │  OK  │
│                                                      └──────┘
│   Date Separator: ○ /   ○ .   ○ ,   ⦿ -   ○ ;   ○ blank   ┌────────┐
│                                                            │ Cancel │
│   Time Format: ○ None    ⦿ 12 hour    ○ 24 hour            └────────┘
│
│       Decimal: ⦿ period   ○ comma    ○ none
│
│  Currency Symbol: [ $ ]   ⦿ Before   ○ After
│
│   Calendar Start: ⦿ Sunday   ○ Monday                ┌──────┐
│                                                      │ Help │
│                                                      └──────┘
└─────────────────────────────────────────────────────┘
```

Figure 3.2
Date preferences

The default is for each week to start on a Sunday but if you want to start each week from Monday simply select Date and International Formats from the Preferences menu. The dialog box that this produces can be used to alter many aspects of date display, including the day that a week starts on, see Figure 3.2.

The project calendar has a conventional layout that is easy enough to understand but its exact appearance depends on the type of graphics display that you are using. This means for example, the number of weeks that you see at a time varies.

The number to the immediate right of each of the day names is simply the length of the standard project working day in hours. The default for this is, of course, 8 hours. When you create a new resource this 8 hour working day is inherited by its calendar but can subsequently be changed. Notice that you can set a shorter or longer workday simply by typing in the new value next to the day name. For example, to define a day as a half working day on a regular basis you would simply enter 4 hours next to its name. In the same way if you want to extend the working day all you have to do is type in the value.

38 Calendars   Chapter 3

```
                Zero length day        Length of working day
              defines a weekend                /
              ┌──────┬──────────────┬──────────────┬─────────┬──┐
              │ 1992 │ Sun (0.0)    │ Mon (8.0)    │ Tue 8.0 │ W│
              ├──────┼──────┬───────┼──────────────┼─────────┼──┤
              │ May  │  03  │ WKND  │ 04           │ 05      │ 0│
              ├──────┼──────┬───────┼──────────────┼─────────┼──┤
              │ May  │  10  │ WKND  │ 11           │ 12      │ 1│
              │      │      │       │    (4.0)     │         │  │
              └──────┴──────┴───────┴──────────────┴─────────┴──┘
                                        Workday override
```

Figure 3.3
The calendar data

Any one-off variations on the length of the working day can be entered into the space just below the relevant date on the calendar. This overrides the standard working day and can be used to create one-off partial or whole holidays or longer working days, see Figure 3.3.

Weekends and holidays

Weekends are indicated by the word WKND appearing next to the date. Any day that is set to a standard working day length of 0 hours is treated as a weekend - see Figure 3.3. This of course allows calendars to be constructed that conform to local custom.

To enter a one-off holiday all you have to do is to type the name or abbreviation of the holiday into the calendar in the line below the date or enter 0 hours for the workday override. (Notice that entering text in the workday override has the same effect as entering 0 hours.)

For example, in Figure 3.4 May 4th has been set as a full day holiday with the name May Day. A quick way of creating a one-off holiday is to press F3 which assigns the default name Holiday - see May 6th in Figure 3.4.

1992	Sun 0.0		Mon 8.0	Tue 8.0	Wed 8.0	Thu 8.0
Apr May	26	WKND	27	28	29	30
May	03	WKND	04 May Day	05	06 Holiday	07

Figure 3.4
Whole day holidays

It is very important to notice that weekends, i.e. periodic whole day holidays, and one-off whole day holidays behave in slightly different ways.

» A weekend is defined by setting a standard day length of zero hours next to the day name. It is only inherited by resources created after the change to the project calendar. Weekends can be changed - both added and deleted - by editing a resource's calendar.

» A one-off holiday is defined by setting the number of work hours on the particular day to zero or by entering the name of the holiday. Project holidays affect all resources, even those created before the change. They can, however, be edited on resource calendars by entering the number of hours that the resource is to work on that day in place of the project holiday name (or the equivalent 0 hours).

A standard calendar

Once you have set up a project calendar then the chances are that you will want to use it with more than one project. To allow you to do this SuperProject provides a command Save as Default in the Edit menu. Notice that this command only appears when you are viewing the project calendar. You can type in a suitable name for the project calendar or accept the default SYSHLDYS.

The calendar that you are using with a particular project is saved with that project and automatically reloaded along with the project. If you want to load another calendar then use the command Load Default in the Edit menu. Again this command is only available when you are viewing the project calendar.

You can maintain a set of different calendars stored on disk to be used with projects as appropriate.

Tasks without resources

The first project model constructed in Chapter 1 involved nothing more than task definitions, durations and constraints. The task durations were estimated in days but this unit was really nothing more than a convenient unit in which to specify the relative durations of tasks.

Now that we know about the existence of calendars it is worth asking exactly what task durations really relate to. As the number of hours in the working day can be changed what exactly does it mean to say that a task will take so many days?

If you haven't allocated any resources to a task then only two types of day are distinguished - working and non-working:

» a working day is any day that has any non-zero number of hours indicated on the project calendar

» a non-working day has zero hours indicated on the project calendar

When a task is scheduled the start and finish dates are adjusted so that they include the same number of working days as the task's estimated duration in days. Notice that it doesn't matter how many hours are indicated on the project calendar - all working days, even partial holidays or days with more working hours than the standard day - are treated as being of equal value. You should try to avoid falling into the trap of giving meaning to the hours worked as indicated on the project calendar when no resources have been allocated.

In other words:

» The estimated duration (in days) of a task that has no resources allocated is interpreted as the number of project working days need to complete the task

For example, if you estimate a task's duration as 5 days and there is a whole day project holiday within the 5 days from its starting date then the task's finishing date will be 1 day later so that 5 working days are included in the period. Notice, however, that the task's duration is still shown as 5 days even though it takes 6 calendar days or more to complete.

The same sort of behaviour applies to partial working days but in this case it seems less reasonable. For example, if you alter the project calendar to show that a Thursday is a half working day, i.e. only 4 working hours, and define a task that needs 5 days - it still needs exactly five working days irrespective of the start date! In other words no allowance is made for the half day off in the scheduling of the task!

This may seem like a mistake but the error lies in the fact that the user is trying to interpret working hours in the absence of resource allocation. If you are not intending to use resources and resource allocation in a project model then restrict yourself to complete project holidays on the project calendar - partial workdays have no meaning in the absence of resources.

Resource calendars

The project calendar defines project wide holidays but it is also possible to define holidays for individual resources. To see a resource's calendar you can select Resource Calendars in the Edit menu. Shortcuts are to type Ctrl-N or, if you are using a Windows version, to click on the double arrows in the icon bar.

A resource's calendar looks much the same as the project calendar. However, holidays defined on the project calendar and inherited by the resource calendar show in a different colour or style on the resource calendar so that you can tell that they are project wide.

While viewing a resource calendar you can create new one-off holidays that apply only to that particular resource. You can even create a periodic holiday for a resource but this will still be called WKND even if this is inappropriate. Notice that any holidays that you create on a resource calendar have no effect on any other calendar. You can edit weekends and holidays as defined on the project calendar to permit a resource to work. If you want to allow the resource to work every weekend then alter the standard work hours from 0 to 8 **next** to the day name. If you only want to override a particular weekend or on-off holiday then enter 8 hours (or how ever many hours you want the resource to be available for) **below** the date.

All this talk of over-riding weekends and standard workdays brings to mind the use of overtime. You can indeed specify the maximum number of hours of overtime that a resource is available to work but only in Advanced mode - more of Advanced mode and overtime later.

Resources and holidays

Now comes the interesting question of how resource holidays affect a task's duration. If you allocate a resource to a task and the resource has a holiday in the period scheduled for the task then the duration of the task is lengthened, or the start date modified, to provide the specified number of resource hours.

For example, if you estimate a task's duration as 3 days it will indeed be scheduled for the next three work days as

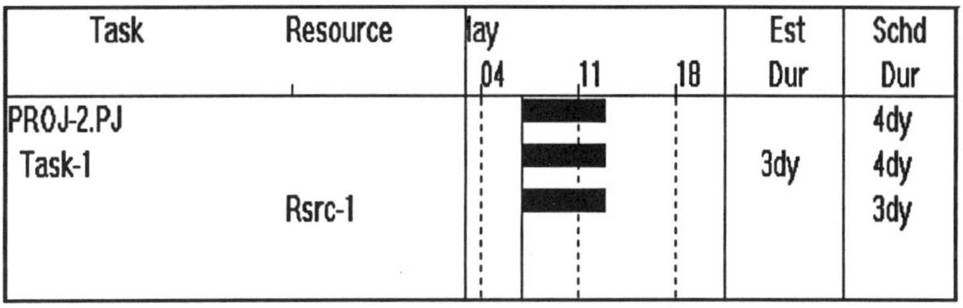

Task	Resource	lay 04	11	18	Est Dur	Schd Dur
PROJ-2.PJ			▬			4dy
Task-1			▬		3dy	4dy
	Rsrc-1		▬			3dy

Figure 3.5
Estimated and scheduled duration in 'expert' mode

indicated on the project calendar. If you now allocate a resource to the task that has a holiday on the second day of the scheduled period then the task's duration will be automatically altered to show 4 days. This is perfectly reasonable behaviour but it sometimes confuses beginners who expect their task duration estimates not to alter!

It is slightly easier to see what is going on if you view the project information in Expert mode. The reason is that in Beginner mode SuperProject uses the single column Schd Dur for you to enter estimated duration and for it to show you the scheduled duration. This double use of a column is intended to reduce the complexity of the display, however it does make it look as if SuperProject is changing values that you enter. If you select Expert Modes, Advanced Planning from the Preferences menu then you will see more clearly what is happening - see Figure 3.5. Now there is an additional column labelled Est Dur which shows the 3 days estimate that the user types in and the 4 days that results due to the need to take into account a resource holiday. You can also see that the resource is only scheduled for 3 days even though the task is to take 4 days.

This behaviour needs a little more clarification. The default task type that SuperProject uses is resource driven. This means that the estimated duration for the task is the number of work days needed by the resources allocated to it to complete it. (Task types are discussed in Chapter 8.)

That is:

» project wide holidays do not affect task duration but do alter start and finish dates

» resource holidays affect both task duration and start and finish dates

Both of these rules are very reasonable and correspond to how you normally think of a project and its relationship to working days.

There is a single special case that is worth mentioning. If a resource holiday falls at the start of a task then the task's duration isn't lengthened, instead the start date is moved to beyond the holiday. For example, a task with an estimated duration of 3 days will still have a scheduled duration of 3 days if the resource it has been allocated has a holiday on the first day on which the task could otherwise start.

Calc

As explained in Chapter 1, SuperProject will not reschedule tasks in response to a change in the model unless you set recalculation to be automatic. In most cases you have to remember to recalculate the schedule manually to see the effect of any changes to the calendars.

To recalculate a project plan select Calculate in the File menu. As a shortcut either press F9 or ! or, if you are using a Windows version, press the CALC button in the top right hand corner.

You should recalculate the project plan whenever you have entered new data, made new links, assigned resources or changed the calendars and need to examine the model in detail.

» If in doubt recalculate!

Workday override - the general case

Now that we know that the standard task type is resource driven and have seen that resource non-working days affect task duration, it is worth examining what happens when the length of the working day is altered on the resource calendar. This brings us to the general case of resource allocation. A whole day holiday is, of course, just the special case of there being 0 resource working hours on a particular day.

What happens in resource allocation is a three-stage process:

» First, the task's duration is used to estimate the resource's allocated hours using the formulae introduced in Chapter 2.

» Second, the resource calendar is examined to discover how many days are needed to provide the number of resource hours calculated in step 1.
(Note: any partial allocation of the working day is taken into account in this step. That is if the resource is only 50% allocated to the task then only 50% of the available hours on any one day will be used - see Chapter 8 for more details.)

» Third, the resource allocation is used to adjust the task's scheduled duration.

The adjustment is fairly straightforward in that the task's scheduled duration is simply set equal to the resource's scheduled duration. If more than one resource is allocated to the task then the scheduled duration is set equal to the longest scheduled resource duration.

For example, suppose you edit the project calendar to show that Thursday is a half working day by editing its standard hours to show 4.0. If you now create a five day task you will see, as described earlier, that this partial holiday has no effect on the scheduling of the task. Without resource allocation SuperProject works in terms of working and

Task	Resource	ay			Est	Schd	Task	Scheduled	Scheduled
		04	11	1	Dur	Dur	ID	Start	Finish
PROJ-1.PJ						6dy	P1	06-05-92> 8:00a	13-05-92 1:00p
Task-1					5dy	6dy	001	06-05-92 8:00a	13-05-92 1:00p
	Rsrc-1					6dy	001	06-05-92 8:00a	13-05-92 1:00p

Figure 3.6
The available work hours affect task duration

non-working days and the 4.0 hour day is treated as a working day on a par with the 8 hour days. Remember: when no resources are allocated SuperProject only makes a distinction between working and non-working days.

If you now allocate a resource to the task and recalculate the model you will immediately see that the scheduled duration has increased to 6 days. The reason is that the resource has a standard working day of 8 hours which means that it has been allocated to the task for 5 days times 8 hours a day, i.e. 40 hours. To find 40 hours of time from the resource calendar, which inherits the half work day on Thursday from the project calendar, it is necessary to use an extra half working day. If you also examine the scheduled finishing time you will discover that it is 1:00pm rather than 5:00pm. (The reason why it is 1:00pm rather than 12:00am is discussed later in the chapter.) The 40 resource hours have been correctly scheduled with reference to the hours indicated on the resource calendar, see Figure 3.6.

To summarise, the task's scheduled duration is however many days it takes to find the allocated number of resource hours on the resource's calendar.

How long is a standard day?

The only mystery in the default scheduling process used by SuperProject is the use of the number of hours in a standard working day. It is clear where all the other quantities come from but where is the standard day defined and where is it stored? The answer to both of these questions is contained in the Details view. You can zoom in to see the current details of the project, any task and any resource. Each Details view shows you everything concerning the object that you have selected including data that can be found in one of the other views and many items of data that cannot.

To switch to a Details view you simply use the command View,Zoom into Details and then select one of - Task Details, Resource Details or Project Details. If you are using the Windows version you can achieve the same result by clicking on the magnifying glass icon while the cursor is positioned on the object in which you are interested. Once you see the Details screen for the given object, you need to be aware that it will generally have a number of windows that can show you different aspects of the object - many of which you will not necessarily understand until you have progressed further in your use of SuperProject. The different aspects of the object can be selected using the Layout,View Subwindows command or by clicking on one of the View Subwindows icons in the Windows version.

For example, if you select Project Details you are presented with a screen that shows a great deal of general information concerning the project and either a list of linked projects - Layout,View Subwindows,Linked Projects - or details of the project working week - Layout,View Subwindows,Project Workday. If you examine the information provided you will see a great many entries that will make sense to you including one at the far right labelled Std Day which specifies the length of the default standard day. Normally this is set to 8 hours but you can change it to any value that is appropriate. This value is inherited by each resource that you create. Each resource can have its own particular

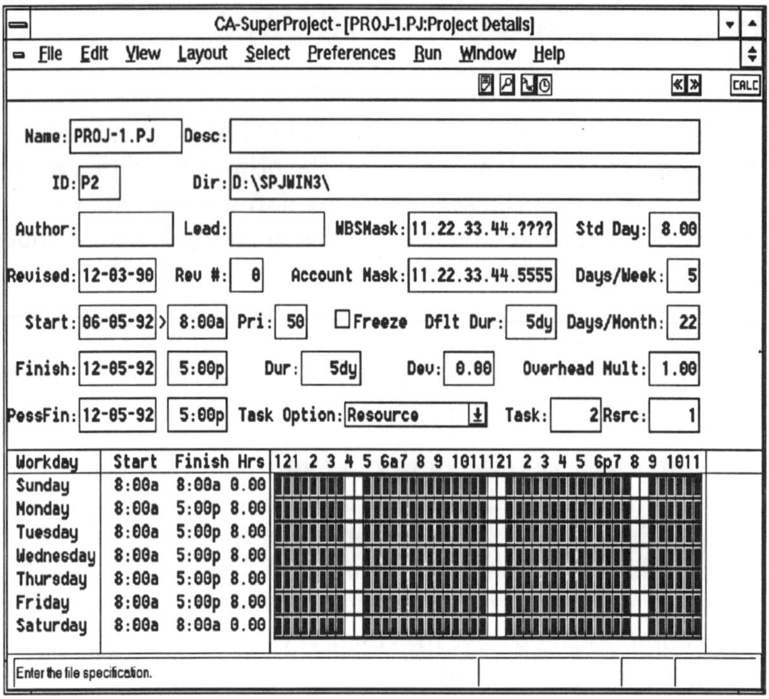

Figure 3.7
The Project Details view

length of standard working day which can be examined in the Resources Details view with the Layout, View Subwindows, Work Periods in force. You can see in Figure 3.7 that the length of the standard day is recorded in the top right. Don't worry too much about all of the other items of data displayed in the Details view, they will all acquire meaning as you expand your knowledge of SuperProject.

Notice that the value of the project's standard working day is inherited by each resource that you create but after this you are free to edit their values. Each time you recalculate the project the current value of the resource's working day is used to work out the number of hours that the resource has been assigned to the task.

Notice also that the number of hours in the standard day has nothing to do with the number of standard working

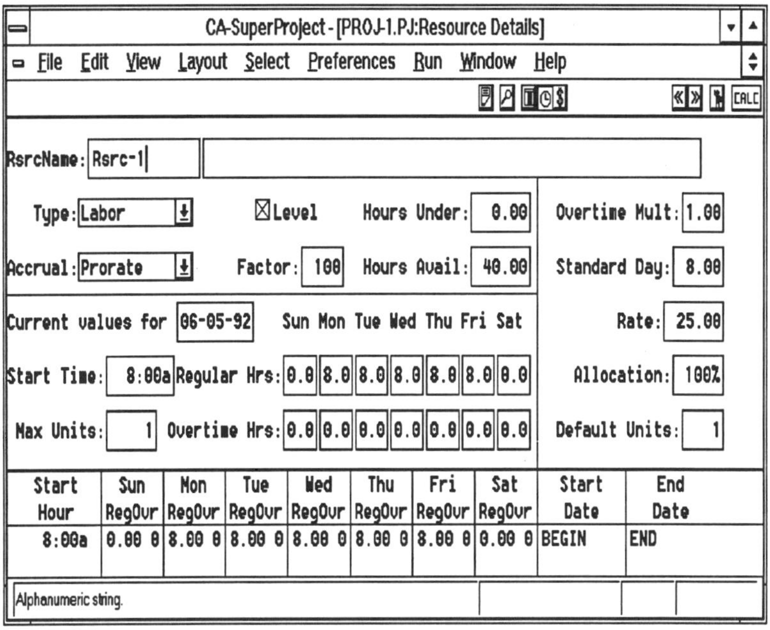

Figure 3.8
The Resource Details view

hours indicated on the calendar for each day. It is quite possible for you to enter a standard working day of 4 hours for a resource and then go and enter a 10 hour working day length on Monday through Friday on each day of the resource's calendar. It is entirely up to you to make sure that the value of the standard working day entered into the Project, and/or Resource, Details is reasonable. Version 2 of SuperProject did try to deduce the standard working day by examining the project and resource calendars but this is in general too difficult and later versions rely on the user to determine the value. For example, what is the standard working day for a resource that works 2 hours for the first three days of the week and 8 hours for the remainder? In nearly all cases it is better that the user takes control and sets the standard working day to a value that they find reasonable.

To give you some idea of the apparently strange results an inappropriate setting can produce, consider the project

Task	Resource	May 04	11		Est Dur	Schd Dur	Alloc /Day	Units Assgn	Sched Rsrc Total Hrs
PROJ-1.PJ						5dy			60.00
Task-1					5dy	5dy			40.00
	Rsrc-1					5dy	100%	1	40.00
Task-2					5dy	3dy			20.00
	Rsrc-2					3dy	100%	1	20.00

Figure 3.9
Changing the standard working day

model shown in Figure 3.9. The reason that Rsrc-2 has only been allocated to Task-2 for 20 hours is that its standard day has been set to 4 hours whereas that of Rsrc-1 is set to 8 hours. What is slightly more puzzling is why Task-2's scheduled duration has been reduced to 3 days? The reason for this is that although Rsrc-2's standard working day has been set to 4 hours its calendar still shows it as available for work for 8 hours each day. This means that the required 20 hours can be found in 2.5 working days which rounds up to 3 scheduled days.

From this example it should be clear to you that the arithmetic of resource allocation and scheduling is simple and rigorous. Whatever value the standard working day has it is used to calculate the number of hours that the resource is allocated to the task and this in turn is used to discover how many resource calendar days are needed to provide the number of hours. Whether or not this procedure is reasonable depends entirely on your setting of the standard working day to be in agreement with the number of hours that the resource is available each day.

If it helps you can think of the standard day as just a convenient multiplier used to convert estimated task duration into number of resource hours.

The standard work pattern

As well as complete and partial non-working days as defined on the project or resource calendar, each day has its own pattern of working hours and breaks. For example, if a resource calendar is set to an 8 hour day this doesn't mean that the resource starts working at 8.00am and continues for a full 8 hours until 4.00pm because there will usually be a 1 hour lunch break at around 12:00am. To get accurate start and finish times for tasks and resource allocations it is important that the patterns of working and non-working hours are correctly set.

Each project has its own project workweek definition. This can be examined and altered in the Project Details view. The project workday information appears in the bottom portion of the screen when you select the Project Workday option in the Layout,View Subwindows menu - refer back to Figure 3.7 and see Figure 3.10. The pattern of solid blocks defines the work and non-work portions of the day. Each block represents 30 minutes and a white block represents a 30 minutes break. You can change a block from black to white and vice versa by double clicking on it. Setting the pattern of work and non-work 30 minute periods can be quite tricky so it is fortunate that once set it doesn't often need to be changed. The default is for 1-hour breaks from 4:00am to 5:00am, 12:00am to 1:00pm and 8:00pm to 9:00 pm.

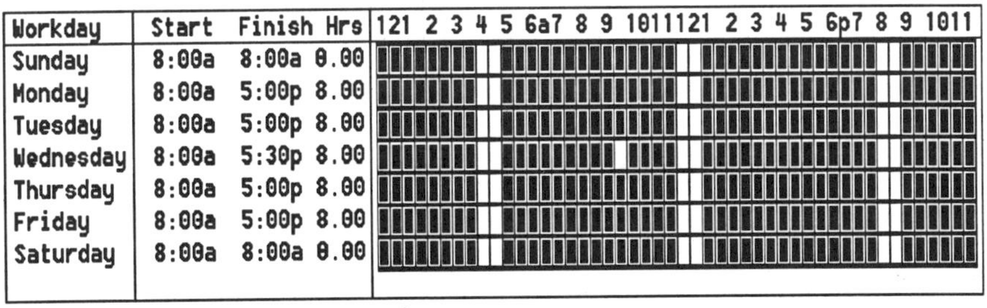

Workday	Start	Finish	Hrs	121 2 3 4 5 6a7 8 9 1011 121 2 3 4 5 6p7 8 9 1011
Sunday	8:00a	8:00a	0.00	
Monday	8:00a	5:00p	8.00	
Tuesday	8:00a	5:00p	8.00	
Wednesday	8:00a	5:30p	8.00	
Thursday	8:00a	5:00p	8.00	
Friday	8:00a	5:00p	8.00	
Saturday	8:00a	8:00a	0.00	

Figure 3.10
The pattern of the working day

As well as the pattern of breaks you also have to specify the standard starting time and the number of hours worked. The number of hours worked on each day is taken from the project calendar but the relationship is two way. That is, if you change the length of the working day in Project Details view, the project calendar will also be changed and vice versa.

The number of hours worked are used in conjunction with the start time and pattern of break periods to work out the finish time. If you look at Figure 3.10 you can see that there is an extra half hour break on Wednesday at 9.30 am and this automatically pushes the finish time back to 5.30 pm. Notice that the start and finish times have no effect on resource availability which is set by the number of working hours specified for each day.

When you create a new resource the start time and the pattern of breaks defined in the Project Details view are inherited along with the holidays and workday durations on the project calendar. If you edit the resource calendar the break periods defined at the project level are still honoured. This explains why for the project in Figure 3.6 the 4-hour work period from 8:00am ends at 1:00pm and not 12:00am as the 1-hour break at 12:00am implies that work cannot begin on the next task until 1:00pm.

You should think of the pattern of work periods and the start time in the Project Details view as defining the standard shift for all resources. However, you can alter the start time on a resource-by-resource basis and create additional shifts. The start time for each resource can be set in its Details view. When you set the start time for a resource the pattern of break periods defined in the Project Details view is used to work out a finish time which is used in all scheduling. Notice that this means that the pattern of breaks applies to all resources in the project. This makes it possible to define a number of shifts but if shifts overlap they must share the same break periods.

Task	Resource	04 11	Est Dur	Schd Dur	Task ID	Scheduled Start	Scheduled Finish
PROJ-1.PJ		▓▓▓		5dy	P2	06-05-92> 8:00a	13-05-92 2:00a
Task-1		▓▓▓	5dy	5dy	001	06-05-92 8:00a	12-05-92 5:00p
	Rsrc-1	▓▓▓		5dy	001	06-05-92 8:00a	12-05-92 5:00p
Task-2		▓▓▓	5dy	4dy	002	06-05-92 5:00p	13-05-92 2:00a
	Rsrc-2	▓▓▓		5dy	002	06-05-92 5:00p	13-05-92 2:00a

Figure 3.11
Two different shifts

For example, in Figure 3.11 you can see that Rsrc-1 is working the standard 8:00am to 5:00pm shift but Rsrc-2's starting time has been altered to 5:00pm. Because of the pattern of breaks, an 8-hour shift starting at 5:00pm will finish at 2:00am which is indeed the scheduled finishing time of the assignment and Task-2.

It is possible to allocate two resources that are working different shifts to a single task but the effect probably isn't quite what you might expect. Each resource is scheduled for the same number of hours and the task's duration isn't reduced - see Figure 3.12. The reason for this is that the task's duration is used to estimate the resource hours needed and this is true even if the resources are working different shifts. How resource allocation can be used to reduce task duration is explained in Chapter 9.

Task	Resource	04 11	Est Dur	Schd Dur	Task ID	Scheduled Start	Scheduled Finish
PROJ-1.PJ		▓▓▓		5dy	P2	06-05-92> 8:00a	13-05-92 2:00a
Task-1		▓▓▓	5dy	5dy	001	06-05-92 8:00a	13-05-92 2:00a
	Rsrc-1	▓▓▓		5dy	001	06-05-92 8:00a	12-05-92 5:00p
	Rsrc-2	▓▓▓		5dy	001	06-05-92 5:00p	13-05-92 2:00a

Figure 3.12
Two different shifts working on the same task

More than one resource

If a task only needs a single resource then it is easy to see how the availability of that resource directly affects the task's duration - but what if more than one resource is allocated to a task?

If more than one resource is allocated to a task then the scheduled duration of the task will depend on the resource that needs the greatest number of days to meet the demands of the task. For example, if two resources are allocated to a 3-day task and one has two non-workdays during the final two days of the task then it is scheduled for 5 days even though the first resource has completed its share of the task in three days, see Figure 3.13. In other words, it is the least available resource which governs how long the task takes to complete. Notice that this implies that some of the resources allocated to a task may become free before the task is completed if there are delays introduced by the non-availability of other resources. You can see in Figure 3.13 that Rsrc-1 is shown as still allocated to the task but not working by the dotted line on the Gantt chart. Also notice that a weekend, that is a periodic project wide holiday, gets in the way of finishing Task-1 and so the completion date is actually pushed back by four days because of two days of resource unavailability. This interaction between holidays producing a longer delay than you would first have imagined is a common occurrence in any project schedule.

Task	Resource	May 04	11	Est Dur	Schd Dur	Alloc /Day	Units Assgn	Sched Rsrc Total Hrs
PROJ-1.PJ					5dy			48.00
Task-1				3dy	5dy			48.00
	Rsrc-1	▪	....		3dy	100%	1	24.00
	Rsrc-2				3dy	100%	1	24.00

Figure 3.13
The least available resource determines the length of the task

Painting a room

As an example of how project and resource calendars affect a project's scheduling, consider the room painting project introduced in Chapters 1 and 2.

Load PAINT2, the version of the project model saved at the end of Chapter 2. There is a company holiday on 11th May and this has to be entered onto the project calendar. If you do this and re-calculate the project model you will find that the total project duration increases by 1 day, even though no task duration is affected.

Next we need to enter the fact that Bill has a day release to attend a college course every Wednesday. Here we meet a slight problem. The easiest way to create a regular non-working day is to enter zero hours next to the day name Wed at the top of the column. This certainly schedules a non-workday every Wednesday but the default label of WKND that appears is a little off putting!. The alternative is to enter the text "College" just below the date on each Wednesday. This is time consuming but in practice you only have to do this for the duration of the project - i.e. Wed 6th, 13th and 20th May. The only danger with this approach is that at a later time the start date for the project is moved without the extra step of entering additional non-working days. Again this is a matter of checking resource assignments for a project very carefully before accepting the model's conclusions.

The effect of the day release non-working days on the project is quite interesting. On the first Wednesday Bill was scheduled to the **Clear room** task which was estimated to take 1 day of Bill and Tom's time. As Bill isn't available on the first day Tom clears the room on his own on day 1 and then Bill clears the rest of the room on his own on day 2. Thus the **Clear room** task now takes 2 days so extending the project by another day. How realistic this scheduling is, I leave you to decide, but it is a perfectly logical consequence of stating that the task needs two resources for 1 day and then only making one of the resources available on the first day. In practice it may be that both Tom and Bill are needed together, to lift heavy furniture say, to complete the clearing of the room and so dividing the allocation in this way does not result in the task being completed.

The effect of the second Wednesday day release is less serious as far as the project finish date is concerned. Originally the **Paint ceiling** task was scheduled for the second Wednesday. (Recall that Bill was reassigned to this task to resolve Tom's over commitment on that day.) As this is a 1-day task and Bill is the only resource allocated to it, making the day into a non-workday for Bill simply moves its start by one day without altering the task duration. Of course, moving its start by one day delays its finish by one

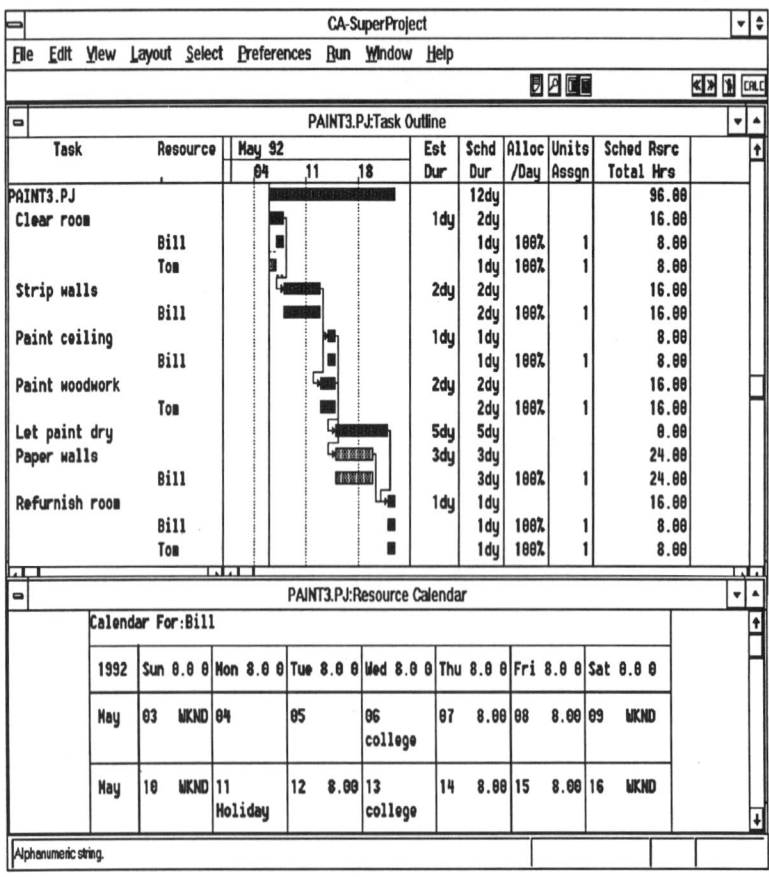

Figure 3.14
The project after the calendar changes

day but as this task isn't on the critical path before the delay this has no effect on the project's duration. However, after the one day delay it is on the critical path so any further delay would increase the total time to complete the project. See Figure 3.14 which shows the total effect of the changes to the Gantt chart and Bill's revised calendar.

The project should be saved for later use as PAINT3.

Resource assignment

If you look carefully at the calendar shown in Figure 3.14 you will see that an additional value is indicated to the right of the date. This is the number of total number of hours that the resource, Bill in this case, has been allocated to tasks on that day. If you look at the project calendar you will see a similar value for each project workday showing the total resource time allocated for each day.

Calendar For:PAINT3.PJ					Range: 14-05-92 To: 14-05-92		
1992	Sun 0.0	Mon 8.0	Tue 8.0	Wed 8.0	Thu 8.0	Fri 8.0	Sat 0.0
May	03 WKND	04	05	06 8.00 Holiday	07 8.00	08 8.00	09 WKND
May	10 WKND	11 Holiday	12 8.00	13 8.00	14 16.00	15 8.00	16 WKND

Task Name		Schd Dur	Alloc /Day	Units Assgn	Sched Rsrc Total Hrs	Sel Flag
Paint ceiling	Bill	1dy	100%	1	8.00	
Paint woodwork	Tom	2dy	100%	1	16.00	

Figure 3.15
Project calendar with assignments

This display of resource time allocated is useful for spotting over-commitment of resources and for examining the effect of holidays but a more detailed breakdown would be useful. You can see a complete listing of the tasks that a resource is assigned to on any day by selecting View Subwindows - Assignments in the Layout menu.

You can also do the same with the project calendar displayed. In this case all tasks that are active on the selected day are listed along with their associated resource assignments - see Figure 3.15. Clearly this is a useful and easy to understand way of discovering what is scheduled to happen on any given day. It can also help spot over-scheduled resources.

If you are using SuperProject for Windows then notice that you can switch to and from the assignment listing by pressing one of the two buttons at the top right next to the magnifying glass icon.

If you would like to list all assignments within a specified period of the selected date then you can use the Input Date Range command in the Edit menu. Notice that this option is only available when the assignment's window is displayed. For example, if you specify a date range of 2 days then all assignments that start within the 2-day period from the current date will be displayed in the assignment window.

Quick ways with dates

There are a number of useful techniques that speed up working with calendars. The first is the Find Date command in the Edit menu. This allows you to enter the date that you are looking for into a dialog box and when you press OK the calendar is arranged to make it the current date. This command can be used in any view and it is worth learning its keyboard shortcut - Ctrl-F.

You can also delete all holidays entered on a calendar by selecting Erase All Holidays in the Edit menu. This will erase all non-workdays from the current calendar. Notice that it will not remove non-workdays from resource calendars that are based on the project calendars. If you are planning to erase all holidays then it might be a good idea to save the calendar beforehand just in case you want to change your mind!

Key points

» Patterns of working and non-working days are specified using calendars which are stored along with the project details. There are two types of calendar - a project calendar which is used to define project wide holidays and resource calendars which are used to define extra holidays that apply to individual resources. The project calendar is used as a template for all of the resource calendars.

» The number of working hours in each day can be set, as can one off, regular and partial holidays.

» The length of the working day can be overridden by entering the number of hours to be worked below the relevant date.

» The default task type used by SuperProject is resource driven. This means that the estimated and scheduled task duration can be different because of resource availability.

» Project whole day holidays affect start and finish dates but not task duration. Resource whole day holidays affect both start and finish dates and task duration.

» If a task has no resources assigned to it then its duration is interpreted as the number of working days to complete it. In this context a working day is simply a project day with any number of work hours available.

» When a task has a resource assigned to it then its duration is converted into resource hours in the usual way. The task is then scheduled for as many days as it takes to find that number of hours on the resource's calendar. If more than one resource is assigned to a task then the least available resource controls the task's duration.

Chapter 4
Complexity Control

Managing a small project is relatively easy. You can keep all the details of tasks, resources and assignments in your head and form an initial plan using nothing but a piece of paper. You can also resolve problems as they arise by knowing the project so well. When a project becomes large enough to outgrow the mental capacity of the average human mind then it is time to use more systematic methods. Obviously, SuperProject's ability to record the details of a project is a great help but even in this case there comes a point where the data and the diagrams that are presented overwhelm the user. Large projects can still become difficult to understand because of the amount of detail presented. The solution is to make use of the traditional techniques of complexity control.

Hierarchies

The main weapon in controlling the apparent complexity of a project is the use of hierarchies of tasks. There isn't a single way of decomposing a project into tasks and the number of tasks that you perceive as making up a project depends on how closely you are looking. At the most coarse level you may be able to see that a project has a number of phases - a start, a middle and an end - which often correspond to getting ready to do the work, doing the work and clearing up! Each of these phases may in turn be decomposable into other phases and so on until you reach a level of decomposition where it isn't an advantage to divide a phase into any smaller steps.

The reason why the final level of sub-division is appropriate for project modelling will vary but usually it corresponds to tasks which have no further structure as far as the model is concerned. For example, in the case of painting a room the sub-division stops at a task level at which it is reasonable to expect the assigned resources to manage the task. The **Paint woodwork** task isn't further sub-divided into **Clean down paint work, Sand paint work, apply undercoat, apply 1st coat of gloss**, etc. because it is assumed that the resource, i.e. the painter, is capable of managing the task without further interference from the project planner. As far as the project model is concerned **Paint woodwork** simply has a duration and resource assignments and any further internal structure it may have is irrelevant.

This idea that there are different levels at which a project can be decomposed into tasks gives rise to a hierarchy of ways of viewing the project. For example, at the first level you would see only the main phases:

      Initial phase
      Middle phase
      Final phase

At the next level you can inquire about the tasks that make up each of the phases:

      Initial phase
            Task 1
            Task 2
      Middle phase
            Task 3
      Final phase
            Task 4
            Task 5

and so on. Notice that at the highest level view the project has the appearance of simplicity, and as you move down each level you reveal increasing degrees of detail and hence complexity.

Notice also the way that indenting has been used to show the level that each task name belongs to. This indenting is a natural notation to show a hierarchy and it is used in many other situations. For example, paragraphs in a contract or other complex documents often use different levels of indent and computer programmers have been using indentation to make the structure of programs clear for many years.

Top down

Although the examples used in earlier chapters were described as if the project decomposed into tasks at a single level, this isn't a good way to work in general. The best way of describing a project, and hence building up a project model, is to work "top down". In other words you should first describe the most general phases of the project. This immediately gives you a complete project model to work on. The next stage is to refine the definition of each of the phases by defining the tasks that make them up. At this stage you shouldn't necessarily try to define the phases in terms of the smallest possible tasks. You should again attempt a decomposition of each phase that has few enough tasks to be easily understandable. The project definition and model should be repeatedly refined in this way until you find that you are working at an appropriate level of task definition.

Notice that using the top down method automatically produces a project model that is hierarchically ordered. It also has the advantage that further refinement, should it become necessary, is a natural extension of the initial project model. It is also important to be aware that not all project phases will necessarily need to be decomposed to the same number of levels.

SuperProject's hierarchy

SuperProject fully supports the hierarchical decomposition of a project into tasks. Indeed all tasks are hierarchical by default with the project's name as the topmost level. When you enter a task's name it is assumed to be in the level immediately below the project name and this is indicated by a single level of indent. SuperProject supports further levels of indent and to move a task into another level all you have to do is use the promote/demote command:

	Menu	Key (MS-DOS version)
Promote	Edit,Position,Right	Shift-Right arrow
Demote	Edit,Position,Left	Shift-Left arrow

Note: The Windows version of SuperProject uses Alt-Shift and a cursor arrow key for promote/demote. The reason for this change is that Shift and a cursor key is used by Windows in marking out text for cut and paste operations.

If you are using the Windows version of SuperProject then you can also promote/demote a task by clicking on the left and right arrows in the icon bar while the task is selected.

The best way of describing how the hierarchy works in SuperProject is via a simple example. First open a new project and type over the default project name to replace it by NEWPRO.PJ. This is the name of the new project and it is the top level heading. Next enter three new tasks **Initial Phase, Middle Phase** and **Final Phase**. These are the three tasks that form the first level of decomposition of the project, as can be seen by the single level of indent below the project name - see Figure 4.1.

The next step in the top down refinement of this project is to define the tasks that make up each of the phases. If the **Initial Phase** is made up of two major tasks, **Task-1** and **Task-2**, then these can be entered below this heading in the usual way. Of course this simply adds the new tasks at the same level as **Initial Phase**. To demote them to be components of **Initial Phase** you have to select each task in turn and give the 'demote' command either by using the

Task	Resource	May 92 04	11	18	Schd Dur	Task ID
NEWPRO.PJ			▓▓▓		5dy	P13
Initial Phase			▓▓▓		5dy	001
Middle Phase			▓▓▓		5dy	002
Final Phase			▓▓▓		5dy	003

Figure 4.1
The first level

menu, by pressing (Alt-) Shift-Right or by selecting the right arrow icon. If you do this you will see **Task-1** and **Task-2** indent to the right and the colour of the heading **Initial Phase** changes to show that it is composed of other tasks. After decomposing **Middle Phase** into **Task-3** and **Final Phase** into **Task-4** and **Task-5** the result can be seen in Figure 4.2.

If any of the tasks at the second level were decomposable into yet smaller tasks then a third level could be established in the same way. If a task is wrongly assigned as a sub-task then it can be promoted up one or more levels using the promote command. Notice that SuperProject will not promote or demote a task to levels that do not make sense. For example, you cannot demote a task an arbitrary number of times but only to one level lower than a task listed above it.

Task	Resource	May 92 04	11	18	Schd Dur	Task ID
NEWPRO.PJ			▓▓▓		5dy	P13
Initial Phase			▓▓▓		5dy	001
Task-1			▓▓▓		5dy	004
Task-2			▓▓▓		5dy	005
Middle Phase			▓▓▓		5dy	002
Task-3			▓▓▓		5dy	006
Final Phase			▓▓▓		5dy	003
Task-4			▓▓▓		5dy	007
Task-5			▓▓▓		5dy	008

Figure 4.2
The second level

Scheduling the hierarchy

One of the advantages of using a top down project hierarchy is that it makes it much easier to establish links between tasks. You can first create the links that are necessary between the sub-tasks that constitute the definition of a heading and then link the headings to determine the project. If there are more levels than two then you simply create the links as required at each level. The duration of any task is determined by the scheduled duration and links of the sub-tasks that make it up. In effect each task acts like a mini-project which is scheduled in the same way as the entire project.

For example, if **Task-1** and **Task-2** in **Initial Phase** have to be sequential but **Task-4** and **Task-5** in **Final Phase** can run in parallel then **Task-1** and **Task-2** should be linked as shown in Figure 4.3. Notice that the scheduled duration of **Initial Phase** is altered to 10 days.

Of course the project model currently shows the three phases as running concurrently which isn't the case. To modify this, links have to be made between each of the phases. You can do this in the usual way but notice that now you are linking, in one operation, all of the sub-tasks - see Figure 4.4. Notice also that now the total project time has increased to 20 days, as you would expect. Creating the

Task	Resource	May 92 04 11 18	Schd Dur	Task ID
NEWPRO.PJ			10dy	P13
Initial Phase			10dy	001
Task-1			5dy	004
Task-2			5dy	005
Middle Phase			5dy	002
Task-3			5dy	006
Final Phase			5dy	003
Task-4			5dy	007
Task-5			5dy	008

Figure 4.3
Linking sub-tasks

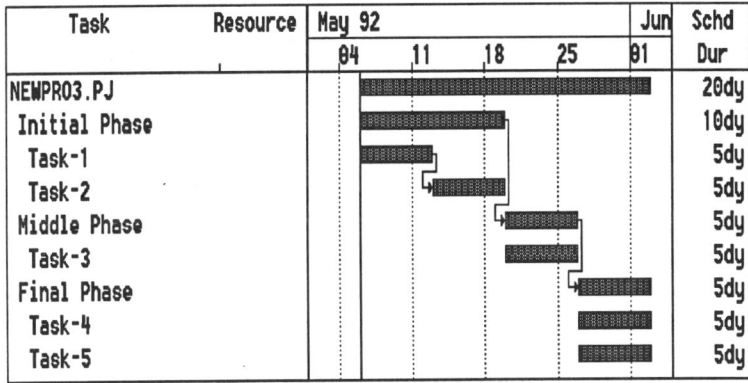

Figure 4.4
Linking headings and sub-tasks

same project model without the use of the hierarchy would have involved using more links because it would have been necessary to link some of the individual sub-tasks across the phases.

A painting hierarchy

The project model of painting a room that we have used since Chapter 1 is an excellent example of how working with a top down hierarchy simplifies things. Although this was introduced as a non-hierarchical project description it isn't difficult to see that there are two clear larger scale phases: preparing the room which consists of **Clear room** and **Strip walls** and painting the room which consists of **Paint ceiling** and **Paint woodwork**. The other tasks, papering the walls and refurnishing the room are not worth dividing down into smaller tasks or organising into larger groupings. The final hierarchy can be seen in Figure 4.5. In this case the original project was edited to add the new tasks **Prepare room** and **Paint room** and then the demote command was used to indent the existing sub-tasks. You can see that the links have also been remade so that the constraints are specified between the higher level headings. This reduces the total number of links needed and makes the Gantt chart look simpler. SuperProject actually prompts the user for permission to remove links that have been made redundant by the introduction of a grouping of tasks under a single heading.

Of course, this example is a little unnatural in that the hierarchical structure should have been imposed from the start but it does demonstrate some of the advantages of using a hierarchy. It also raises a number of interesting and subtle questions.

Why, for example, is the **Let paint dry** task not included under the **Paint room** heading? Logically it has something to do with painting the room and and so would seem to fit naturally under this heading. To understand the reason why **Let paint dry** isn't suitable for inclusion under the heading you have to look at the way that constraints are specified. The **Paper walls** task can start as soon as the painting is complete without having to wait for the paint to dry, but the **Refurnish room** task is constrained by both the end of the **Let paint dry** task and by the end of the **Paper walls** task. What this means is that if **Let paint dry** is included

Task	Resource	ay 04	11	18	2	Schd Dur	Task ID
PAINT4.PJ						12dy	P1
Prepare room						4dy	017
Clear room						2dy	001
	Bill					1dy	001
	Tom					1dy	001
Strip walls						2dy	002
	Bill					2dy	002
Paint room						2dy	018
Paint ceiling						1dy	003
	Bill					1dy	003
Paint woodwork						2dy	004
	Tom					2dy	004
Let paint dry						5dy	005
Paper walls						3dy	006
	Bill					3dy	006
Refurnish room						1dy	007
	Bill					1dy	007
	Tom					1dy	007

Figure 4.5
The paint project as a hierarchy

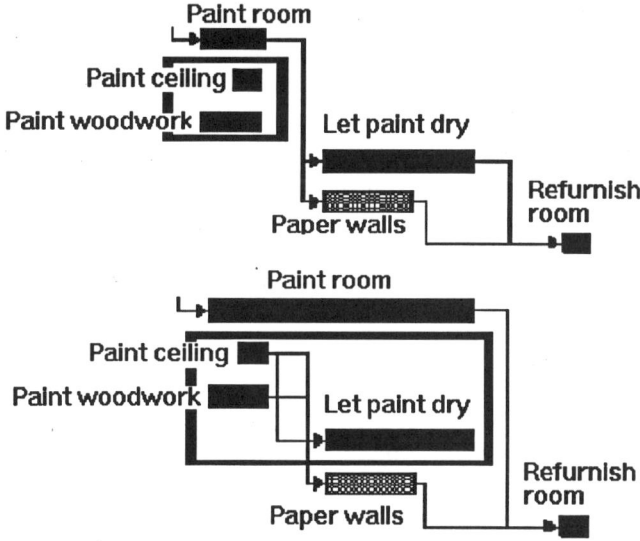

Figure 4.6
Two ways of drying paint!

under the heading **Paint room** links have to be made from tasks within the grouping to tasks outside the grouping, that is from the ends of the **Paint ceiling** and **Paint woodwork** tasks to the **Paper walls** task. If the **Let paint dry** task is excluded from the **Paint room** heading then the links between tasks are simpler, see Figure 4.6.

If possible you should try to avoid links between sub-tasks under different headings. This results in a project model that is simpler to understand and work with. However, there are lots of times when it is useful to break this guideline because it produces a simplicity in some other aspect of the model. For example, if the paint drying stage is in some way the responsibility of the same resources as are used to paint the room then it might simplify the organisation of the work to have all three tasks grouped under the same heading. There are also lots of occasions when a project is so complex that not allowing links between sub-tasks under different headings would effectively mean abandoning all attempts at a hierarchical organisation! The most that can be said is that restricting links to strictly within and between headings produces the maximum simplification.

Of course it goes without saying that SuperProject will make links between tasks irrespective of which heading they are grouped under and you still have complete freedom in creating your project model whether you make use of hierarchies or not.

Viewing hierarchies

The main advantage of organising tasks into a hierarchy is to allow them to be worked with at more than one level. SuperProject will allow you to alter the display of the project model so that the lower levels are hidden. To hide all of the levels below a given heading all you have to do is select the heading and press the - (minus) key or alternatively use the command Hide Lower Level in the Edit menu, or if you are using the Windows version click on the - (minus) button in the icon bar. Each time you press the - (minus) key one level - the lowest - of sub-tasks is hidden. The first press hides the assignment data, the second the lowest level sub-tasks, then next any sub-tasks that remain and so on.

When all of the levels below a heading are hidden the heading is displayed as if it was a single task without any further structure. The most compressed view of the entire

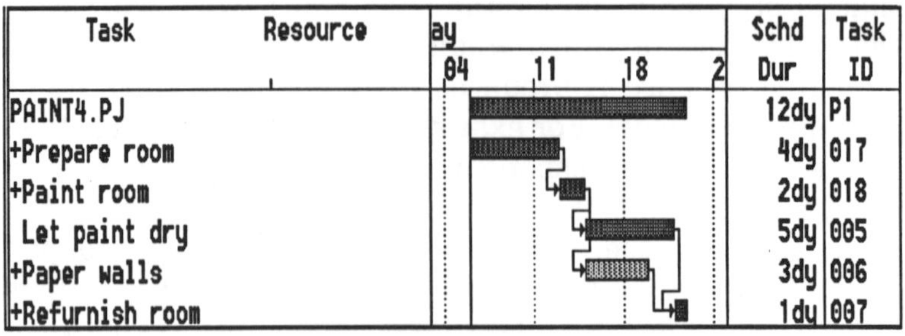

Task	Resource	ay				Schd Dur	Task ID
		04	11	18	2		
PAINT4.PJ						12dy	P1
+Prepare room						4dy	017
+Paint room						2dy	018
Let paint dry						5dy	005
+Paper walls						3dy	006
+Refurnish room						1dy	007

Figure 4.7
The collapsed view of the paint project

project can be achieved by selecting the project heading and pressing the - (minus) key enough times to hide all of the levels in the project. For example, in the case of the room painting project the result of selecting the project name and pressing - (minus) twice can be seen in Figure 4.7. Viewing a project model in this collapsed form is one of the best ways of gaining an understanding of its general structure.

Of course once you have an understanding of its general structure you can 'unfold' detail. To expand a heading so that it shows the sub-tasks below it all you have to do is select the heading and press the + (plus) key or give the command Show Next Level in the Edit menu or click on the + (plus) button in the icon bar. Each time you expand a heading the tasks at the next level appear until you finally reach the lowest level sub-tasks or the resource assignments. By expanding the headings selectively you can tailor the display to show just the detail you require. To show all of the project in all of its detail simply select the project name and press + (plus) until all levels are fully expanded.

Editing task position

So far it has been assumed that you will create a project in a top-down manner but in reality you will tend to add tasks, and even additional phases, at different levels. You will also want to move existing tasks. To make this possible there are two commands that allow tasks to be moved vertically within the hierarchy. The command Edit,Position,Up or (Alt) Shift-Up arrow and Edit,Position,Down or (Alt) Shift-Down arrow will move the current task one row up or down respectively. The only restriction is that a task will only move within its existing level and if you try to move a heading then all of the sub-tasks beneath the heading move as well. That is, the position commands can only be used to rearrange headings or tasks within their existing level.

This sounds simple but in practice it can be quite confusing if the project has an extensive hierarchy. Suppose for example, you have placed a task under the wrong heading. You cannot simply use the up or down movement keys to reassign it because they will only move the task under its existing heading. To move it to a new heading you have to first move the task to be the last item at its current level. You can do this by repeatedly pressing (Alt) Shift-Down until the task doesn't move any further down. Next you have to promote it to the level of the heading under which you want to place it using (Alt) Shift-Right arrow. If you had not already moved it to the end of the list of items under the existing heading it would have become a new heading for all the items below it and they would have moved with it! Next you can use (Alt) Shift and the up and down arrow keys to move it to just below its new heading. Finally you demote it to join the other items grouped below the heading.

If you are still unsure of the way the positioning keys work try the following exercise:

1) Starting from a new project create six tasks and using the (Alt) Shift-Right arrow demote Task-2, Task-3, Task-5 and Task-6 to produce the hierarchy shown in Figure 4.8.

2) Starting from the hierarchy shown in Figure 4.8 try to move Task-5 to be under the Task-1 heading.

If you try to do this by simply pressing (Alt) Shift-Up arrow you will discover that it will not move because it is already at the top of its particular level under Task-4. If you promote

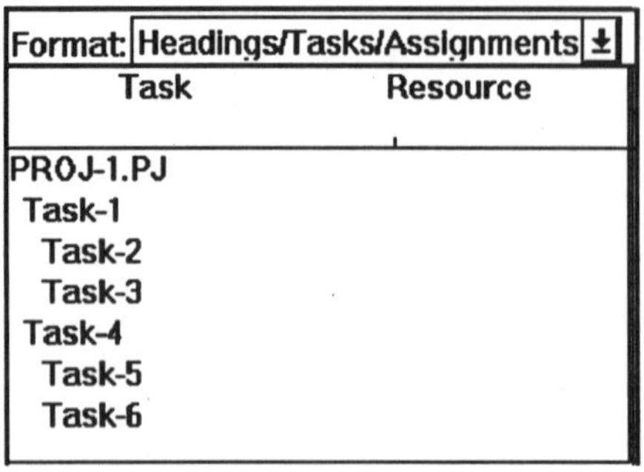

Format:	Headings/Tasks/Assignments ±
Task	Resource
PROJ-1.PJ	
Task-1	
Task-2	
Task-3	
Task-4	
Task-5	
Task-6	

Figure 4.8
The example hierarchy before editing

Editing task position 73

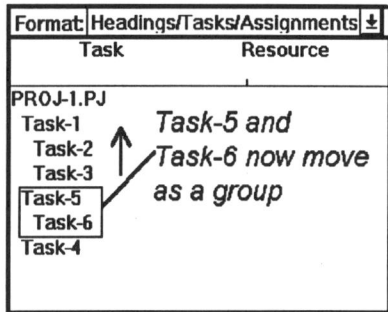

Figure 4.9
The example hierarchy before editing

it using (Alt) Shift-Left arrow then it will then move up but it will take Task-6 with it, see Figure 4.9.

The correct way to move the task is to first move it to the bottom of the list of sub-tasks below Task-4. Next promote it to the same level as Task-1 and Task-4. Move it using (Alt) Shift-Up arrow to just below Task-1 and then demote it using (Alt) Shift-Right arrow. You can then use the (Alt) Shift-Up arrow to move it to another position within the list of sub-tasks below the Task-1 heading. You can see the complete sequence of operations in Figure 4.10. Even after some practice it is still possible to make a muddle of a hierarchy by not noticing exactly what it is you are moving.

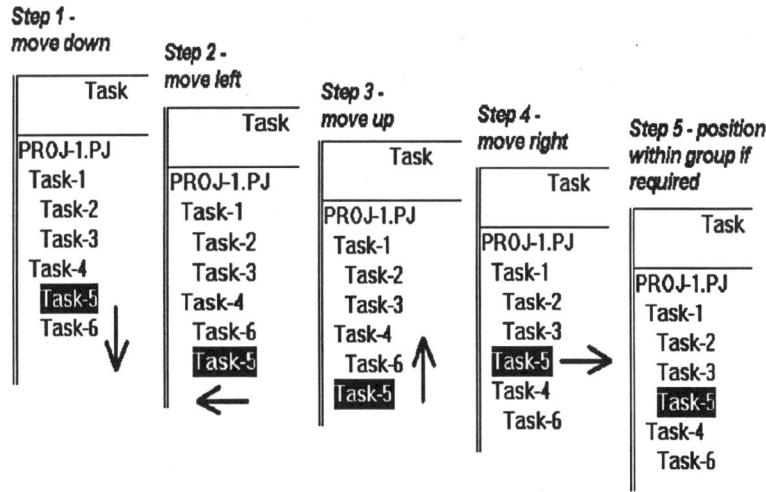

Figure 4.10
The example hierarchy before editing

Cut and Paste - Windows only

As well as moving tasks within the hierarchy using the positioning commands, you can also use the Windows cut and paste facilities to move blocks of tasks. To cut or copy a block of tasks all you have to do is drag over the task names that you want to select. In practice this can be harder than it sounds. The first time you click on a task name it becomes the current task and is shown in reverse colours. The second time you click it is selected for editing and an editing cursor appears. At this point you can edit the task name in the usual way. In addition you can also drag with the mouse to select a block of text. The most reliable way of doing this is to position the text cursor at the end of the word and drag back to the start of the word. Once it is selected, you can cut or copy the text to the Clipboard using the Edit, Cut or Edit, Copy commands. You can then place the editing cursor somewhere else in the task list and copy the contents of the Clipboard back into the task list using Edit,Paste.

Using cut and paste you can move chunks of the hierarchy from one place to another in one operation. There is a good deal more to say about selecting tasks and objects in general but this is postponed until Chapter 9.

Milestones

Milestones are another useful weapon in the fight against complexity. A milestone is simply a task of zero duration that is used to mark the achievement of some project goal. For example, completing the roof of a building is often regarded as a milestone in a project because it signals a psychological change in the project's state of development as well as indicating a change in the type of work that is needed to complete it.

You can enter a milestone into SuperProject simply by specifying that a task has a duration of 0 days. Milestones are shown on the Gantt chart using a special symbol - a square with a hole in it by default.

Another use for milestone tasks is to model events that have little or no duration as far as the project is concerned. For example, you can use a milestone to mark the fact that materials or other resources need to be ordered. Such a task doesn't really have a zero duration but it often isn't worth assigning a real duration and resources to it! In short milestones are used to mark the achievement of a particular state or as event markers.

Resource assignment

The use of a hierarchical project structure doesn't really affect the way that the assignment of resources is handled. The only real difference is that resources can only be assigned to tasks at the lowest level. In other words you cannot assign resources to headings. This is a very reasonable restriction as the heading only derives its meaning from the sub-tasks grouped beneath it and as such cannot directly own resources. The only time that this restriction causes a problem is when you are trying to edit an existing project model to promote sub-tasks into headings so that their description can be further refined. In this case resource allocation will be lost and resources will have to be assigned to the newly defined sub-tasks.

Key points

» The main weapon in controlling complexity is the use of a hierarchical organisation of tasks under headings. A project model is best created in a 'top down' fashion. First identifying the major phases of the project and then refining the definition by assigning sub-tasks to the phases and so on. In practice most project models are best constructed using a mixture of top down and bottom up.

» The lowest level of sub-task corresponds to the level of decomposition at which responsibility for the task falls to the resources allocated to the task. At this level the task has no further structure as far as the model is concerned.

» SuperProject supports hierarchical organisation by way of the demote (Alt) Shift-Right arrow key and promote (Alt) Shift-Left arrow commands. These correspond to a right and left indent respectively.

» Constraints can be specified more simply by linking separate headings. The ideal hierarchical decomposition of a project would involve links within headings and between headings but not between sub-tasks under different headings. This is usually not possible.

» Layers below a given heading can be hidden by pressing the - (minus) key while the heading is selected. Layers can be expanded by pressing the + (plus) key while the heading is selected.

» You can edit the order of tasks using (Alt) Shift-Up arrow and (Alt) Shift-Down arrow.

» Milestones are tasks of zero duration that are used to mark the achievement of some project state or the occurrence of an event.

Chapter 5
Views and Outlines

A project model contains information about tasks and resources. In many ways this data is more fundamental than any one given way of visualising it. So far we have concentrated on using the Task Outline view with its tabular summary of tasks and the resources assigned to them, but SuperProject offers a number of other views including the Resources Outline view that was introduced in Chapter 2. In this chapter the focus shifts to examine the idea of using different views of the same project model, and here the Task, Resource and Date Outline views are discussed in some detail. The PERT and Work Breakdown Structure views are covered in the next chapter.

The Views menu

In Beginner mode the View menu offers a total of six different views of the project model. These are:

> Task Outline
> Resource Outline
> Date Outline
> PERT Chart
> Work Breakdown Chart

and

> Calendars

In Expert mode two additional menu selections become available:

                Account Outline
and   Zoom into Details

If you are using the Windows version of SuperProject then the Zoom into Details option is also available irrespective of the current mode by clicking on the 'zoom' icon (the small magnifying glass) in the icon bar.

Of these views the Task, Resource and Calendar views have already been discussed but not in full detail. Each view has its own set of menu options that are appropriate to the operations that make sense in that view. This causes some confusion if you try to find a menu item that isn't available in the current view. It can leave you thinking that you have lost a menu option or that your imagination is working overtime. The solution to nearly all such missing menu options is that a different view has been selected in which the option doesn't appear. (If this isn't the case then the only remaining possibility is that you are in Beginner mode when you think that you are in Expert mode!)

The Layout menu

The format of each of the views is controlled by the Layout menu. A layout is a complete specification of the data to be included, its format, colour, symbols used etc., and is stored on disk. As will be explained in Chapter 14 you can create your own custom layouts and save them to disk for later use. This is one of the most powerful features of SuperProject but it can be confusing when you are just starting to learn how to use it. To make life easier in these initial stages a selection of pre-defined layouts is supplied for you to use. You have already been making use of these layouts without realising it because one is designated as the default layout. For example, the default layout in the Task Outline view is Task Outline (in Version 2 it is GANTT-1 Chart with Beginner mode symbols.)

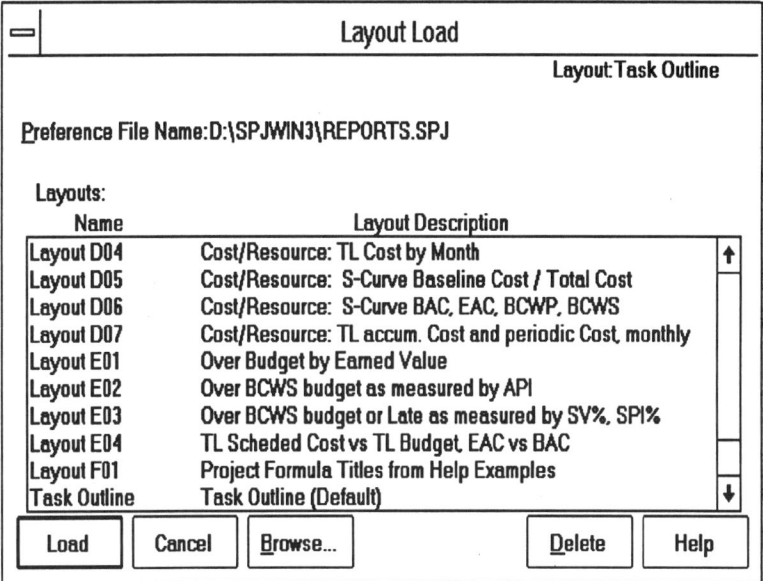

Figure 5.1
The Layout Load dialog box

To load a new layout all you have to do is select Load from the Layout menu which results in the display of the Layout Load dialog box - see Figure 5.1. In this dialog box you can see a complete listing of all of the layouts currently available for use along with a brief description.

Notice that in Version 3 the number of layouts available is greatly increased. If you are upgrading from Version 2 then you might find the name changes and the bewildering number of possible layouts confusing. However, the change is very much for the better because the new layouts are not only designed to make examination of the project model easier but also to make particular data entry and editing tasks easier. You could say that in Version 3 there is a layout for every occasion and activity.

If you select one of the layouts then it will be used for the current view until you select a new one or restart SuperProject. Don't worry too much if some of the layout descriptions use terms and ideas that you don't recognise, many of them are concerned with some of the more advanced options in SuperProject. These will be described in later chapters. For the moment all that is important is that you have grasped the idea of loading a layout from disk.

For example, the Painting a room project has been viewed in the default layout in previous chapters but if you want to see rather more detail on the Gantt chart then an alternative layout might be preferable. If you use the command Layout Load and select B09 (or if you are using Version 2 GANTT-2 Chart w/Float, Delay and other Advanced planning symbols) the result should be something like Figure 5.2. In this case the only addition to the original Gantt chart is the appearance of symbols to mark the float time available on the **Paper walls** task. Float time is just the extra time that a task can take without it affecting the total duration of the project, that is, without it becoming a critical task.

If you are simply interested in seeing what the project data looks like using each of the possible layouts then you can use the command To Next Layout in the Layout menu. This simply cycles through the layouts in the order in which they are listed in the dialog box. The keyboard shortcut Ctrl+T for this command provides an even quicker way of sampling layouts!

Notice that Layout not only affects the Gantt chart but can determine which columns of data show and in what order. It is even possible to restrict the objects - tasks, resources, assignments - on view to a particular selected set.

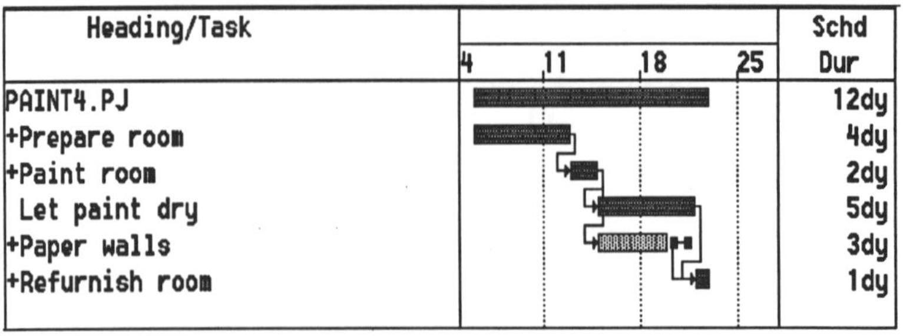

Heading/Task	4	11	18	25	Schd Dur
PAINT4.PJ					12dy
+Prepare room					4dy
+Paint room					2dy
Let paint dry					5dy
+Paper walls					3dy
+Refurnish room					1dy

Figure 5.2
The B09 layout

Making a layout the default

If you select a new layout then the selection will only affect the current session since once you quit SuperProject and restart it the original default layout will be used. You can select a layout and make it a new default by simply saving the preferences file. The preferences file SYSPREF.SPJ stores a wide range of default values that are used to set SuperProject's behaviour when it first starts running. If you load a new layout and then give the command Save Preferences in the Preferences menu then the layout will become the new default as long as you don't change the name of the preference file from SYSPREF.SPJ. The only problem with modifying the preference file is that you have to be careful not to save changes to other defaults when you only intend to modify the default layout.

Controlling Task Outline view

Although Task Outline view has been the one that has been used most so far there is still much to say about it. As well as being able to modify the layout of this view you can also choose to remove or alter the Gantt chart. If you select Gantt Window Commands in the Layout menu you are presented with a further sub-menu. Some of the options will be greyed out and unavailable because they do not apply to the current Gantt chart layout, in particular all of the options that relate to Cost/Rsrc. These options are only used when cost charts are added to the Gantt chart and are described later.

In the case of a simple Gantt chart the most important options are Full/Narrow Gantt width. If you want to see a Gantt chart embedded in the usual columns of data then select Narrow. The Full option gives the whole of the screen over to the chart. The options to increase and reduce Gantt scale can be used to progressively change the time scale. Each time you select the increase or decrease option the scale changes by one day per plotted unit. You can use the

82 *Views and Outlines* Chapter 5

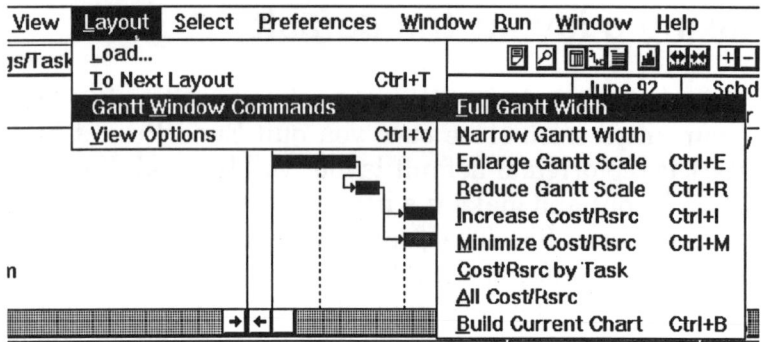

Figure 5.3
The Gantt Window sub-menu

shortcut key presses Ctrl-E for Enlarge or Ctrl-R for Reduce or the double headed icons in the menu bar. Scaling the Gantt chart has a similar effect to moving up and down the project hierarchy in that it allows you to view the project in increasing and decreasing detail in time.

View options

In both the Task and Resource Outline views you can choose exactly what combination of headings, tasks and resources are displayed in the first column of the table. This is a simple enough idea - you select what you want to appear from the Layout View Options sub-menu - see Figure 5.4.

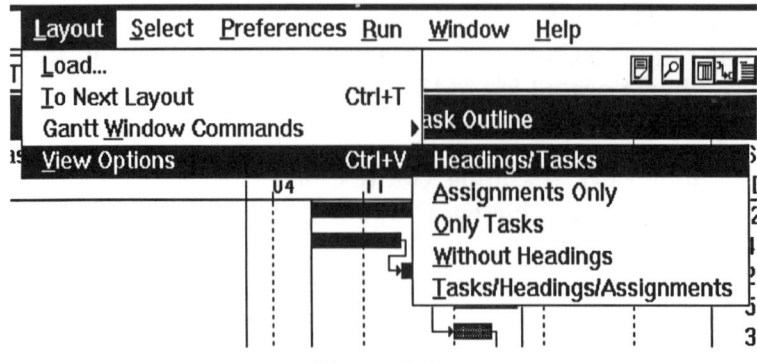

Figure 5.4
The View Options sub-menu

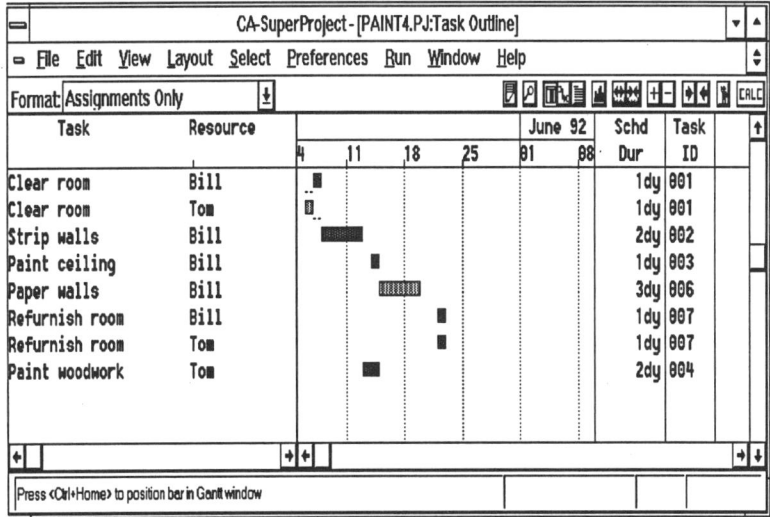

Figure 5.5
Viewing the table with Assignments Only

The same selection of options is also available in Resource Outline view and is made available in an additional pull-down menu in the Windows version.

Viewing the table with Assignment Only selected is a good way to see the resource allocation in a compact form - see Figure 5.5. The Gantt chart also changes to show only the resource bars. The only subtle point is that if you ask to see Tasks/Headings/Assignments what you actually see will depend on how you have used the + (plus) and - (minus) keys to expand and hide the hierarchy. If you have hidden the resources assigned to a task then they will still be hidden when you select Tasks/Headings/Assignments.

Resource Outline

The Resource Outline view has also been briefly described in earlier chapters but, as in the case of Task Outline view, there are many features that deserve closer attention. Many of the ideas introduced with respect to Task Outline view also apply to Resource Outline view. For example, you can load any one of a number of possible layout definitions.

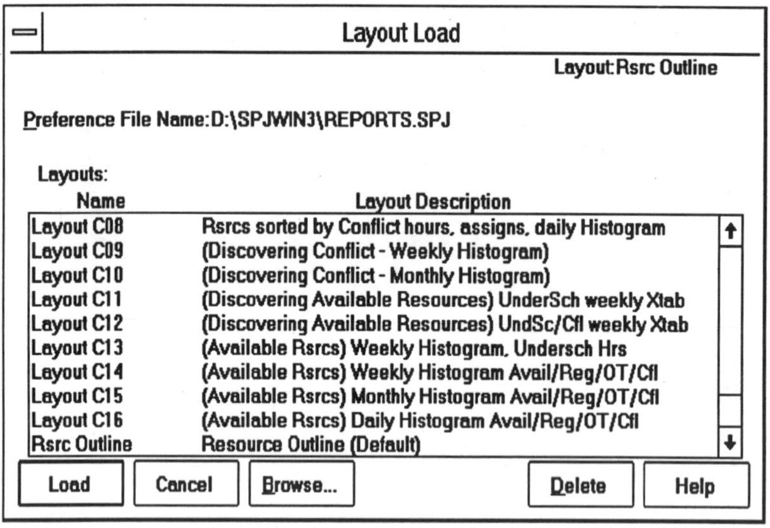

Layout Load

Layout: Rsrc Outline

Preference File Name: D:\SPJWIN3\REPORTS.SPJ

Layouts:

Name	Layout Description
Layout C08	Rsrcs sorted by Conflict hours, assigns, daily Histogram
Layout C09	(Discovering Conflict - Weekly Histogram)
Layout C10	(Discovering Conflict - Monthly Histogram)
Layout C11	(Discovering Available Resources) UnderSch weekly Xtab
Layout C12	(Discovering Available Resources) UndSc/Cfl weekly Xtab
Layout C13	(Available Rsrcs) Weekly Histogram, Undersch Hrs
Layout C14	(Available Rsrcs) Weekly Histogram Avail/Reg/OT/Cfl
Layout C15	(Available Rsrcs) Monthly Histogram Avail/Reg/OT/Cfl
Layout C16	(Available Rsrcs) Daily Histogram Avail/Reg/OT/Cfl
Rsrc Outline	Resource Outline (Default)

[Load] [Cancel] [Browse...]   [Delete] [Help]

Figure 5.6
Resource Outline standard layouts

Chapter 14 describes how you can define your own layouts but in many cases choosing from the standard layouts supplied will be sufficient, see Figure 5.6. The default layout is the standard Gantt chart plus histogram of resource hours. Once again you should not be worried by the fact that some of the layouts involve terms and concepts that we have not yet dealt with. As in the case of the Task Outline view there are many new layouts introduced in Version 3. For example layout B05, as shown in Figure 5.7, is particularly useful for examining resource allocations.

You can also control the layout of the Gantt chart using the Gantt Window Commands sub-menu in the Layout menu, see Figure 5.3. In this case you can alter the time scale of the Gantt chart and the hours scale used for the resource utilisation histogram at the bottom of the screen. The Increase Cost/Rsrc option makes the vertical scale larger by 1 unit and so increases the proportion of the total screen that the histogram occupies. Selecting Minimize Cost/Rsrc returns the histogram to its original size. Notice that the time scale on the histogram is always the same as that used on the Gantt chart.

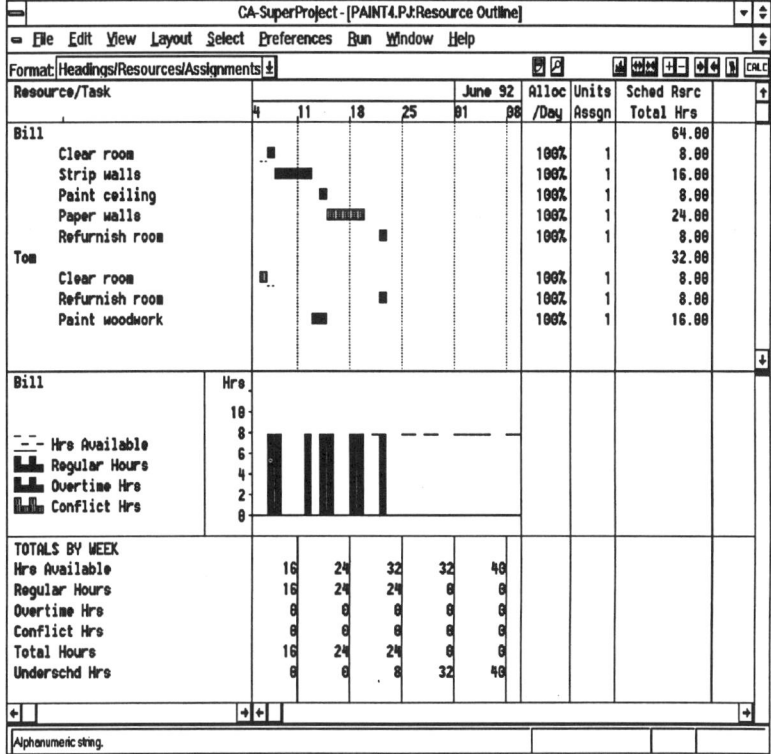

Figure 5.7
Resource Outline Layout B05

If you are using the Windows version of SuperProject you can adjust the size of the histogram window by dragging the 'split bar' that divides the scroll bar into two portions, see Figure 5.8.

The final three options in the sub-menu are unique to the Resource Outline view. If you select the Cost/Rsrc by Resource option then the histogram will automatically change to show the details of the resource associated with the line that the cursor is currently on. By contrast if you select All Cost/Rsrc then the histogram shows details of the resource's allocation to the task that the cursor is currently on or its entire allocation when the cursor is positioned on the resource itself. You should use All Cost/Rsrc when you need to see a detailed breakdown of the resource's

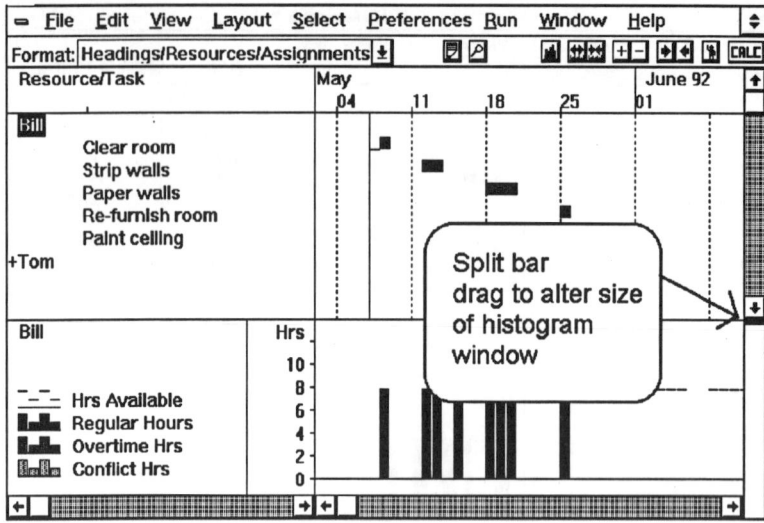

Figure 5.8
The Split bar

commitments. Finally, if you select Build Current Chart the histogram will only be updated for the current cursor line when you press Ctrl-B. This gives you control over when a new histogram is drawn, but be careful not to interpret an out of date histogram simply because you have forgotten to press Ctrl-B to update it!

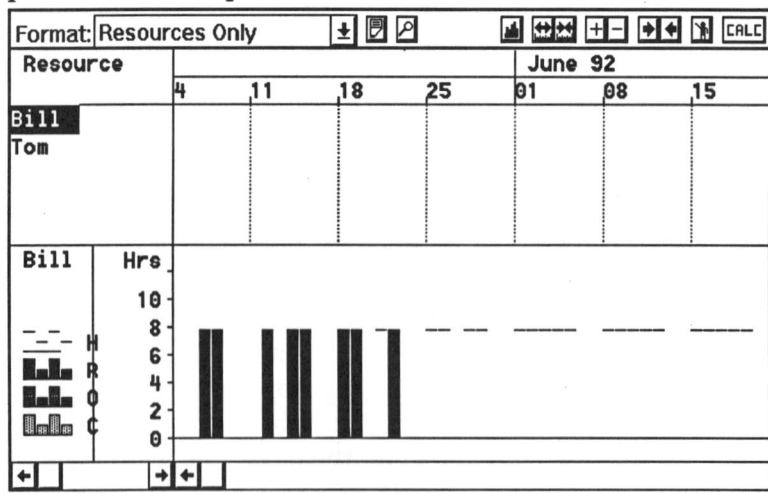

Figure 5.9
Resources Only

Resource Outline 87

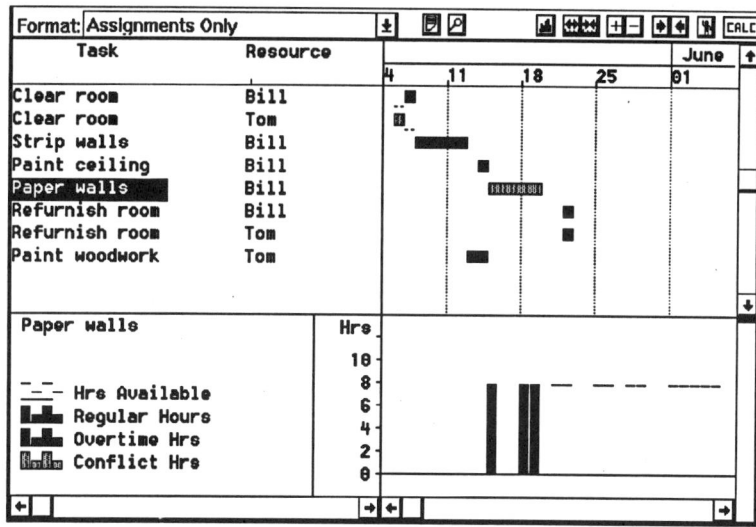

Figure 5.10
Assignments Only

As in the case of the Task Outline view you can use the Layout, View Options menu or the equivalent drop down list in the Windows version to control what information is displayed in the table. Selecting Resources Only provides a compact listing that can be used to examine resource

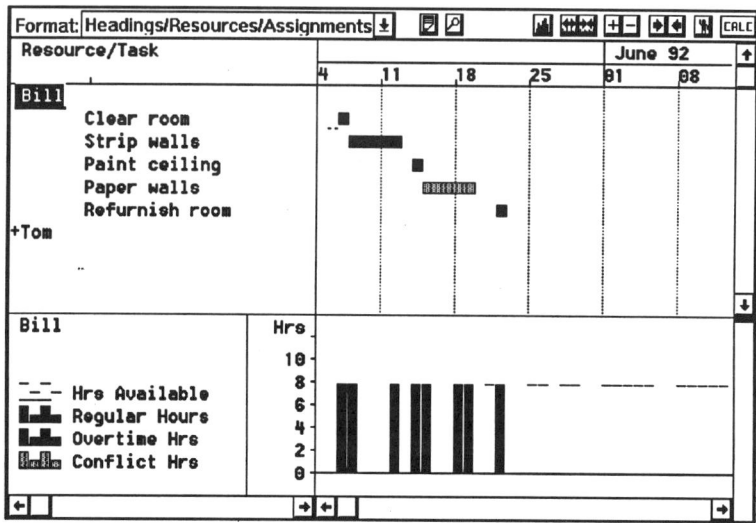

Figure 5.11
Using the hierarchy in Resource Outline view

utilisation but notice that in this case the Gantt chart will be blank! See Figure 5.9. Selecting Assignments Only allows you to study resource assignment by task, see Figure 5.10.

Notice that if you select an option that displays resources and tasks you can make use of the hierarchy to hide and expand levels in the usual way - only now the detail is organised by resource. For example, in Figure 5.11 you can see that the tasks to which Bill is assigned are expanded but Tom's are hidden.

Date Outline view

Date Outline view is the simplest of the three views discussed in this chapter. It is just a listing of tasks and resources ordered by date. You can control the fineness of

Date	Task	Resource	Schd Dur	Task ID	Scheduled Start		Scheduled Finish	
1992								
1st Qtr '92								
2nd Qtr '92								
April 92								
May 92								
Week-18								
Week-19								
	Clear room	Bill	1dy	001	07-05-92	8:00a	07-05-92	5:00p
	Clear room	Tom	1dy	001	06-05-92	8:00a	06-05-92	5:00p
	Strip walls	Bill	2dy	002	08-05-92	8:00a	12-05-92	5:00p
Week-20								
	Strip walls	Bill	2dy	002	08-05-92	8:00a	12-05-92	5:00p
	Paint ceiling	Bill	1dy	003	14-05-92	8:00a	14-05-92	5:00p
	Paint woodwork	Tom	2dy	004	13-05-92	8:00a	14-05-92	5:00p
	Let paint dry		5dy	005	15-05-92	8:00a	21-05-92	5:00p
	Paper walls	Bill	3dy	006	15-05-92	8:00a	19-05-92	5:00p
Week-21								
	Let paint dry		5dy	005	15-05-92	8:00a	21-05-92	5:00p
	Paper walls	Bill	3dy	006	15-05-92	8:00a	19-05-92	5:00p
	Refurnish room	Bill	1dy	007	22-05-92	8:00a	22-05-92	5:00p
	Refurnish room	Tom	1dy	007	22-05-92	8:00a	22-05-92	5:00p
Week-22								
June 92								
3rd Qtr '92								
4th Qtr '92								

Figure 5.12
Date Outline view

the dates listed using the same hierarchical control methods introduced for tasks i.e. demote/promote. If you place the cursor on the year and use demote i.e. (Alt) Shift-Right arrow then you will see the four quarters. A second demote shows the months, a third the weeks and finally the days. You can also select individual time units and promote or demote them to show more or less detail. You can also use + (plus) and - (minus) to expand and hide levels in the date hierarchy.

Unlike the other two views described in this chapter, there is only one default layout for the Date Outline view. There is also very little you can do by way of customisation other than alter the fineness of the date hierarchy. In Expert mode you can alter which columns of data are visible and the sort order for tasks that are listed under the same date classification - see Chapter 14.

Column widths

One aspect of layout that is too useful to leave until later is the ability to alter the width of each data column. This feature was introduced with Version 3. To alter the width of a column all you have to do is position the cursor over the dividing line between columns next to the column title. When you have positioned the cursor correctly it will change its shape to a 'split bar'. While the split bar is showing you can drag the column divider to the position you want. Notice that you can make a column too narrow to display its data properly.

Advanced layout and reporting

The use of the Layout menu is only the start of the control that you have over the way SuperProject presents information. In Chapter 14 you will discover not only how to tailor its on-screen output to your liking but also how to produce printed reports.

Key points

» SuperProject supports a number of views of the same project data.

» Each view is controlled by the information stored in a layout file. Which layout is used can be determined by using the Layout Load command.

» While layouts can be completely customised each view has a range of standard layouts supplied.

» The Gantt chart that accompanies the Task and Resource view can be altered in scale and extent.

» You can select what data is listed in both Task and Resource view choosing headings, tasks, resources or any combination.

» In Resource Outline view you can histogram the resource's total commitment or on a task-by-task basis.

» Date Outline view can be used to see a date-ordered listing broken down by quarter, month, week or day.

» You can alter the width of any data column by dragging the column dividing line at the top of the column. (This feature was introduced in Version 3.)

Chapter 6
PERT and WBS Charts

There are two standard graphical views of the project model's data - the PERT chart and the Work Breakdown Structure chart. Although these two views emphasise different features of the project it is convenient to deal with them together because they involve similar commands.

The PERT chart

The PERT (Project Evaluation and Review Technique) chart is one of the best known graphical tools used in project management. All graphical representations of a project involve some sort of network diagram that shows the relationships between tasks. A network diagram is composed of nodes and arrows connecting the nodes. In a standard PERT chart each node represents a task and the arrows represent task dependencies. This is very similar to the Gantt chart representation of the project data except that there is no attempt to represent the task duration in a PERT chart. That is, in a Gantt chart the node representing the task has a size that corresponds to its duration and a position fixed by its start date. In a PERT chart all task nodes are the same size and their position carries no meaning. In practice of course nodes are positioned so that the relationships between the tasks is clear. Indeed this is the main advantage of the PERT chart in that it reveals the relationships between the project tasks that might be difficult to see on the Gantt chart because of the additional information displayed.

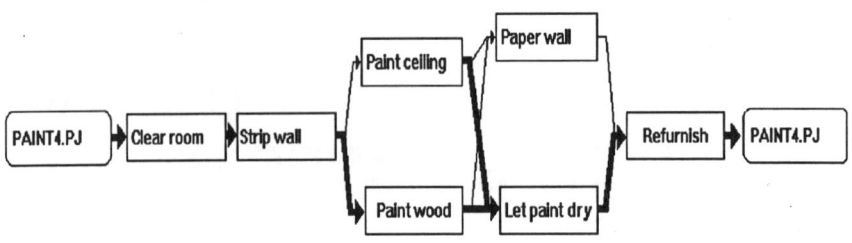

Figure 6.1
PERT chart of paint project

For example, if you look at the PERT chart of the project to paint a room before it was organised into a hierarchy then you can see clearly the relationship between the painting tasks and the subsequent tasks - see Figure 6.1. Notice also that the critical path through the project is also clear to see.

The PERT diagram can also be condensed and simplified by using the hierarchical breakdown of the project. For example, you can see the paint a room project PERT diagram using a hierarchical organisation in Figure 6.2. Notice that the levels have been hidden and the **Prepare room** and **Paint room** tasks are shown as single boxes.

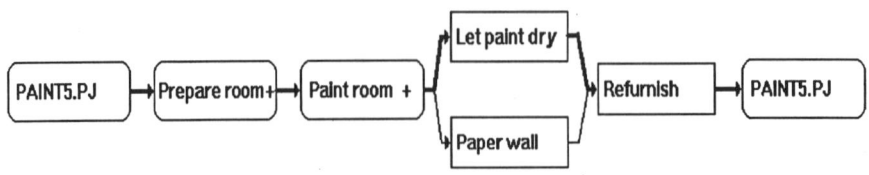

Figure 6.2
Condensed PERT chart of paint project

Notice that the lines drawn in the PERT chart to connect the tasks together are only concerned with the logical sequence of tasks. That is the links show which tasks have to follow a given task. It is quite possible for two tasks to be shown on the PERT chart as being able to run concurrently but when you view the Gantt chart they actually run sequentially. The reason for this apparent anomaly is that one of the tasks may be delayed by resource shortages and this is not a logical constraint on the scheduling of the tasks. If the resource conflict was resolved then the tasks would indeed run in parallel as indicated on the PERT chart.

SuperProject's PERT view

To see the project data as a PERT chart all you have to do is select PERT Chart view from the View menu. The PERT chart will be immediately drawn showing the currently visible headings and tasks in the Task Outline view. That is, if the tasks below a heading are hidden then only a single box will appear on the PERT chart and the sub-tasks will be hidden. Any box that represents a level that can be expanded is displayed with a small + (plus) sign in the corner. Selecting this box and pressing the + (plus) key will immediately expand it to show the sub-tasks that make it up. In the same way you can hide the sub-tasks by selecting one of them and pressing the - (minus) key.

The default layout for the PERT produces a rather large display and it is unlikely that you will be able to see it all on the screen at one go, however you can gain a good idea of the project's structure by scrolling to see the chart in sections. The default layout displays a range of information with each task box - the Task Id number, Task name, start date, and duration, see Figure 6.3.

The lowest level of tasks are drawn using rectangular boxes and higher levels in the hierarchy are drawn with rounded edges. If you expand a higher level then it is represented on the chart as two boxes - one marking the start and one marking the finish of the phase. You can think of this pair

94 *PERT and WBS Charts* Chapter 6

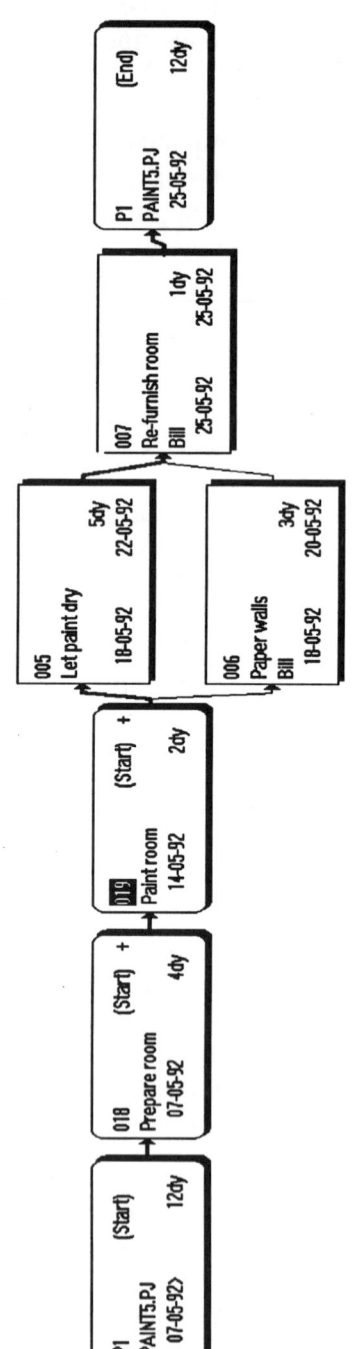

Figure 6.3

The complete default PERT diagram

Editing 95

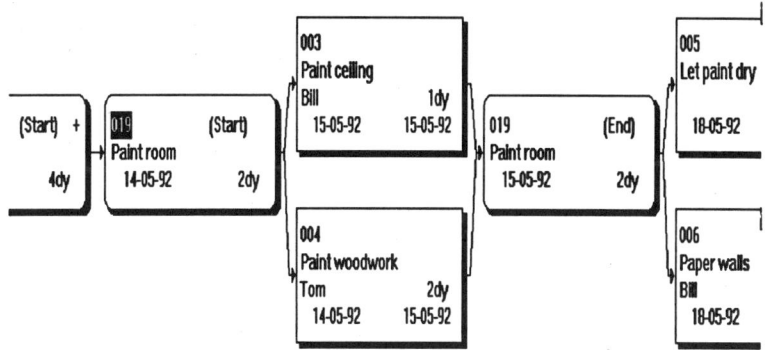

Figure 6.4
The Paint room phase expanded into its sub-tasks

of boxes as a pair of brackets enclosing the sub-tasks that make up that phase of the project, see Figure 6.4.

Editing

You can edit the project data while in PERT Chart view but in most cases it is easier to work in Task Outline view. You can introduce new tasks in the usual way - F3, or select the Create option from the Edit menu. New tasks are always

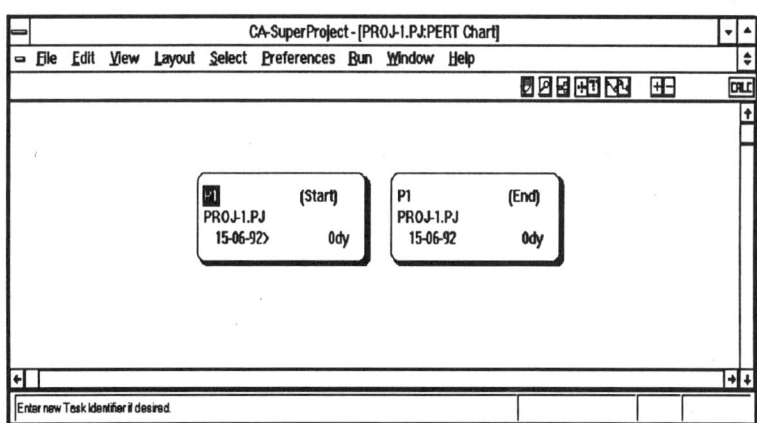

Figure 6.5
The project PERT chart before any tasks have been created

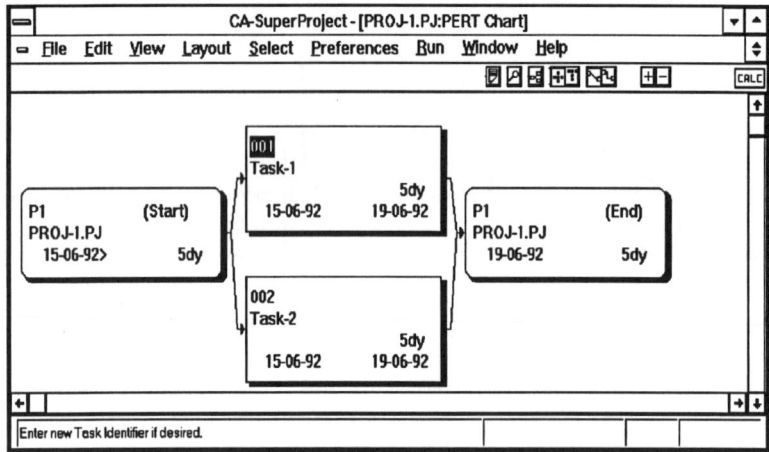

Figure 6.6
After creating two tasks

added without any constraints or links so they are added to the PERT chart as a new box connected to the start and end of the entire project. You can create links by selecting a box and dragging a link to a second box or by pressing F2 and filling in the details. Similarly tasks and and links can be deleted.

Editing a project using the PERT chart is one way of making absolutely sure that you understand the relationship between this and other views of the project data. Starting with a completely new project the PERT chart looks like

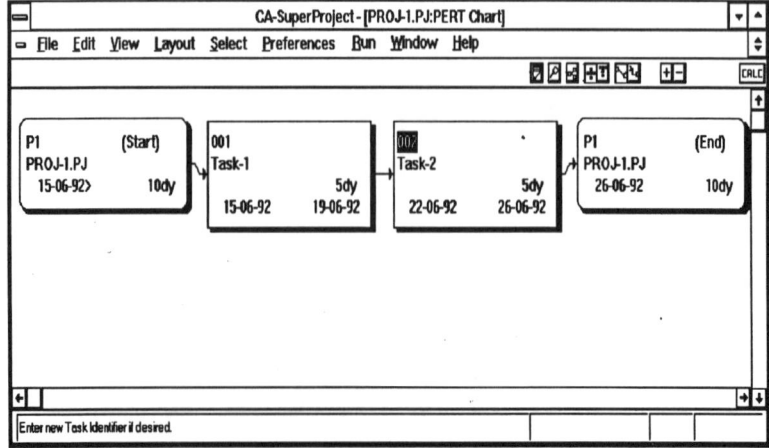

Figure 6.7
After linking Task-1 to Task-2

Figure 6.5. Creating two new tasks results in the PERT chart shown in Figure 6.6. The two new tasks are created with links between the start and finish of the project. Selecting Task-1 and dragging to Task-2 or alternatively pressing F4 and entering Task-2 creates a link that specifies that Task-1 must be completed before Task-2 can be started. This produces the PERT chart in Figure 6.7.

Layouts

As in the case of the other views, the format of the PERT Chart view is determined by layout files. In this case, however, it is much more important to investigate the standard set of supplied layouts. The reason is simply that the PERT Chart is usually so large that you have to select other layouts to view it properly on the screen. There are a number of standard layouts (see Figure 6.8) that make it easy to see the overall structure of the project, if not the fine detail. Perhaps the most compressed of all the layouts is A04 (Tiny Box Style in Version 2) - see Figure 6.9.

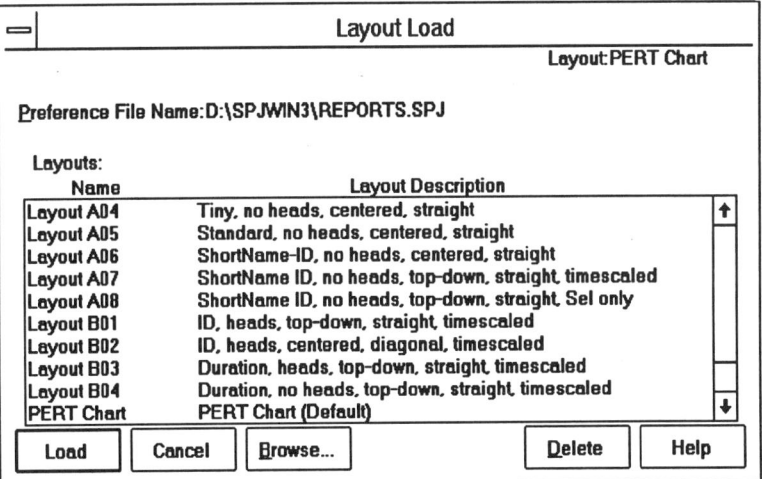

Figure 6.8
Standard PERT layouts

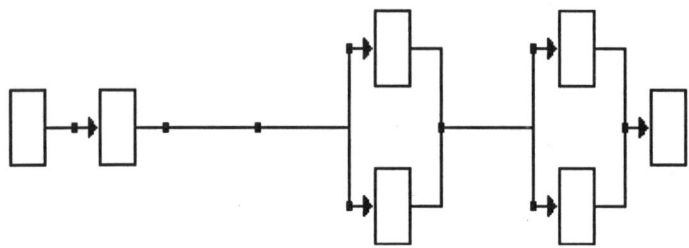

Figure 6.9
Tiny Box Style

The best way to discover the usefulness of each of the layout styles is to use Ctrl-T to move to the next layout in the list. You can carry on cycling through the possible layouts in this way until you find one that suits your purpose. It is also possible to modify a PERT chart by moving the boxes on the screen. If you accidentally disturb the order of the PERT chart use the Arrange Chart option in the Edit menu (or Ctrl-A which is equivalent).

A number of new features were added in Version 3 that makes the PERT chart even more flexible. You can opt to restrict the connecting lines between the boxes to horizontal or vertical lines only (also in Version 2.1) and to space the boxes on the horizontal axis in proportion to the time between their starting dates. You can see both of these new features used together in Figure 6.9. The PERT layout options are described in more detail in Chapter 14.

Work Breakdown Structure Chart

The Work Breakdown Structure (WBS) chart is used to display the hierarchy of tasks that make up a project. If you don't use a hierarchical decomposition of a project then the WBS chart will look very boring - being little more than a left to right listing of the tasks, see Figure 6.10. When you

Work Breakdown Structure Chart 99

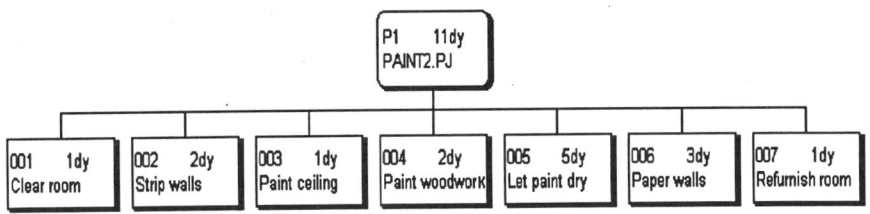

Figure 6.10
WBS Chart for a non-hierarchical project

view a WBS chart for a project that has a hierarchical structure then what you see is exactly that hierarchical structure in the form of a tree diagram, see Figure 6.11.

The WBS chart view supports the use of layout definitions in the same way that all of the other views do. The default layout shows the same sort of information that the PERT chart does - task id, task name, task duration, start date and finish date. However, you might prefer to use a more condensed view of the hierarchy as provided by the layout's Short Names Box. You can also select between a number of possible orientations for the WBS chart - top to bottom, left

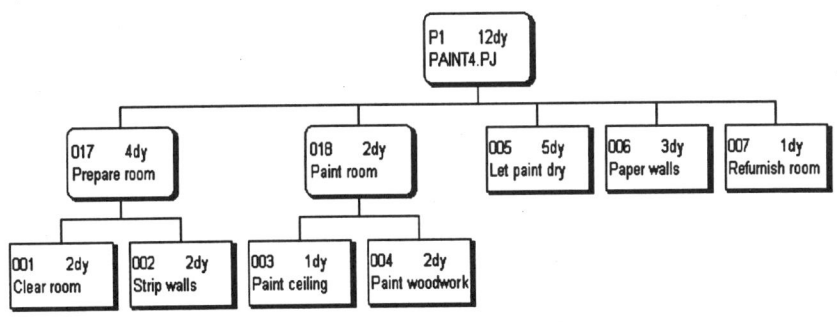

Figure 6.11
WBS Chart for a hierarchical project

to right and so on. Use whichever of these you feel most at home with. You can, of course, also use the +(plus) and -(minus) keys to collapse and expand the hierarchy shown on the chart. In addition you can also move whole sections of the hierarchy to the left, right, up or down by selecting the appropriate option from the Edit, Position sub-menu. Moving tasks to the right or left simply rearranges the chart to make it easier to understand. Moving tasks up or down is a more serious business in that it actually restructures the hierarchy. That is, it is the WBS equivalent of the promote and demote operations in Task Outline view and so should be used with great care. You can also add and delete tasks.

Using the WBS

The value of the WBS chart depends very much on how you perform the hierarchical breakdown of the project. If your breakdown reflects the work unit or group structure of the resources needed to tackle the sub-tasks gathered under a heading then the WBS is indeed a work breakdown structure. For example in the case of the Paint Room project shown in Figure 6.11 the **Clear room** and **Paint room** headings could each be taken to be the responsibility of different work units. In a larger project a layer of headings could be included that corresponded to the project's management structure. You can even incorporate additional information such as costs and WBS codes to make summarising and controlling the work structure easier. But even in this case the effectiveness of the tool depends on how you create the project hierarchy.

To give you an example of how general the WBS chart is with respect to the way it represents the project hierarchy consider Figure 6.12. This shows the management hierarchy of a company. Each management level was entered as if it was a task and the promote/demote commands were used to create the appropriate indenting to represent the hierarchy. To avoid the task durations

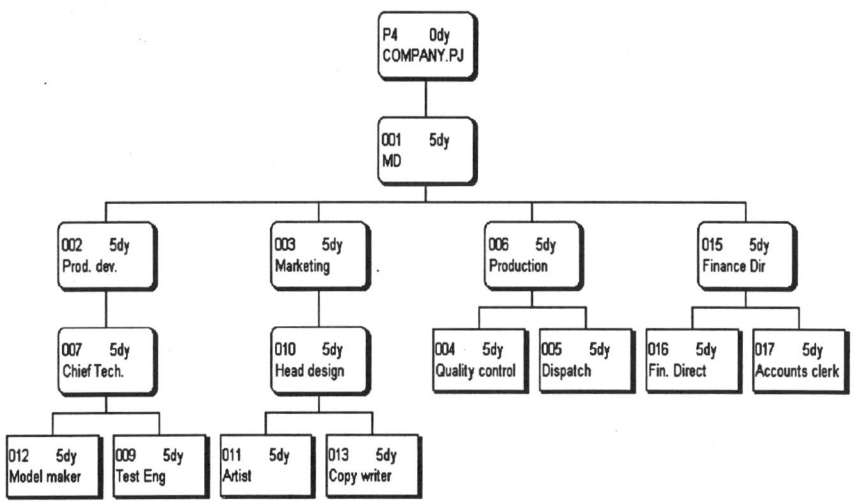

Figure 6.12
A company hierarchy

shown here appearing on the chart a suitable layout has to be defined, see Chapter 15. Although this isn't a perfect representation it does emphasise the completely general nature of the hierarchy and the WBS chart.

Key points

» The PERT chart shows the relationships and constraints that exist between the tasks that make up a project.

» The scheduled dates for a task do not affect the look of a PERT chart. If two tasks are shown as running in parallel this simply means that there are no logical constraints between them.

» You can edit the project by adding/deleting tasks and links on the PERT chart.

» There are a range of layouts that help with the sometimes difficult task of seeing the general structure of the project.

» You can expand and contract the different levels of the hierarchy within the PERT diagram.

» The WBS chart shows the pure hierarchy of the project irrespective of constraints or scheduled dates.

» The WBS chart can make use of a range of layouts.

» What the WBS chart shows depends very much on the organising principles that you have used in creating the hierarchical decomposition of the project.

» You can use the WBS chart to show almost any hierarchy of names - not just tasks within a project.

Chapter 7
Advanced Tasks

If you haven't already done so, now is the time to set SuperProject into Expert Mode using the command: Preferences,Expert Modes,Advanced Planning. All the descriptions and figures in this and later chapters use Expert rather than Beginner mode.

SuperProject's ability to help you accurately schedule and manage a project depends firstly on the realism of the project model that you build. At the moment there are many types of task and relationships between tasks that we simply have no way of including in the model without a great deal of manual intervention. For example, the only sort of constraint that we can currently apply between tasks is a Finish-to-Start link but it isn't uncommon to need to model tasks that are linked so that they always start at the same time - i.e. a Start-to-Start link. You could find a way of representing such tasks within the existing framework but you would have to sacrifice some other aspect of the model's accuracy. Fortunately there is no need to do this because SuperProject allows you to use Start-to-Start links, as well as any of a large selection of task behaviours, with respect to scheduling requirements and resource allocation.

One of the problems of having such a large range of task and resource characteristics is that it can be difficult to select the correct combination to accurately model the project. In the early stages this often doesn't matter because of the limited ways in which the project model is used. If something needs to be changed to optimise the schedule then it is usually possible to remember that a particular task has special requirements and modify the model to keep it true to life.

The danger of this 'fix-it-up' approach is that later in the life of the project you may have forgotten the details that were so fresh in your mind at the time you first created the project model. Even if this is not the case it is possible that someone else will attempt to alter the model without your deeper insights into the way it should work.

What all this means is that you should always attempt to build into your project models an adequate level of fidelity. If you succeed in doing this then you can be confident in the results that any changes to tasks or resource assignment may produce. It is also worth making the point that many such modifications will be made at short notice as you make use of the model to control the progress of the project.

Link types

The default link type between tasks is Finish-to-Start or FS. This is the type of link that is produced if you drag between two bars on the Gantt chart or if you accept the defaults in the Link dialog box. SuperProject also allows you to make links between tasks that use the start date of each task or the finish date of each task. These are called, not unreasonably, Start-to-Start (SS) and Finish-to-Finish (FF) links. To set the link type simply enter FS, SS or FF in the Type field of the Link dialog box, see Figure 7.1.

If you have already made the link between the tasks, perhaps by dragging an FS link between them on the Gantt chart, then the simplest way of setting the link type is to select the 'From' task, press F4 and edit the details that appear in the Link dialog box. Some users prefer to make

Figure 7.1
The Link dialog box

links between tasks by dragging between boxes on the Gantt chart and then edit the few link types that need changing.

The behaviour of the three types of link is a little more subtle than you might expect due to the asymmetric nature of the link. In each type of link there is a predecessor task i.e. the From task, and a successor task, i.e. the To task. In the case of an FS link this difference is obvious in that the predecessor's Finish is linked to the successor's start. However even for SS and FF links there is a difference in the way that the predecessor and successor are treated. It helps to think of a link as having a From-To direction even in cases where they appear to be symmetrical SS and FF links. The reason is that SuperProject always calculates the successor's schedule on the basis of the predecessor. For an SS link this results in the successor being able to start at the same time or after the predecessor. For an FF link the successor can finish at the same time or later than the predecessor. In other words the SS link is better thought of as a 'do not start before' link and the FF link as a 'do not finish before' link.

Notice that you cannot make a link from task A to task B then a link from B to A. Such a situation is called a circular dependency and SuperProject will display an error message if you try to, or accidentally produce, a chain of tasks that have a circular dependency on one another.

This may sound complicated but there is a great deal of regularity in the handling of links that the following summary should help make clear:

» **FS link** The predecessor task must finish before the successor can start.

» **SS link** The predecessor task must start before the successor can start.

» **FF link** The predecessor task must finish before the successor can finish.

A link example

To make sure that you understand exactly how the different types of link work you might like to try the following exercise. Starting with a new project create four tasks - Task-1 to Task-4.

Make:
>an SS link from Task-2 to Task-3,
>an FF link from Task-3 to Task-4
>a default FS link from Task-1 to Task-2.

The result, after pressing F9 to recalculate the schedule if necessary, should look like Figure 7.2. If it doesn't look like this then the chances are that you have made some of the links in the wrong order.

For example, if you reverse the SS and FF link so that Task-3 is linked to Task-2 and Task-4 is linked to Task-3 the result is as shown in Figure 7.3. As you can see this still obeys the link rules in that Task-2 doesn't start before Task-3 but it probably doesn't correspond to what was required of the SS link in this case. The lesson is that FF and SS links are not symmetrical and it does matter which task is the successor and which the predecessor.

Notice also that the reason that the difference between the two models is so noticeable is that Task-2 is FS linked to Task-1. This pushes its start date forward leaving Task-3 behind. If it was Task-3 that was FS linked to Task-1 then

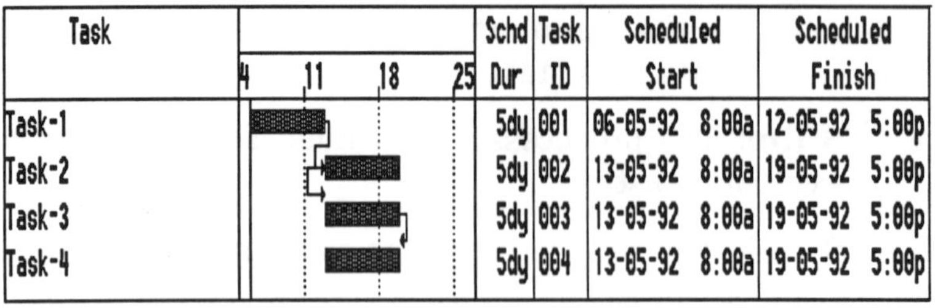

Task	4	11	18	25	Schd Dur	Task ID	Scheduled Start	Scheduled Finish
Task-1					5dy	001	06-05-92 8:00a	12-05-92 5:00p
Task-2					5dy	002	13-05-92 8:00a	19-05-92 5:00p
Task-3					5dy	003	13-05-92 8:00a	19-05-92 5:00p
Task-4					5dy	004	13-05-92 8:00a	19-05-92 5:00p

Figure 7.2
A link example

Task				Schd Dur	Task ID	Scheduled Start	Scheduled Finish
	4	11	18 25				
Task-1				5dy	001	06-05-92 8:00a	12-05-92 5:00p
Task-2				5dy	002	13-05-92 8:00a	19-05-92 5:00p
Task-3				5dy	003	06-05-92 8:00a	12-05-92 5:00p
Task-4				5dy	004	06-05-92 8:00a	12-05-92 5:00p

Figure 7.3
Changing the order of links

Task-2 would be moved forward with it. What this means is that you may not notice a logical error in the linking of tasks until you make a change in the model which brings it to light.

PERT links

The three types of links are shown on the PERT as well as the Gantt chart. Each of the link types is actually drawn from the start or finish, that is the left or right end of the boxes, as appropriate. However as the default PERT chart doesn't offset boxes that are arranged in a straight line this can be difficult to see. To make sure that you can tell the difference between the three types of link the type of connection to the box is marked with an 's' for Start and 'f' for Finish, see Figure 7.4.

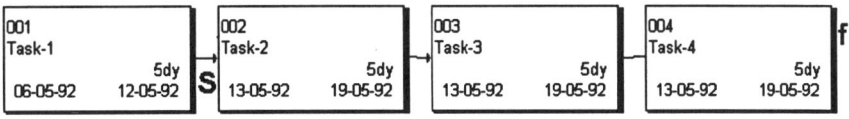

Figure 7.4
Links on a PERT chart

108 *Advanced Tasks* Chapter 7

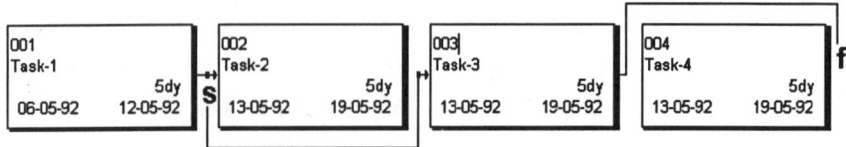

Figure 7.5
Links on a PERT chart using straight connections

A better way of seeing FF and SS links is to select the 'straight links' option introduced in Version 3. You can do this by clicking on the icon just before the plus and minus. By using only horizontal and vertical connecting lines the links make a detour around the PERT boxes and so are visible, see Figure 7.5.

Lag

As well as the strictly logical relationships between task finish and starts, a constraint very often takes the form of a given period of time that must elapse between tasks. For example, it might be that a soak test has to be conducted on some electronic assembly for a given number of days before it is built into the next module. In this case the two tasks are linked by an FS relationship but there is also a specific lag between the end of the 'build assembly' task and the start of the 'incorporate into module' task. One way of dealing with this problem is to create a dummy task that has a duration equal to the lag between the two real tasks. This is the approach taken in the Paint a room project where the **Let paint dry** task was used to create a lag.

Although the additional task method can be used to good effect, it is often better to recognise a delay between tasks as a lag rather than as a dummy task that needs no resources. You can enter a lag in days, hours or even as percentage of the task's duration in the Link dialog box as shown in Figure 7.1. Each link from a task can have a different lag defined so it is possible to set up complex relationships with more than one task.

How a lag is treated depends on the type of link:

» **FS link** The lag is added to the finish date to determine the start date of the next task.

» **SS link** The lag is added to the start date of the predecessor to give the successor's start date.

» **FF link** The lag is added to the finish date of the predecessor to give the finish date of the successor.

These are very reasonable rules as long as you think of the lag as being a delay built into the link between the two task dates. See Figure 7.6 for an example of each type of link with delay.

Version 3 allows you to specify negative lags. These can be used for example, to start a task a given time before another finishes.

One of the problems with lags built into links is that they are specified in terms of working days. That is if you specify a lag of 1 day and the next day is a weekend then the lag

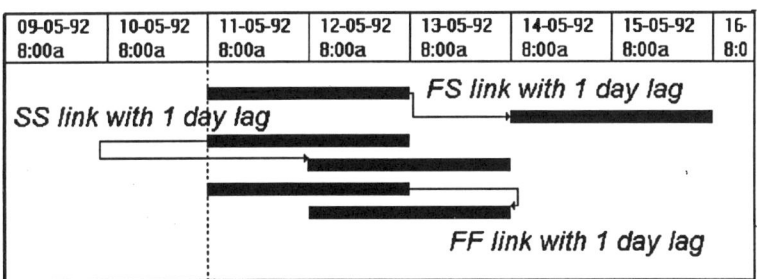

Figure 7.6
Links with delays

will still be applied on the Monday, making Tuesday the start of the next task. Equally if a resource is unavailable for the start of a task the lag will still be applied to the start of the already delayed task. For example, if you specify a lag of 3 days and a resource allocated to the task is unavailable for 3 days then the total delay to the task will be 6 days. In other words, the lag is added to the starting date of a task that would result if it were scheduled without the lag.

This makes a using a lag suitable for modelling a delay of a given number of working days. For example, if you don't want to follow up a client contact until 10 working days have elapsed then specify an FS lag of 10 days. However, specifying a lag can be an unsuitable model for processes that depend on elapsed time, such as drying or curing, where a work or non-work day should be treated equally. The error in ignoring non-workdays may be reasonable as long as the lag time is large and estimated in working weeks. For example, if the time to cure concrete is specified as 4 working weeks or 20 days then at least weekends will not cause an unnecessary delay in starting the next task. A better model for a strictly elapsed time process such as drying is to use an Elaspsed time task - see Chapter 8.

It is also important not to use a lag to model a delay due to the unavailability of a resource. For example, if the next task cannot start because a resource has a day off or is being used somewhere else then mark the day as a holiday on the resource calendar rather than specify a 1 day lag. The effect will be the same on the schedule but only by marking the resource holiday can you hope to understand, and perhaps modify, the situation in the future. The only situation in which a lag could be used to model a resource unavailability is if the resource needs x working days recuperation after completing one task and starting the next one!

Task schedule type

So far it has been assumed that all tasks should be started as soon as possible and any delays are undesirable. This sort of task is referred to as an As Soon As Possible or ASAP task. Most, but not all, tasks within a project are ASAP tasks and SuperProject provides a range of alternative task scheduling types. To make use of these you have to move into Expert mode.

If you are in Expert mode Task Outline view and move the cursor across the data columns you will eventually reach the Task Type column. This offers a list of task types from which you can select an appropriate choice. The task types fall into two groups - general conditions and 'must' dates restrictions. The first group is:

» **ASAP** - As Soon As Possible. The task is scheduled as soon as possible taking account of links and resource availability.

» **ALAP** - As Late As Possible. The task is scheduled to start as late as possible but without delaying the overall project. What this means is that if the task is on the critical path the ALAP setting will not have any effect. If the task is not on the critical path then its start will be delayed so that there is no gap between the task finish and the next task.

It is interesting to compare the difference between an ASAP and an ALAP task. If you look at Figure 7.7 you can see quite clearly the effect of changing a task's type from ASAP to ALAP. In the upper part of the diagram the task is scheduled as an ASAP task. The critical path is determined by Task-3. Task-2 starts immediately after Task-1 ends and the 'spare' time at the end of Task-2 is shown as 'float'. In the lower part of the diagram Task-2 is ALAP and in this case its start is delayed as late as possible without increasing the total duration of the project.

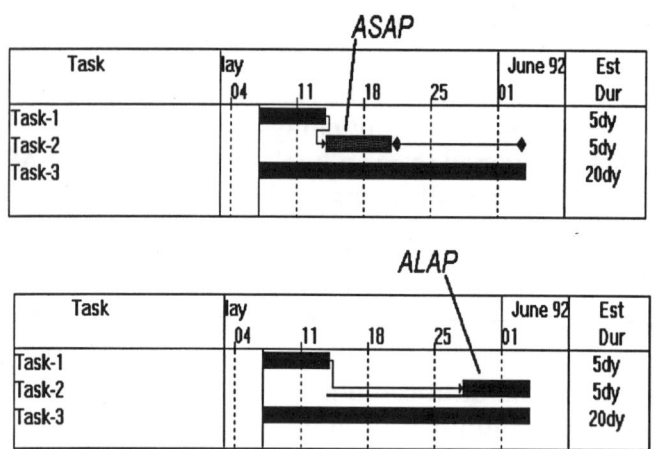

Figure 7.7
ASAP v ALAP tasks

A typical ALAP task is the ordering of material or resources that are needed for a subsequent task. By making this an ALAP task the material or resource is kept in store or is unused for the minimum time.

Just in time

An interesting application of the ALAP combined with a link-specified lag is in the application of 'Just-In-Time' inventory management. The JIT principle is that stock is ordered from suppliers so that it arrives as it is needed. This of course has the advantage of minimising the average holding of stock items. The method works as long as a good control method is used to ensure that orders are placed in time to ensure delivery when the items are required.

You can model a JIT management system using SuperProject by making the event of ordering the item an ALAP task with 0 days duration and then link it to the task that uses the item with a lag that is the delivery time in working days.

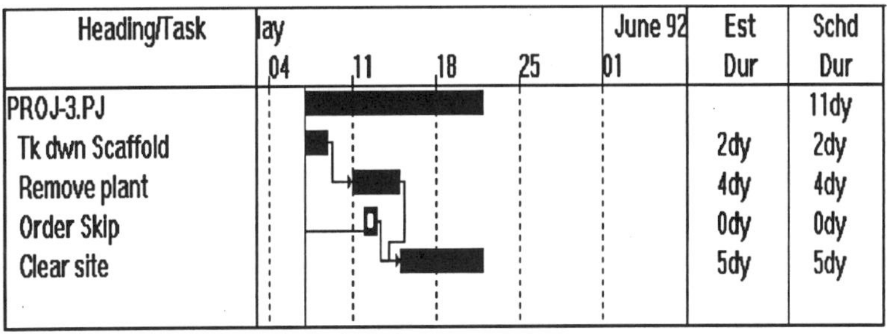

Heading/Task	ay 04	11	18	25	June 92 01	Est Dur	Schd Dur
PROJ-3.PJ							11dy
Tk dwn Scaffold						2dy	2dy
Remove plant						4dy	4dy
Order Skip						0dy	0dy
Clear site						5dy	5dy

Figure 7.8
Using ALAP and lag to order resources

For example, suppose a project needs to hire a waste disposal skip to arrive on the day that site clearance starts. If the delivery time for a skip from the order being received is 3 working days then the lag between the **Order skip** task and the **Clear site** task should be set to 3 days. You can see this idea in use in Figure 7.8. Notice the way that **Order skip** is delayed until the point where it results in the skip being delivered just in time to start **Clear site** which is an ASAP task FS linked to the **Remove plant** task. It doesn't matter how you change the project model, the use of the ALAP task and the lag will always produce the correct schedule. The only potential for error is the late delivery of the skip!

Also notice that the **Order skip** task is shown on the Gantt chart using a diamond symbol. The reason for this is that a task with 0 duration is referred to as a Milestone task. Milestones are normally used to mark the completion or achievement of some project sub-goal or target. In this case the 0 duration task has a rather more important role than just a symbolic marker - it initiates an action.

Must dates

The second group of task types, after ASAP and ALAP, involve the specification of date constraints on the scheduling. You can make use of the the symbols =, < and > to impose restrictions on scheduled dates. There are two special columns relating to must dates - Must Start and

Must Finish (Expert mode only). You can use these columns to enter dates and one of the constraint symbols.

For example, if you wanted a task to start after the 10-05-92 you would enter 10-05-92> in the Must Start column. You can think of >, the greater than sign, as meaning 'on or after'. In the same way <, the less than sign, means 'on or before' and the =, equals sign means on the given date. By using the Must Start and Must Finish dates in combination with <, > and = it is possible to specify a wide range of conditions that the scheduled date must meet. For example, if you set the Must Start date to 11-05-92> and the Must Finish date to 29-05-92< then the task has to be scheduled within this period of time.

Entering Must dates can be quite difficult. It can be made much easier by realising that the date column is divided into three parts - the date, the constraint symbol and the time. If you place the cursor on the date then pressing tab or right arrow moves the cursor to the constraining symbol and then to the time. If you you enter a constraint symbol in the correct position and then press Enter then SuperProject will transfer the current scheduled start or finish date, as appropriate to the column. You can use this as the basis for editing or just accept it if it is appropriate.

As an alternative way of entering Must dates you can make use of the options in the Task Type column. These take the form of English descriptions of the type of constraint and selecting one of them places the correct symbols in the Must date columns. For example, if you select Start After in the Task Type column then the current scheduled date is inserted into the Must Start column along with the > symbol. It is important to notice that selecting the Work Between option is the only way you can specify a period of time that the task should be scheduled in. The reason for this is that SuperProject will not let you enter both a Must Start and Must Finish date directly as a precaution against errors.

The complete set of options are:

» Must start/finish on   *date*=
» Must start/finish before *date*<
» Must start/finish after   *date*>
» Work between   start *date*> and finish *date*<

The Must date symbols <, > and = also appear in the scheduled start and finish date columns to make sure that you know that there is a constraint on the scheduling.

You can also set a Must Start on date by double clicking on a bar in the Gantt chart and then dragging its left-hand end. The date to which you drag the Gantt bar becomes the Must Start on date. After dragging a bar like this the only way that you can change its Must date constraint is to select a different task type. Simply deleting the = sign next to the date will not work.

Clearly, Must dates are important in modelling many projects. They allow you to build in many realistic constraints on when a task can or should happen. The only danger is in making too much use of them. Each Must date constraint that you add to a project makes it that much more difficult for SuperProject to schedule it efficiently. You can even add so many date constraints that it becomes impossible to arrive at a consistent schedule at all!

The project start and finish date

One fundamental use of a Must date is to set the proposed start date for the project. When you create a new project the Must Start date is set to the current date, i.e. today, with an on or later than symbol. This simply means that the first project task has to be scheduled to start today or, if there are other constraints, later.

The simplest way to modify the proposed start date is to use the Project Details view. If you enter a date into the Start field then SuperProject will insert it as 'must start on or later' start date for the project heading. The project will then be rescheduled and the project finish date field will be automatically filled in. Notice that any Must dates that you have entered will not be altered by changing the project's start date and this can result in error messages to the effect that the start date is that the Must dates cannot be honoured. In this case you either have to change the start date or edit the must dates.

As well as being able to set a project start date and have SuperProject work out the finish date you can set a desired finish date and allow SuperProject to work out the required start date. All you have to do is enter the finish date in the Project Details view and the appropriate start date will be automatically entered. Notice that all that happens is that the project finish date is entered into the Must Finish column as a 'on or before' date.

If you are working in Beginner mode then you can set the project start date by editing the date shown in Scheduled Start which sets the Must Start date automatically.

The Civic Xmas tree

Most projects are complex because they have a great many inter-related tasks and resource assignments and it is the total number of things to be considered that makes management difficult. In this example, the complexity is generated by the number of constraints to be met. The project itself may be small but it is still surprisingly complicated.

The project is to arrange the setting up and switching on of the Civic Xmas tree. The tasks are:

        Meeting of Xmas tree committee
        Order tree
        Tree arrives
        Clear site
        Test decorations

The Civic Xmas tree

Set-up of tree
Decorate tree
Switch on party

This seems simple enough but there are some date constraints to take into account. The committee can only meet in the week 16-11-92 to the 20-11-92 and the tree must be switched on in the first week in December i.e. 01-12-92 to 04-12-92. The added complication is that the tree takes 5 working days to be delivered from the nursery and it must not be left standing around before being set up at the site.

If you enter the task names, suitably abbreviated, and move to the Must dates columns you should see something like Figure 7.9. Notice that you will not be able to see the Task Type and Must dates columns on the screen at once, as shown in the figure, unless you load layout B08. If you are using Version 2 or earlier then you will have to customise the Task Outline layout to achieve the same result - something which is not described until Chapter 14. As well as the specified Must dates, the project start date has also been constrained to be on or after the 16-11-92.

The next step is to enter the task durations as shown in Figure 7.10. If you examine the resulting schedule, after recalculation if necessary, you should see a Gantt chart displayed in Figure 7.10. This schedule is quite reasonable in that the Must dates are easily satisfied for the tasks that are so constrained. However, the project model isn't of much

Heading/Task	Task Type	Task ID	Must Start	Must Finish
XMAS.PJ		P8	16-11-92> 8:00a	
Meeting	Work Between	009	16-11-92> 8:00a	20-11-92< 5:00p
Order Tree	ASAP	001		
Tree arives	ASAP	035		
Setup Tree	ASAP	003		
Decorate Tree	ASAP	002		
Clear site for tree	ASAP	004		
Test decorations	ASAP	005		
Switch on party	Work Between	033	01-12-92> 8:00a	04-12-92< 5:00p

Figure 7.9
Task Types and Must dates

118 *Advanced Tasks* Chapter 7

Task	Resource	mber				December 9	Est Dur	Schd Dur
		09	16	23	30	07		
XMAS.PJ			▓▓▓▓▓					11dy
Meeting			▪				1dy	1dy
Order Tree			▫				0dy	0dy
Tree arives			▫				0dy	0dy
Setup Tree			▪				1dy	1dy
Decorate Tree			▓				2dy	2dy
Clear site for tree			▪				1dy	1dy
Test decorations			▓				2dy	2dy
Switch on party						▫	0dy	0dy

Figure 7.10
The Gantt chart before linking

use because it doesn't yet take into account the delivery time for the tree and there are no suitable links between the tasks.

The links that have to be entered are:

        Order tree -> Meeting SS link
        Order tree -> Tree arrives FS link 5 day lag
        Tree arrives -> Set-up tree FS link
        Set-up tree -> Decorate tree FS link
        Clear site -> Set-up tree FS link
        Test decorations -> Decorate tree FS link
        Decorate tree -> Switch on party FS link

If you enter all of these links and recalculate the project you should see the Gantt chart shown in Figure 7.11. If you examine this project plan you will find that it satisfies all of the constraints. The meeting and the switch on party are on the first possible day of their respective ranges and the tree is delivered in time for the subsequent tasks. However, the project model fails because the tree is ordered on the 16th, delivered on the 20th and finished on the 25th. It then waits around five days until the 1st before the lighting up party. What is needed is a schedule that minimises the time between completing the tree and the party.

Heading/Task	ber				Decemb	Est Dur	Schd Dur
	09	16	23	30	0		
XMAS1.PJ			▓▓▓▓▓▓▓▓▓▓▓▓				11dy
Meeting		▓				1dy	1dy
Order Tree		▫				0dy	0dy
Tree arives			▫			0dy	0dy
Setup Tree			▓			1dy	1dy
Decorate Tree				▓▓▓		2dy	2dy
Clear site for tree		▓				1dy	1dy
Test decorations		▓▓▓				2dy	2dy
Switch on party					▫	0dy	0dy

Figure 7.11
Gantt chart after linking the tasks

This requirement could be built into the model by making **Decorate tree** an ALAP task but this has the undesirable effect of leaving the tree standing undecorated for five days! The correct solution is to make the **Order tree** task ALAP. With this change the schedule becomes that shown in Figure 7.12. This seems very reasonable as now the meeting is scheduled for the 19th, when the tree is ordered, and it arrives on the 25th. This gives just enough time to complete the project in time for a 1st December switch on.

The only anomaly is the way that the site is cleared and the decorations are tested on the 16th. The problem with this is that **Clear site for tree** and **Test decorations** should be in some sense 'close' to the setting up of the tree. Otherwise the site would probably have to be cleared again and the decorations retested. It isn't difficult to see that both of these tasks should be ALAP as well. With these changes the final project model, and its schedule, can be seen in Figure 7.13. In this case everything happens at a reasonable time to ensure that the switch on party is on the 1st December.

The Xmas tree project model is quite sophisticated but it still doesn't completely capture the essence of the real project. To find out in what respects it is deficient all you have to do is change the week that the committee meeting

120 *Advanced Tasks*   *Chapter 7*

Heading/Task	Dece 16 23 30	Est Dur	Schd Dur	Task ID	Scheduled Start
XMAS1.PJ			11dy	P8	16-11-92 8:00a
Meeting		1dy	1dy	009	19-11-92> 8:00a
Order Tree		0dy	0dy	001	19-11-92 8:00a
Tree arives		0dy	0dy	035	25-11-92 5:00p
Setup Tree		1dy	1dy	003	26-11-92 8:00a
Decorate Tree		2dy	2dy	002	27-11-92 8:00a
Clear site for tree		1dy	1dy	004	16-11-92 8:00a
Test decorations		2dy	2dy	005	16-11-92 8:00a
Switch on party		0dy	0dy	033	01-12-92> 8:00a

Figure 7.12
The schedule after changing Order Tree to ALAP

can be held in to 23-11-92 to 27-11-92. In this case the meeting is scheduled for the 23rd but ordering the Xmas tree is still scheduled for the 19th! The reason is that the SS link from Order tree to the Meeting task allows the meeting to happen later than the ordering of the tree. In other words the link doesn't specify that the two tasks should happen at the same time. You might think that the solution is to use a single task for both activities - a combined meeting and order tree task. This certainly keeps

Heading/Task	Dece 16 23 30	Est Dur	Schd Dur	Task ID	Scheduled Start
XMAS1.PJ			8dy	P8	19-11-92 8:00a
Meeting		1dy	1dy	009	19-11-92> 8:00a
Order Tree		0dy	0dy	001	19-11-92 8:00a
Tree arives		0dy	0dy	035	25-11-92 5:00p
Setup Tree		1dy	1dy	003	26-11-92 8:00a
Decorate Tree		2dy	2dy	002	27-11-92 8:00a
Clear site for tree		1dy	1dy	004	25-11-92 8:00a
Test decorations		2dy	2dy	005	25-11-92 8:00a
Switch on party		0dy	0dy	033	01-12-92> 8:00a

Figure 7.13
After changing Clear site and Test decorations to ALAP

Heading/Task		16	23	Decemb 30	8	Est Dur	Schd Dur	Task ID	Scheduled Start
XMAS1.PJ			▓▓▓▓▓			8dy		P8	23-11-92⟩ 8:00a
Meeting			▫			1dy	1dy	009	23-11-92⟩ 8:00a
Order Tree			▫			0dy	0dy	001	23-11-92 8:00a
Tree arives				▫		0dy	0dy	035	27-11-92 5:00p
Setup Tree				▓		1dy	1dy	003	30-11-92 8:00a
Decorate Tree				▓▓		2dy	2dy	002	01-12-92 8:00a
Clear site for tree				▪		1dy	1dy	004	27-11-92 8:00a
Test decorations				▓▓		2dy	2dy	005	27-11-92 8:00a
Switch on party					▫	0dy	0dy	033	02-12-92⟩ 5:00p

Figure 7.14
The revised schedule

the two together but now you cannot specify both a Work Between task type and an ALAP task type.

A sort of solution can be obtained by reversing the precedence of the link from:

> Order Tree -> Meeting

to:

> Meeting -> Order Tree

This makes sure that the **Order Tree** event cannot occur before the meeting. In this case the schedule that results can be seen in Figure 7.14. It is still quite reasonable only now the meeting has to be on the first possible day, i.e. the 23rd November, and the switch on party is on the second possible day, i.e. 2nd December. Notice that changing the precedence of the tasks in the link between **Meeting** and **Order Tree** isn't a complete solution because there are now situations in which the meeting will be scheduled before the ordering of the tree. The point is that SuperProject doesn't have a way of exactly modelling the project constraints, i.e. a single task that has a work between and an ALAP condition. The moral of the story is that you can only trust your project model's scheduling if it is accurate - and most models are only approximations to reality. You must rely on your own intelligence to provide the necessary additional behaviour.

Key points

» Links between tasks can be any one of three types:
    FS - Finish-to-Start
    SS - Start-to-Start
    FF- Finish-to-Finish.

» All links have an implied direction **From** one task, the predecessor, **To** another, the successor. A link affects the predecessor and successor tasks differently in that a successor can never be scheduled earlier than a predecessor.

» You can build a lag, specified in working days, into a link.

» Tasks can be ASAP or ALAP or constrained to be scheduled in particular date ranges.

» The date ranges are specified using the symbols = for 'on a specified date', > for 'on or before' and < for 'on of after'.

» It is important to ensure a project model has as much correspondence with the nature of the real project's task types as possible.

Chapter 8
Resource and Task Types

Using a range of task and link types to build an accurate project model is only half of the picture. The other half relates to the accurate modelling of resources and the effect that resource assignment has on task duration. There is no doubt that tasks behave very differently to changes in resource allocation. For example, some tasks show no change in the time to complete if you allocate more resources and others take less time. Obviously in reality the behaviour of tasks to the allocation of more resources can be complex. It is well known that the time to complete a programming task does become less the more programmers allocated to the task. It is equally well known that beyond a certain point the effect of the additional allocation becomes less and might even turn round and increase the task duration. Such subtleties are generally not built into project models for many reasons and simple task/resource behaviour is generally sufficient.

Modelling

By building in the effect that resources have on tasks, you can use the model to see what happens to the project plan when you alter resource assignments. You can even ask SuperProject to modify resource assignments automatically to correct problems. However, notice that you do not have to model resources this accurately if you only want to see the effect of altering task durations. It might be that you consider task durations as the fundamentals of your model and control the real project to produce those task durations in ways which are external to the model. For example, in situations where management control was limited to specifying task durations, modelling resources would be pointless. It might be quite sufficient to pass on to a sub-contractor the required task duration and let him solve the resource allocation problem needed to meet the schedule. In other words, when the resources and their allocation are beyond your control there is no point in including them in your project model. Under such circumstances task durations become the fundamental quantities.

Scheduled duration

SuperProject allows you to work with five different types of task/resource characteristics. The key to understanding the way that these work is to realise that there are two types of time estimate that can influence a task's scheduled duration - the task's estimated duration and the scheduled resource hours. There may be a list of scheduled resource hours associated with a task depending on how many resources have been allocated to it. The difference between the types of task/resource characteristics lies in how the resource hours alters the scheduled task duration. This picture is slightly complicated in that in most cases the allocated resource hours are calculated from the estimated task duration. That is:

    Estimated task duration ->
        Resource allocation in hours ->
            Scheduled task duration

For example, you type in an estimated task duration of 2 days and the resource's allocated hours are calculated to be 2 days times the number of hours in the resource's standard day which by default is 8 hours - giving 16 hours. Depending on the type of task, this requirement for 16 hours of resource time might then have an effect on the scheduled task duration.

At this point you might be a little puzzled. As the number of hours that the resource is allocated is calculated from the estimated duration, how can this result in a different scheduled duration? That is, if the estimated duration is 2 days and the allocated resource time is 16 hours surely this is just another way of saying 2 days? The answer is that the resource allocation has to be interpreted as a requirement for 16 hours of resource time before the task can be completed. If the resource calendar shows that there is a resource holiday or short time working on any of the days within the scheduled period then the task's scheduled duration could be longer than estimated.

To summarise:

» Estimated task duration is used to calculate resource hours need and this in turn is used to discover the number of calendar days needed to complete the task.

Task options

Of the five types of Task/Resource characteristic:

>   Resource driven
>   Workday driven
>   Effort driven
>   Elapsed
>   Span

only the first three - resource, workday and effort driven - are affected by the availability of resources and these are worth examining in detail.

Resource driven

A resource driven task is the default and it is the type of task that has been used in examples and descriptions in all previous chapters. A resource driven task can finish early or late because of the availability of the resources allocated to it.

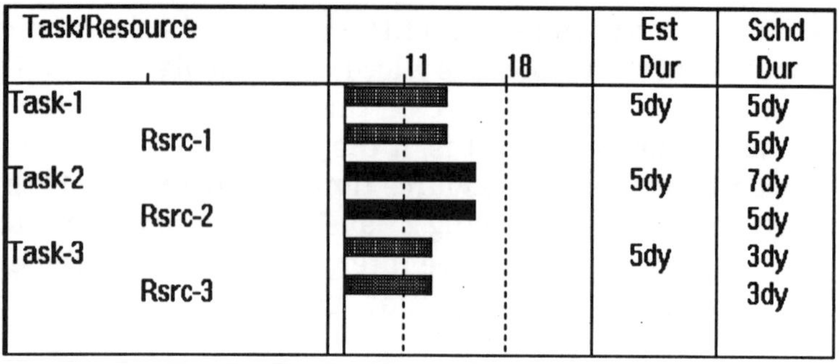

Task/Resource	11	18	Est Dur	Schd Dur
Task-1			5dy	5dy
Rsrc-1				5dy
Task-2			5dy	7dy
Rsrc-2				5dy
Task-3			5dy	3dy
Rsrc-3				3dy

Figure 8.1
Three resource driven tasks with the same estimated duration

For example, if you look at Figure 8.1 you can see three resource driven tasks each with a different resource allocated to them. Each has the same estimated duration of 5 days and so each resource is allocated to its task for the same 40 hours.

In the case of Task-1, Rsrc-1 is available for 8 hours on each of the project working days and so Task-1's scheduled duration is also 5 days.

In the case of Task-2, Rsrc-2 is taking a long weekend and there are two resource holidays marked on its calendar. To obtain the full 40 hours of resource time it takes 7 project work days and so the scheduled duration is longer than the estimated duration.

Finally, in the case of Task-3, Rsrc-3 is available for 16 hours on two of the days within the task's duration. The result is that the 40 resource hours can be found in only 3 project working days making the scheduled duration shorter than the estimated duration.

In the case of resource driven tasks, think of the estimated duration as the resource hours needed to complete the task.

Workday driven

A workday driven task is a sort of halfway house between a task that is influenced by resource and one that is scheduled in terms of project workdays. For a workday driven task the estimated duration is taken to be the scheduled duration, unless a resource allocation cannot be met in that time. That is, resource availability can make the scheduled duration longer but not shorter. You should use a workday driven task when the duration of the task is governed by resources and factors that are not included in your project model. In this case one of the allocated resources could still lengthen the task's duration but even if all of the allocated resources could complete in less than the estimated duration, some other factor not in the model would still make the task take its estimated duration.

If you look at Figure 8.2 you can see the effect of making a task workday driven. The resource calendars are the same as in Figure 8.1 i.e. Rsrc-1 is fully available, Rsrc-2 has two resource days holiday and Rsrc-3 works two double length days. You can see that the resource availability is reflected in the respective Gantt chart bars and in each resource's scheduled hours. However, only the unavailability of the resource in the case of Task-2 has any effect on the scheduled task duration, and it results in lengthening it.

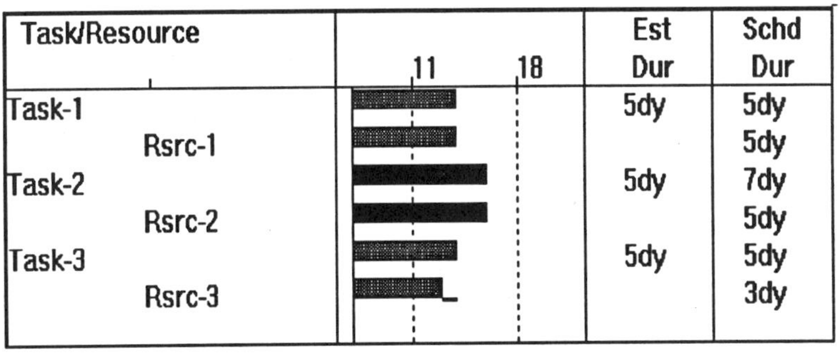

Task/Resource	11	18	Est Dur	Schd Dur
Task-1			5dy	5dy
Rsrc-1				5dy
Task-2			5dy	7dy
Rsrc-2				5dy
Task-3			5dy	5dy
Rsrc-3				3dy

Figure 8.2
Three workday driven tasks with the same estimated duration

Effort driven

Effort driven is the most complicated of the resource influenced task types. In the case of an effort driven task the estimated duration of the task is taken to be the total resource requirement of all the resources allocated. For example, if the estimated task duration is 2 days then this is equivalent to 2 days times the number of hours in the standard working day, i.e. a total of 16 resource hours. So far this looks identical to a resource driven task but notice that the 16 hours now represents the total number of hours that all the resources assigned to the task must work to complete it. You can see the difference quite clearly in Figure 8.3. Task-1 and Task-2 are both effort driven and have the same estimated duration of 6 days. In both cases this means that a total of 6 times 8, i.e. 48 resource hours. Task-1 has a single resource assigned to it which is available for 8 hours per day and so it has a scheduled duration of 6 days. Task-2 has two resources assigned to it both of which are available for 8 hours per day and so it has a scheduled duration of 3 days. That is, assigning more resources to an effort driven task decreases its scheduled duration - as long as the assigned resources are available.

It is a mistake to assume that assigning more resources to an effort driven task always results in a shorter scheduled duration. The same method of scheduling is used for all SuperProject task types and this means that an effort driven task can be slowed down by a resource which is unavailable. For example, if you have a 5-day effort driven task it will be completed in 5 days if a single resource is

Task	Resource	08	15	Est Dur	Schd Dur
Task-1				6dy	6dy
	Rsrc-1				6dy
Task-2				6dy	3dy
	Rsrc-1				3dy
	Rsrc-2				3dy

Figure 8.3
Assigning resources to an effort driven task reduces its scheduled duration

assigned to it that is available 8 hours a day for 5 consecutive days. If you allocate a second resource to the task in an attempt to reduce the scheduled duration then the total number of resources hours needed, 40, will be split between the two resources making a demand of 20 hours from each. At best this will reduce the scheduled duration to just less than 3 days but if the second resource is on holiday for the first 2 days the scheduled duration will still be 5 days. Even worse, if the second resource is on holiday for the whole working week the scheduled duration increases to 8 days. However, notice that each of the resources still only works for 20 hours. You can see that by a careful choice of resource calendar you can make any amount of extra resource assignment increase the scheduled duration of the effort driven task!

The key point is that the only difference between an effort driven task and a resource driven task is that the estimated resource hours are treated as the total number of resource hours.

Once you know that the estimated duration is the total resource hours needed to complete an effort driven task its behaviour is fairly simple. What is slightly more complicated is its use in building a project model. In most cases the assignment of additional but different resources to a task do not shorten the time taken to complete it. For example, if you allocate one painter to a painting task then allocating an additional carpenter doesn't in general shorten the task's duration (unless the carpenter is willing to be a painter as well). However, if you model this task using a SuperProject effort driven task then allocating an additional carpenter will have exactly the same effect as allocating an additional painter. It is up to you to make sure that the effect of additional resource allocation is sensible within the context of the model.

The default resource type is Labor which has the property of reducing the time that an effort driven task takes. If you change the resource type to Other, either using the Resource Details view or the pop-up editor (see later), then its allocation will not affect an effort driven task. That is, a resource of type Other does not shorten an effort driven task. This allows you to be flexible in the way that assigned resources interact with effort driven tasks.

Elapsed

If you define a task duration for an elapsed time task then the scheduled duration will be the same. The time that you specify is taken to be a complete number of 24 hour days and 30 day months. For example, a task duration specified as 3dy is exactly 72 hours and 1mo is exactly 30 days irrespective of the number of days in the calendar month. Neither the duration nor the starting/finishing dates of an elapsed time task are affected by project holidays. For example, in Figure 8.4 you can see that the elapsed time task Task-1 runs through the weekend period but the resource driven Task-2 doesn't. This makes elapsed time tasks suitable for modelling strictly time dependent processes such as concrete curing, paint drying, and so on.

The rules for what happens if you assign a resource to an elapsed time task are not quite what you might think so it is worth examining them carefully. When you make such an assignment the resource's calendar is consulted in the usual way to see how the requisite number of resource hours can be obtained. What this means is that the resource scheduling can make the elapsed time task take longer or shorter. For example, if you allocate a resource to Task-1 in Figure 8.4 then its scheduled duration immediately increases to 7 days because of the need to take into account

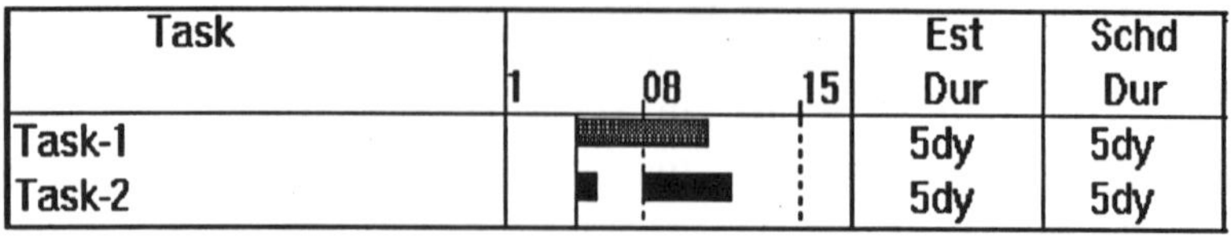

Task	1	08	15	Est Dur	Schd Dur
Task-1				5dy	5dy
Task-2				5dy	5dy

Figure 8.4
An elapsed time driven task Task-1 compared to a resource driven task Task-2

the resource's weekend. Equally if a resource can work for more hours per day on the elapsed time task it will finish early! This is surprising behaviour indeed. For example, if you assign a resource to check the curing conditions for concrete each day then normally you wouldn't expect the lack of inspection on a weekend to lengthen the total curing time but it does if you model this task/resource interaction using SuperProject!

The difficulty is caused by SuperProject applying its standard rules for calculating a resource's allocated time to a task and then using the resource calendar to find this time. The only real solution to the problem is to not assign a resource to a strictly elapsed time task.

Span

The final task/resource interaction is span. This is the simplest of all. The scheduled duration of a spanning task is simply the difference between the start and finish of its successor and predecessor task. In other words, a spanning task starts when its preceding task is finished and continues until the next task is started. This means that a spanning task can have a 0 scheduled duration. Spanning tasks are obviously intended to be used to model tasks which have to be done between two other tasks. For example, you might add the task 'guard site' between two phases of construction. No matter how the two phases of construction are scheduled or re-scheduled the spanning task occupies the time between them.

One subtle point is that the spanning task occupies the whole of the time between the two tasks. That is if the second task starts at 8 am the spanning task finishes at 8 am the same morning. If a resource is allocated to the spanning task it is only scheduled for the hours that it normally works.

Partial allocation

One of the most complicated parts of SuperProject's modelling facilities is the way it uses partial allocation. However, as long as you keep in mind the basic intention of this facility you should be able to see what is going on. Again it is important to remember the two stage process that SuperProject uses:

1) the estimated duration is used to calculate resource hours needed

2) the resource calendar is then consulted to discover how many resource days are needed to meet this requirement.

When partial allocations of the working day are involved the estimated task duration is used in the obvious way to estimate the number of resource hours. If the allocation per day is a percentage then this is interpreted to be a percentage of the standard working day. For example, 50% allocation is 4 hours if the standard working day is 8 hours. If you specify the allocation in hours then this is used without modification. In either case the number of allocated hours is simply:

> estimated duration in days x number of hours per day

For example, if a task's estimated duration is 3 days and a resource is allocated to the task for 50% of its working day, i.e. 4 hours, then clearly its allocated hours will be 3 days times 4 hours, or 12 hours.

So far so good, but the next step involves a second use of the allocation per day. Once SuperProject has the number of hours that the resource has to work it next looks up the resource's calendar to see how many days are necessary for it to complete that number of hours of work. However, if a partial allocation is specified then only this amount of the working day will be used on any given day. If the resource is allocated to the task for only 50% of the time then only 50% of the time available on each day of its calendar will be used. In the case of the previous example, SuperProject will look for 12 work hours on the resource calendar but it will never use more than 50% of the working hours on any day.

This behaviour should be contrasted with what happens if you specify the actual number of hours to be worked in Alloc/Day. In this case each day on the resource calendar is examined to see how many resource hours it can supply. If the resource is available for more hours than specified in Alloc/Day then that amount is used on the task. If the resource is available for fewer hours then only the available hours are used on the task. Thus the resource will work for as many hours as it is available on the calendar up to the specified allocation per day. The task duration is then set to the number of resource days it takes to accumulate the total number of resource hours.

For example, if a task's estimated duration is 3 days and a resource is allocated to it for 2 hours per day the total resource hours required to finish the task is 3 times 2 hours or 6 hours. If the resource calendar shows that it is available for 8 hours on the first day then 2 hours will be used on the task. If the calendar shows that it is available for only 1 hour on the next day then this 1 hour will be used even though it falls short of the daily allocation of time. This process continues until a full 6 hours of resource time have been used.

Both of these interpretations of partial allocation are reasonable and meaningful but there is a potential trap. If you make use of partial allocation of the same resource to more than one task then the resource scheduling for each task is done independently. This means that the resource calendar is examined for each task and resource hours are allocated without reference to how they might have already been allocated to the other task. The exact effect depends on whether you have made the partial allocation as a percentage or as an absolute number of hours.

If you are using percentage allocation and the percentages allocated to each task add up to 100% then this works perfectly. For example, if a resource is 25% allocated to

Task-1 and 75% to Task-2 then whatever time is shown on the resource's calendar will be split between the two tasks accordingly. However, if you allocate 50% of a resource's time to Task-1 and 75% to Task-2 the relevant portions of time will still be taken from the time indicated on the resource calendar even though this results in more time than the resource actually has available being allocated. This over-allocation will be indicated in Resource View on graphs showing resource allocation. The point to make here is that it is up to you to ensure that the percentage of time allocated to each task adds up to 100%.

The situation is slightly worse if you make partial allocations in terms of hours. In this case each task will take the number of hours it needs up to the limit indicated on the resource calendar without reference to the hours used by other tasks. Thus if a resource is allocated 2 hours to Task-1 and 3 hours to Task-2 and its calendar shows that it is available for only 1 hour it will be scheduled to work for 1 hour on both tasks, producing an over-commitment of 1 hour.

Both sorts of over-scheduling can be detected and steps can be taken to put the matter right. But you shouldn't assume that just because you have set a partial allocation that the whole allocation will necessarily be consistent.

Effort driven partial allocation

The previous discussion is completely general and applies to resource, workday, effort driven and elapsed tasks. When working with effort driven tasks and partial allocation there is one additional complication. If you assign two resources to an effort driven task the total resource hours needed are distributed between the two resources in proportion to their allocation. For example, if an effort driven task has an estimated duration of 5 days, then it needs a total of 40 hours resource time in total. If Rsrc-1 is allocated to the task for 75% of its working day and Rsrc-2 for 50% of its working day then the 40 hours is distributed between the two tasks in the ratio 75 to 50. In other words, Rsrc-1 is allocated for:

$$\frac{40 \times 75}{(75+50)}$$

which works out to 24 hours and to Rsrc-2 for:

$$\frac{40 \times 50}{(75+50)}$$

which works out to 16 hours. If 75% of Rsrc-1's working day is 6 hours the 24 hours that are allocated will take 4 of its days. If 50% of Rsrc-2's working day is 4 hours the 16 hours allocated to it will also take 4 of its days. Of course this is no coincidence - the total hours are divided so as to make sure that all the resources working on an effort driven task work for the same number of days.

The same sort of calculation applies if the allocation per day is defined as a given number of hours. For example, if Rsrc-1 works for 5 hours per day and Rsrc-2 works for 3 hours per day the total allocation is divided between the resources in the ratio 5 to 3.

Notice that the equality of days worked by each resource only applies if they have the same number of hours available on each day. If their calendars are different the result could be that they have to work different numbers of days to meet their commitments to the task. For example, if Rsrc-1 works a 4-hour day it will take twice as many days to complete its proportion of the task as a resource that works a standard 8-hour day.

Task/Resource	1	08	15	22	Est Dur	Schd Dur	Task ID	Alloc /Day	Sched Rsrc Total Hrs
Task-1					5dy	8dy	001		40.00
Rsrc-1						8dy	001	75%	24.00
Rsrc-2						4dy	001	50%	16.00

Figure 8.5
Dividing the work in an effort driven task

Estimating resource time

You may be puzzled as to why resource time is always calculated from task duration. Why not enter the number of resource hours a task is estimated to need and allow SuperProject to use this information to calculate an estimated task duration? This is indeed possible but, before explaining how, it is worth saying a few words on why the standard scheme of estimating resources from tasks is so useful.

SuperProject encourages the view that the allocation of a resource to a task is for the full estimated duration of the task. It might be that the resource's calendar prohibits it from working for some days when it would otherwise be needed, but it is still allocated to the task for the non-working days. In the same way if another resource prolongs a task beyond the task's estimated duration the other resources are still allocated to the task even though they may not be working on it. Even if you make use of partial allocation a resource is still partially allocated to the task for its full duration. For example, if you 10% allocate a manager to a task, then 10% of the manager's working day is allocated to the task for the task's entire duration.

This implies that when you are creating a project model you should try to find tasks that need the allocation of a resource for the entire duration of the task. If a task is such that one resource is needed for the first third of the task and another for the final two thirds, then this task should be sub-divided into two tasks that make exclusive use of the two resources.

This 'total' resource allocation means that it is indeed reasonable to use the task's duration to estimate the number of resource hours needed. Indeed, if each resource is allocated for the full duration of a task then the only possible variations are in partial allocation or the use of effort driven as opposed to resource driven tasks.

However reasonable it is to estimate resource hours needed from task duration, there will be times when it is easier to estimate the time each type of resource will need to spend on a given task. In this case, or indeed in any case, there is nothing stopping you from moving along to the scheduled resource total hours column and entering a value. This value will then be used in exactly the same way as if SuperProject had calculated it. That is, it is used, along with any partial allocation per day, to look at the resource calendar and find the number of resource days needed to supply the specified number of hours. Resource hours that are entered rather than calculated are shown in a different colour or shading.

For example, if you assign Rsrc-1 to Task-1 with an estimated duration of 10 days, then it will be scheduled for 80 hours of resource time. If, however, you place the cursor in the column headed 'Sched Rsrc Total Hrs' and type in 40.00 the scheduled duration for the task will change to 5 days, even though the estimated duration still shows 10 days (assuming that Rsrc-1 is available for 8 hours per day for each of the 5 days) - see Figure 8.6.

If you enter the number of hours needed for a list of resources then each resource will be scheduled accordingly. Each resource calendar will be used in turn to discover how many resource days are needed to supply the specified number of hours. Each resource works from the start of the task until it has completed the required number of hours. If a resource completes its allocated hours it remains assigned to the task but, of course, assigning it to another task for this period will not cause over-commitment. It is

Task/Resource	08	15	Est Dur	Schd Dur	Sched Rsrc Total Hrs
Task-1			10dy	5dy	40.00
Rsrc-1				5dy	40.00

Figure 8.6
Entering the resource's scheduled hours directly

even possible to introduce a delay into the resource's start date so that it can work for any portion of the task, but this causes other complications - see Partial Allocation in Chapter 13.

For example, if you assign Rsrc-1 to Task-1 and enter its number of hours directly as 40 hours and then assign Rsrc-2 and enter 56 hours directly then the task is scheduled for 7 days (assuming that both resources are available). You can see in Figure 8.7 that Rsrc-1 isn't used for the last two days of the task but it is still assigned, as the two-day long dash on the Gantt chart indicates.

Of course you can mix calculated and directly entered resource scheduled hours. The only danger is that you will forget to enter a sensible estimated task duration for the one resource in the list for which you haven't entered a scheduled duration directly. Direct entry of resource hours is particularly useful if you have no idea how long a task will take but can work out how long each assigned resource will take to complete its component of the task. However, if you find that you are making use of this method often the chances are that you are not defining the tasks in your model appropriately. Ideally a task should be defined to ensure that all assigned resources work for the same period on the task if they are available.

If you want to delete a scheduled duration that you have entered directly and revert to a calculated duration then all you have to do is to delete the entry and recalculate the schedule.

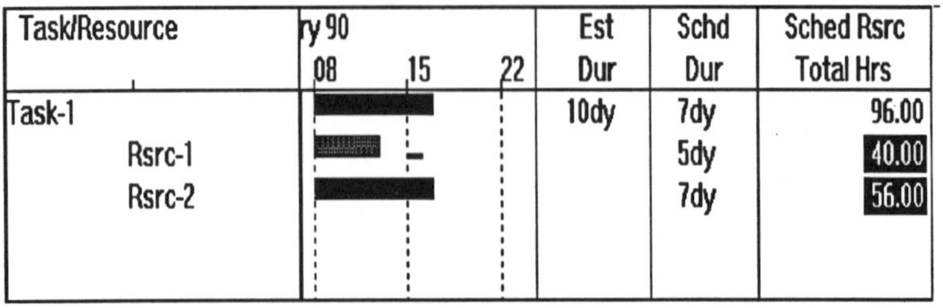

Task/Resource	ry 90 08 15 22			Est Dur	Schd Dur	Sched Rsrc Total Hrs
Task-1				10dy	7dy	96.00
Rsrc-1					5dy	40.00
Rsrc-2					7dy	56.00

Figure 8.7
Two resource allocations entered directly

The pop-up editor

One of the most difficult aspects of using SuperProject is the need to enter data into many different columns which are often widely spaced. One solution to this problem is to select an appropriate layout that groups the columns of data used to complete a particular data entry task. An alternative is to use the pop-up editing window introduced in Version 3.

You can make the pop-up editor appear by double clicking on any object, either task or resource, by selecting the command Edit,Popup Edit Form or by clicking on the icon to the left of the magnifying glass. There is a version of the pop-up edit form for tasks, assignments and for resources. Each one makes available the data concerning the object selected in a form that is easier to use than the column layout. The only disadvantage is that you can see data for one only object at a time.

Although the pop-up editor is useful for all stages of model preparation and editing, it contains many data fields and options that are only relevant once you have moved to expert mode. Indeed there are many task and resource data fields and options that are not described until later chapters.

You can see the task pop-up edit form for a typical task in Figure 8.8. You should be able to recognise most of the entries on the form - the duration, start and finish dates and the resource hours allocated to it. The three buttons to the left - Scheduled, Actual and Baseline - can be used to select which set of data is displayed. Actual and Baseline data are described in Chapter 11 so for the moment only Scheduled data will be discussed. You can make entries or edit the data shown on the form and when you select the Close button the data will be stored back in the relevant columns for that task.

If you click on the button labelled Effort then the Task Effort editing form appears - see Figure 8.9. This contains

```
┌─────────────────────────────────────────────────────────────┐
│ ═                        Task - Short Form                  │
├─────────────────────────────────────────────────────────────┤
│ Task Name:│Paper walls    │  ID:│006│  WBS:│01.04.00.00.0006│  ┌─────┐
│                                                              │  │Close│
│ Description:│                                   │            │  └─────┘
│                                                              │  ┌──────┐
│   Duration:│ 3dy │ Start:│15-05-92││8:00a│ Finish:│19-05-92││5:00p│ │Effort│
│                                                              │  └──────┘
│        ⦿ Scheduled    %Complete:│ 0.00 │   Priority:│    │    │  ┌─────┐
│        ○ Actual                                              │  │Costs│
│        ○ Baseline   Sched Effort Hours: 24.00  Status:Schd   │  └─────┘
│                                                              │  ┌────┐
│                                                              │  │User│
│                                                              │  └────┘
└─────────────────────────────────────────────────────────────┘
```

Figure 8.8
The Task pop-up editor

all of the data concerned with the resource allocations to the task. You can change the task's type using the Options box towards the middle of the form. The columns of data labelled Actual, Remaining and Baseline correspond to data fields that are described in Chapter 11. There are two other editing windows corresponding to the Costs and User

```
┌─────────────────────────────────────────────────────────────┐
│ ═                       Task - Effort Form                  │
├─────────────────────────────────────────────────────────────┤
│ Task Name:│Paper walls   │  ID:│006│  WBS:│01.04.00.00.0006│  ┌─────┐
│                                                              │  │Close│
│ Description:│                                   │            │  └─────┘
│                                                              │  ┌─────┐
│   Est.Dur.:│ 3dy │ Start:│15-05-92││8:00a│ Finish:│19-05-92││5:00p│ │Short│
│                                                              │  └─────┘
│     Effort:⦿ Hours    %Complete:│ 0.00 │   Priority:│    │   │  ┌─────┐
│            ○ Days                                            │  │Costs│
│            ○ Weeks      Options:│Resource ▼│                 │  └─────┘
│                                                              │  ┌────┐
│              Scheduled   Actual   Remaining   Baseline       │  │User│
│   Regular:     24.00      0.00      24.00                    │  └────┘
│   Overtime:     0.00      0.00       0.00
│   Conflict      0.00
│   Total:       24.00      0.00      24.00       0.00
└─────────────────────────────────────────────────────────────┘
```

Figure 8.9
The Task Effort pop-up editor

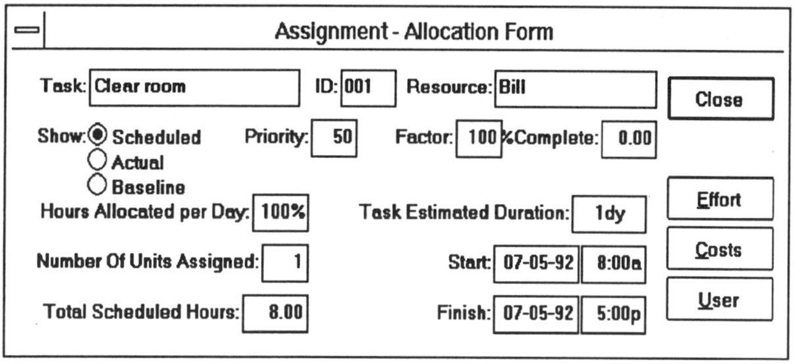

Figure 8.10
The Assignment pop-up editor

buttons. The data fields listed in these windows are described in Chapters 12 and 13 respectively.

If you ask for the pop-up editor window while a resource is selected in Task Outline View then you will see the Assignment editor - see Figure 8.10. As in the case of the Task pop-up editor window there are additional windows corresponding to Effort, Costs and User data.

To see the Resource pop-up editor window you all you have to do is ask for the pop-up editor when a resource is selected in Resource View, see Figure 8.11.

Notice that the pop-up editor adds nothing new to the data fields or options, it simply makes them easier to examine and edit.

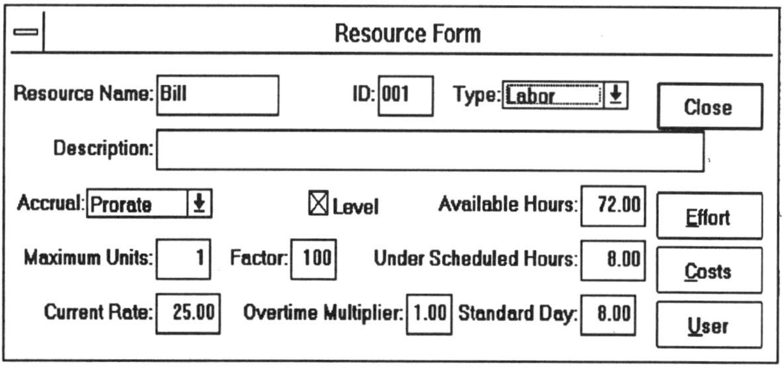

Figure 8.11
The Resource pop-up editor

Key points

» Resource assignments affect task scheduled durations in different ways.

» There are 5 types of task and in each case the estimated task duration is used to calculate the number of resource hours needed using:
　　estimated task duration x hours allocated per day
where hours allocated per day is either specified as a given number of hours or as a percentage of the standard working day.

» For a resource driven task the number of days on the resource calendar needed to provided the resource hours becomes the task's scheduled duration.

» The number of resource hours needed applies to each assigned resource separately and the least available resource determines the scheduled duration.

» A workday driven task behaves in the same way as a resource driven task but its scheduled duration is never less than its estimated duration.

» In the case of an effort driven task the calculated resource hours are the total number of resource hours needed spread over all the assigned resources.

» Elapsed time driven tasks behave in the same way as resource driven tasks but project holidays are ignored. If a resource is assigned then its availability does affect the scheduled duration.

» A span task has a duration that fills the time between its predecessor task finishing and its successor task starting.

» You can enter a resource's scheduled time allocation as an alternative to allowing SuperProject to work it out.

Chapter 9
Large Models

Although there is still much to learn about using SuperProject, the time has come to look at a rather larger example. In this chapter a project model for the development of a software package is presented. Rather than just going to a completed project model it will presented in stages that roughly correspond to what might really happen.

Stage 1 - Roughing out the hierarchy

The first stage in the construction of any project model is to enter a broad outline of the project's structure. Unless you are very familiar with the type of project - i.e. unless you have done it before - it is best to use SuperProject as a way of interactively creating an overview of the project. Don't become too functionally fixed at this early stage and be prepared to re-structure your model several times before finding a reasonable hierarchy.

In the case of the software project it was decided to split the topmost hierarchy into product development, product production and product launch. This roughly corresponds to the three teams of people who will work on the project and also provides a rough sequencing in that the majority of development tasks must occur before production and both must precede the launch.

Task	Resource	May 92 04　　11　　18	Schd Dur	Task ID
WORD.PJ		▆	5dy	P1
Product		▆	5dy	011
Software		▆	5dy	021
Manual		▆	5dy	022
Packaging		▆	5dy	023
Production		▆	5dy	024
Disk duplication		▆	5dy	025
Manual printing		▆	5dy	026
Packaging production		▆	5dy	027
Packing		▆	5dy	028
Launch		▆	5dy	029
Advertising		▆	5dy	030
Press conf		▆	5dy	031
Press pack		▆	5dy	032
Review copies		▆	5dy	033

Figure 9.1
The first hierarchy

The final hierarchy can be seen in Figure 9.1. Notice that there is no suggestion that this was arrived at in a single step. In practice you can expect to refine a hierarchy even quite late on in a project's life as tasks have to be introduced and reorganised. At this stage the project model's major utility is in helping the project planner organise.

Stage 2 - Refining the hierarchy

In practice refining the hierarchy is in itself a number of steps that often merge with the initial creation and later modification of the hierarchy. However, the availability of a large scale structure for the project allows you to concentrate on the details under the headings. To make this as easy as possible it is worth making use of the Hide/Show level commands to fold all but the section of the hierarchy that you are working on.

As you can see in Figure 9.2 the first part of the hierarchy that has been refined is the software development. The **Production** and **Launch** headings have been contracted.

Task	Resource	May 92 04　　11　　18	Schd Dur	Task ID
Product		▬▬▬	5dy	011
Software		▬▬▬	5dy	021
Design		▬▬▬	5dy	036
Coding		▬▬▬	5dy	037
Beta test		▬▬▬	5dy	038
Gamma test		▬▬▬	5dy	039
Production disk		▬▬▬	5dy	040
Manual		▬▬▬	5dy	022
Packaging		▬▬▬	5dy	023
+Production		▬▬▬	5dy	024
+Launch		▬▬▬	5dy	029

Figure 9.2
Refinement of product development

Stage 3 - Task definitions

Once you reach a low enough level of the hierarchy the time has come to start to define the logical task constraints and to enter some estimated task durations. Again at this stage you do not have to attempt to be exact about figures such as task durations but it does help to try to make task dependencies as accurate as possible. This is the time to think hard about the relationship of one task to another. If you form a logical constraint between two tasks that do not need to be so constrained then you necessarily risk losing some freedom in the organisation of the project. Such an error can be difficult to correct later in the life of the project simply because the tasks have been organised to suit the constraints implied by the model. For example, in Figure 9.3 you can see that coding, i.e. actually writing the program, and the two external phases of testing are shown to run sequentially. This may be reasonable but it introduces a barrier between coding and testing that might be unrealistic.

Notice also that some estimated task durations have been entered in Figure 9.3. The only problem here is that some of the durations are in months and so make it necessary to

Defining tasks

One of the most difficult parts of building any project model is actually identifying tasks. There are many ways to break a project down into tasks and there is no absolute right or wrong way to do it. In the end the only judge is the appropriateness of the resulting project model. Here are some guidelines to help:

» A task should have a duration that is short with respect to the overall duration of the project. It is more difficult to estimate durations for long tasks and they tend to hide a great deal of detail.

» You shouldn't include tasks that do not affect the schedule or cannot be effected to alter the schedule - no matter how vital to the project the task is. For example, any task that it is reasonable to suppose a resource will complete as part of the larger task assigned is best left out of the model.

» Tasks should be precisely definable. If a task specification is vague then it makes it more difficult to control and to assign resources to.

» Always remember to include a complete range of tasks concerned with a phase - including reviews and re-workings of earlier tasks. The possibility of a variable number of reviews and re-workings is one of the most difficult project features to model adequately.

» Do not break down any tasks that are outside of your control. For example, do not split any task that is sub-contracted into smaller stages unless this helps you check its progress.

» A task should be appropriate for resource assignment. If a task needs the entire workforce then the chances are that it should be split into smaller sub-tasks! Also the resources allocated should be required for the full duration of the task.

Stage 4 - Phase 1 details

Task 6 Days Per Column	Resource		92 Apr	May	Jun	Jul	Aug	Sep	Oct	N	Est Dur	Schd Dur
WORD3.PJ				▬	▬	▬	▬	▬	▬			115dy
Product				▬	▬	▬	▬	▬	▬			115dy
Software				▬	▬	▬	▬	▬	▬			115dy
Design				▬							1mo	1mo
Coding					▬	▬	▬				3mo	3mo
Beta test								▬			1mo	1mo
Gamma test									▪		1wk	1wk
Production disk									◆		0dy	0dy
Manual			▪								5dy	5dy
Packaging			▪								5dy	5dy
+Production			▪									5dy
+Launch			▪									5dy

Figure 9.3
Refinement of product development

alter the Gantt chart scale. Also notice the introduction of a milestone task - the creation of a production disk. Although this task only takes moments, its handover to the production team marks the end of a distinct phase of the entire project.

Figure 9.4 shows the rest of the project phases broken down into tasks complete with initial links and task durations. Once again it is important to notice that at this stage most aspects of the project model are almost 'experimental'. The **Launch** heading has not been expanded and this emphasises one of the advantages of the hierarchical approach in that we can choose to leave layers of the project for definition at a later time. A rough idea of how the **Launch** task integrates with the rest of the project could initially be obtained by fixing its duration and linking it with the other tasks in the project.

Stage 4 - Phase 1 details

After completing a rough model of each of the phases the next step is to try to include details of the relationships between the phases of the project. Clearly the product

148 Large Models Chapter 9

Task 6 Days Per Column	Resource	92 May	Jun	Jul	Aug	Sep	Oct	No	Est Dur	Schd Dur	Task ID
WORD4.PJ										115dy	P1
Product										115dy	011
Software										115dy	021
Design										1mo	1mo	036
Coding										3mo	3mo	037
Beta test										1mo	1mo	038
Gamma test										1wk	1wk	039
Production disk										0dy	0dy	040
Manual											30dy	022
Design										1wk	1wk	044
Develop text										5dy	5dy	045
Layout										2wk	2wk	046
Proof										5dy	5dy	047
Correct										5dy	5dy	048
Packaging											13dy	023
Design										1wk	1wk	052
Mock-up										3dy	3dy	053
Trial										2dy	2dy	054
Final design										3dy	3dy	055
Production											5dy	024
Disk duplication											5dy	025
Obtain quotes										5dy	5dy	059
Select supplier										0dy	0dy	061
Place order										0dy	0dy	062
Delivery of stock										0dy	0dy	063
Manual printing											5dy	026
Obtain quotes										5dy	5dy	064
Select supplier										0dy	0dy	065
Place order										0dy	0dy	066
Delivery of stock										0dy	0dy	067
Packaging production											5dy	027
Obtain quotes										5dy	5dy	131
Select supplier										0dy	0dy	132
Place order										0dy	0dy	133
Delivery of stock										0dy	0dy	134
Packing										3dy	3dy	028
+Launch											5dy	029

Figure 9.4
The complete task list with initial links and duration estimates

development is the first phase that has to be defined. Within product development software, manual and packaging development can proceed more or less concurrently. However, this doesn't mean that the writing of the manual and the design of the packaging can proceed independently of the software development. For example, if the packaging was designed at the start of the project it would certainly fail to capture the fine detail of the yet-to-be-developed product and might not even convey its overall concept. The same is true, if not more so, of the manual. In both cases it is reasonable to model each task as ALAP (As Late As Possible) and link the finish of each to the end of the software development. Unfortunately SuperProject will not let you make an FF link between project headings and so it is necessary to make the links between the last tasks in each phase. At this point is seems sensible to add milestone tasks to the manual and packaging phases and move all three milestones - production disk, manual and packages to the top level of the hierarchy.

Linking the production disk task to the other two production milestones with FF links does ensure that disk, manual and packaging are all ready on the same day but this really isn't what is required. The lead time on disk duplication is less than that for printing and packaging production. As a result it seems safer to link the manual and packaging milestones to the production disk milestone

| Task   Resource | 92 | | | | | | | Est | Schd |
6 Days Per Column	May	Jun	Jul	Aug	Sep	Oct	Nov	Dur	Dur
WORD.PJ									115dy
Product									115dy
+ Software									115dy
Production disk								0dy	0dy
+ Manual									30dy
Production manual								0dy	0dy
+ Packaging									13dy
Production package								0dy	0dy
Production									5dy
+ Disk duplication									5dy
+ Manual printing									5dy
+ Packaging production									5dy
Packing								3dy	3dy
+ Launch									6dy

Figure 9.5
Product development defined

and add a 1 month lag for the manual and a 2 week lag for the packaging. If you do all of this the result can be seen in Figure 9.5.

Stage 5 - Production

The next phase of the project to be defined is production and clearly the links should be between the milestones that define the availability of each part of the product and the placing of the order for each. To make sure that the quotes for each phase of production are up to date these should be ALAP tasks and there should be a lag between requesting quotes and placing the order, to allow time for production firms to quote for the job. You also have to remember to build in the lags between placing the orders and receiving the finished products. If you do all of this correctly the result should be as in Figure 9.6.

If you feel that the level of complexity of the project model is becoming too great to cope with, then all you need to do is remember that any of the levels can be collapsed back.

Task 6 Days Per Column	Resource	92 May	Jun	Jul	Aug	Sep	Oct	Nov	Est Dur	Schd Dur
WORD6.PJ										128dy
Product										115dy
+ Software										115dy
Production disk										0dy	0dy
+ Manual										30dy
Production manual										0dy	0dy
+ Packaging										13dy
Production package										0dy	0dy
Production										35dy
Disk duplication										15dy
Obtain quotes										5dy	5dy
Select supplier										0dy	0dy
Place order										0dy	0dy
Delivery of stock										0dy	0dy
Manual printing										32dy
Obtain quotes										5dy	5dy
Select supplier										0dy	0dy
Place order										0dy	0dy
Delivery of stock										0dy	0dy
Packaging production										20dy
Obtain quotes										5dy	5dy
Select supplier										0dy	0dy
Place order										0dy	0dy
Delivery of stock										0dy	0dy
Packing										3dy	3dy

Figure 9.6
Production defined

| Task | Resource | 92 | | | | | | | Schd |
6 Days Per Column		pr	May	Jun	Jul	Aug	Sep	Oct	N	Dur
WORD6.PJ										128dy
+Product										115dy
+Production										35dy
+Launch										6dy

Figure 9.7
A simple view of the project model

The simplest possible view of the project can be seen in Figure 9.7.

Stage 6 - Assigning resources

Although the details of the product launch are still to be defined, doing this will be postponed until later. The next step is to assign resources to each task. This is fairly straightforward but quite a lot of work. The assignments for software development can be seen in Figure 9.8. Other assignments are just as obvious and simple at this stage.

| Task | Resource | 90 | | | | | | | Schd | Task | Scheduled | |
6 Days Per Column		Jan	Feb	Mar	Apr	May	Jun	Jul	Dur	ID	Start	
WORD7.PJ									128dy	P1	08-01-90	8:00a
Product									115dy	011	08-01-90	8:00a
Software									115dy	021	08-01-90	8:00a
Design									1mo	036	08-01-90	8:00a
	Chief Prog.								1mo	036	08-01-90	8:00a
Coding									3mo	037	07-02-90	8:00a
	Chief Prog.								3mo	037	07-02-90	8:00a
	Snr Prog								3mo	037	07-02-90	8:00a
	Jnr Prog.								3mo	037	07-02-90	8:00a
Beta test									1mo	038	10-05-90	8:00a
	Chief Prog.								1mo	038	10-05-90	8:00a
	Snr Prog								1mo	038	10-05-90	8:00a
	Jnr Prog.								1mo	038	10-05-90	8:00a
	Test Mng								1mo	038	10-05-90	8:00a
Gamma test									1wk	039	11-06-90	8:00a
	Chief Prog.								1mo	039	11-06-90	8:00a
	Snr Prog								1mo	039	11-06-90	8:00a
	Jnr Prog.								1mo	039	11-06-90	8:00a
	Test Mng								1mo	039	11-06-90	8:00a
Production disk									0dy	040	15-06-90	5:00p
+ Manual									30dy	022	05-04-90	8:00a
Production manual									0dy	150	17-05-90	8:00a
+ Packaging									13dy	023	16-05-90	8:00a
Production package									0dy	151	04-06-90	8:00a
+Production									35dy	024	17-05-90	8:00a
+Launch									6dy	029	08-01-90	8:00a

Figure 9.8
Software development assignments

Model validity

The project model can be completed by spending time entering more data but at some point you should stop and evaluate the accuracy of the model. In practice this is an on-going activity in which you should be constantly on the look out for anomalous scheduling. When you first complete a project model it may seem perfectly accurate and reasonable but this may be due to the way that you have set up the model to work correctly with the initial data. It is still possible for the model to produce grossly invalid results in response to changes in the data.

For example, in the large model presented in this chapter the schedule seems reasonable but if at a later date you assign more programming resources in an effort to reduce the time needed for the Coding task - you will find that nothing happens. The reason is of course that the task is defined to be resource driven when it is clearly effort driven. When you first establish the model the distinction between resource and effort driven tasks isn't important as long as you are estimating the task's duration and allowing SuperProject to work out the resource commitments. The task type only reveals itself as important later when you try to adjust the task's scheduled duration by altering resource assignments. In other words, a project model can give correct results even if it doesn't faithfully copy every aspect of behaviour of the real project's tasks and resources.

Given that no project model can be accurate enough to incorporate every aspect of reality how hard should we try to ensure validity? In every case where a model is found to be less than perfect there are always two choices. You can attempt to correct inadequacies in the model manually each time the project data changes, or you can try to improve the model's accuracy and so account for the changes automatically. For example, in the case of Coding we could choose not to make the change to an effort driven task as long as each time a resource was assigned the task's estimated duration was manually adjusted. This may seem

Estimating task durations

Estimating task durations is another difficult operation and the predictions made by the model are clearly dependent on good task duration estimates. One of the skills that you have to learn is how to estimate durations without being swayed by factors that are already built into the model. Indeed just being confronted by a partly completed model can bias estimates in itself! Here are some guidelines to help:

» Consider each task in isolation and don't be influenced by task durations already estimated.

» Don't build into your estimates considerations of resource availability if you are going to assign resources as a later step. If you add a week because resource x is on holiday and then SuperProject adds another week when you actually assign resource x then your model will certainly lack accuracy.

» Always assume normal working conditions and don't estimate short durations in an effort to force resources to work harder!

» Don't include extra time in your estimates 'just in case'. Your overall project model will be more accurate if each task duration is estimated accurately and without extra time built in.

» Always try to get the people doing the job to estimate how long it will take. Management are nearly always less accurate.

» If possible base estimates on the evidence of the actual time it takes to complete similar tasks.

» A more accurate estimate of duration can be made from an optimistic, pessimistic and most likely estimate using:
(optimistic + 4 x most likely + pessimistic) / 6
See Chapter 10 for more details.

unsatisfactory but it is exactly what happened when the model was first constructed. Then it seemed perfectly reasonable to say that **Coding** would take three months but this estimate must have been on the basis of the resources that were about to be assigned to the task.

If you add features that make the model more accurate then you do not have to remember to make manual 'fix-ups' when you change the project data. The only cost of adding features in this way is that the model itself becomes more complex and so potentially more prone to subtle errors. If you don't add such features then you must remember to make manual adjustments to the schedule to compensate and this in itself is an error-prone procedure.

Working with large models

Part of the problem of validating large models is simply their size. It can be difficult to see where links have been made, what type of tasks and what resource allocations have been made. In reality project models can be many times larger than the example in this chapter and in this case minor difficulties become acute. The best weapon at your disposal for controlling such complexity is most certainly the hierarchical decomposition of your project but even after this has been used there is often a need to control the presentation of the project data more accurately. In the next few sections the commands that deal with organising and selecting data are described. It is important that you master these but you might want to leave this until you really have a large project model of your own to work with!

Column layout

SuperProject presents data in the form of a table. If you include all of the possible data fields this table can have over 200 columns which makes working with it very difficult. However, you can select precisely which columns you would like to see. As long as you are working in Expert mode you

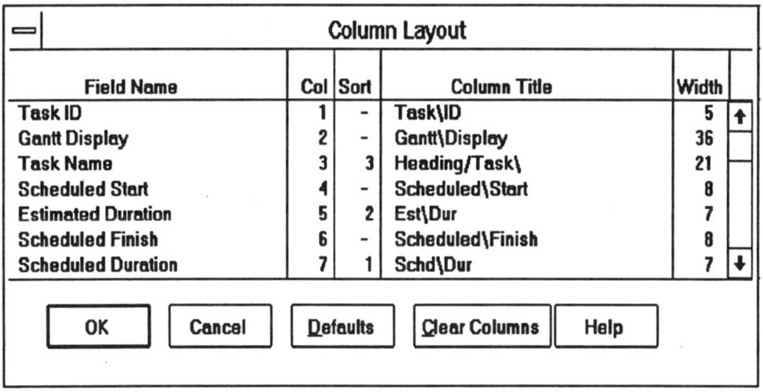

Column layout

Field Name	Col	Sort	Column Title	Width
Task ID	1	-	Task\ID	5
Gantt Display	2	-	Gantt\Display	36
Task Name	3	3	Heading/Task\	21
Scheduled Start	4	-	Scheduled\Start	8
Estimated Duration	5	2	Est\Dur	7
Scheduled Finish	6	-	Scheduled\Finish	8
Scheduled Duration	7	1	Schd\Dur	7

[OK] [Cancel] [Defaults] [Clear Columns] [Help]

Figure 9.9
The column layout dialog box

can select Column layout from the Layout menu and use the dialog box that appears, see Figure 9.9, to determine not only which columns show but the order in which they are presented. In Version 3 you can also set the column width and enter a custom title for each column.

The number entered under the Column heading determines the order of display. If you do not want a column to display then simply enter a - (minus sign) or press the space bar. Any column to which you assign a number will display at that position and the other columns will be re-numbered to take account of this change. You can also use (Alt)-Shift-Up and (Alt)-Shift-Down arrow keys to move a selected column up or down in the order. (Note: the Alt key is needed only if you are using the Windows version.)

Each outline view can have its own column layout details and these are stored when you use the command Layout, Save. You can restore the default layout by simply pressing the button labelled Defaults. This makes it possible to use the column layout facility to reduce the number of columns to just the few that you are trying to inspect or enter data to on a temporary basis. Notice that the list of columns in the dialog box is unlikely to be the complete 130 possible columns because some of them have to be enabled using the Preferences, General Options command.

Task ID	90 Jan	Feb	Mar	Apr	May	Jun	Jul	Task 6 Days Per Column	Scheduled Start		Est Dur
065						⊡		Select supplier	31-05-90	8:00a	0dy
132							⊡	Select supplier	18-06-90	8:00a	0dy
061							⊡	Select supplier	18-06-90	8:00a	0dy
143	⊞							Launch	15-01-90	8:00a	1dy
136	▮							Obtain rates	08-01-90	8:00a	1dy
137	⊞							Plan	09-01-90	8:00a	1dy
054					⊞			Trial	28-05-90	8:00a	2dy
055					▮			Final design	30-05-90	8:00a	3dy
053					⊡			Mock-up	23-05-90	8:00a	3dy
028							▪	Packing	02-07-90	8:00a	3dy
032	▮							Press pack	08-01-90	8:00a	3dy
033	▮							Review copies	08-01-90	8:00a	4dy

Figure 9.10
A custom column layout and sort order

The third column in the Column Layout dialog box can be used to sort the rows into order. For example, you could sort the tasks into order on Task Id number, Estimated duration, etc.. All you have to do is type 1,2 or 3 into the sort column to indicate which column you would like to sort on first, second and third. For example, the Column Layout dialog box shown in Figure 9.9 produces the layout shown in Figure 9.10. Notice that the sort order that you specify is only honoured when headings are not being displayed. The reason for this is that sorting temporarily destroys any hierarchical structure that you have created and so to show headings would be a waste of time. If you add rows to the table you can re-sort it at any time using the command Select, Sort Layout.

It is also worth noting that you can always make use of the Edit, Go To Column command, or Ctrl-C to find any column by name.

Selection filters

As well as reducing the number of columns and sorting on rows, you can also select a subset of 'objects' to work on. There a number of different ways of selecting an object or set of objects. The simplest, if you are using a mouse, is to drag a selection across the objects concerned. Selected objects show on the screen in a different colour or shading to distinguish them from unselected objects. You can move the cursor from one selected object to another using Ctrl-N for Next Selected object and Ctrl-P for Previous object.

You can also select any object using the Select,Select Object command or by pressing F7 and typing in the name of the object. However, in many cases you will want to select objects using selection criteria. If you give the command Select,Enter Criteria the selection dialog box appears, see Figure 9.11. By filling in this form you can specify exactly what objects should be selected.

First you should tick the boxes at the top of the form to indicate which type of object should be selected - tasks, resources, assignment or accounts (described in Chapter 12). You can tick more than one box to select more

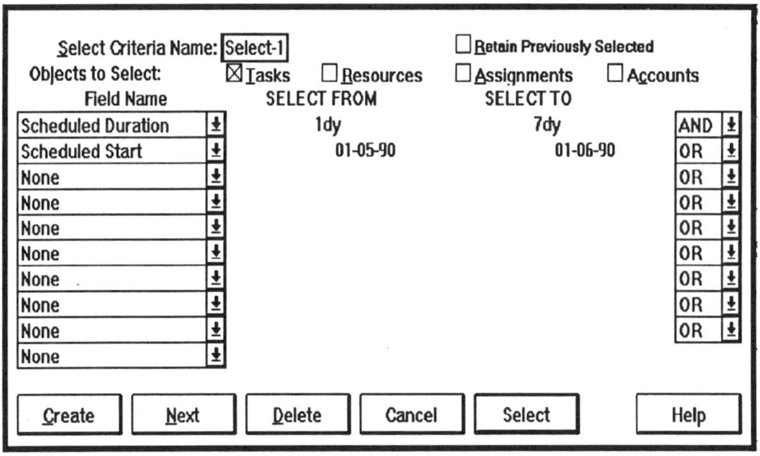

Select Criteria Name:	Select-1		☐ Retain Previously Selected	
Objects to Select:	☒ Tasks	☐ Resources	☐ Assignments	☐ Accounts
Field Name		SELECT FROM	SELECT TO	
Scheduled Duration		1dy	7dy	AND
Scheduled Start		01-05-90	01-06-90	OR
None				OR
None				OR
None				OR
None				OR
None				OR
None				OR
None				OR
None				

[Create] [Next] [Delete] [Cancel] [Select] [Help]

Figure 9.11
The selection dialog box

than one type of object. Notice that not all object types will necessarily show on the current outline view.

The next step is to select a set of fieldnames and conditions. If you click on the arrow to the right of any of the boxes labelled None then a complete list of fieldnames drops down. You can select a fieldname from this list and then enter a condition in the pair of columns to its right. You can enter a single value in the first column or a pair of values that define a range. You can see examples of conditions in Figure 9.11. These conditions can be connected together to make an overall condition using the boxes to the far right to select either AND, OR or NOT. In Figure 9.11 the conditions are connected using AND so they both have to be true for an object to be selected. If you type in a single value then this has to be matched exactly for the object to be selected. You can make use of the symbols ? and * to build more complicated conditions. ? matches any single character and * matches any number of characters. So for example, S* matches all words starting with S, Design* matches all words starting with Design, Task-? matches all words of the form Task- followed by one character and so on. You can obviously use a pair of conditions to specify a range but be careful to make sure that the starting value is smaller than the finishing value. In particular, when using dates, ensure that you use an earlier date followed by a later date.

If you then press the Select button the dialog box vanishes and you will see the previous view but with all of the selected objects highlighted in a different colour or shade. For example, the selection dialog box in Figure 9.11 would select all tasks with an estimated duration in the range 1 to 7 days within a one-month date period as specified.

You can define a number of selection conditions each one identified by a name. The name can be typed in at the top left-hand corner or you can simply accept SuperProject's default naming - Select-*n*. To create a new set of conditions click on the Create button. Any sets of conditions that you have defined are saved along with the project file.

```
┌─────────────────────────────────────────────────────────────────┐
│ Task Outline Layout              Layout:Task Outline            │
│                                                                 │
│   View Options:○ Headings/Tasks      ○ Assignments Only         │
│                ⦿ Tasks Only          ○ Tasks/Assignments        │
│                ○ Headings/Tasks/Assignments                     │
│                                                                 │
│   Outline Options:☒ Show Only Selected    ☒ Show Gantt          │
│                                                                 │
│   Column Options:⦿ All Columns       ○ Task Notes               │
│                  ○ Predecessor/Successors                       │
│                                                                 │
│         Totals:○ Subtotal Headings   ⦿ Rollup                   │
│                ○ None                ○ Subtotal Assignments     │
│                ○ Subtotal Lowest Level                          │
│                                                                 │
│  ┌──────┐  ┌────────┐  ┌──────────┐              ┌──────┐       │
│  │  OK  │  │ Cancel │  │ Crosstabs..│            │ Help │       │
│  └──────┘  └────────┘  └──────────┘              └──────┘       │
└─────────────────────────────────────────────────────────────────┘
```

Figure 9.12
The Task Outline Layout box used to show only selected objects

You can activate any condition by clicking on the Next button which steps you through the defined conditions one by one. You can also delete any existing conditions by pressing the Delete button while it is on screen.

Once you have a set of objects selected they can be subjected to some operations as a group. If you are using the Windows version you can cut, copy and paste a selected group of objects to and from the Clipboard. This is very useful for example, where sections of a project model are repetitious. In the software project model copying and pasting was used to create some of the resource assignments. In addition to clipboard operations you can also delete all selected objects using the Select,Delete All Selected command. To cancel a selection simply use the Select,Unselect All command.

As well as being able to work on particular subsets you can also opt for only selected objects being displayed in any view. As long as you are working in Expert mode, you can use the command Layout, Outline Layout to produce the Task Outline Layout dialog box, see Figure 9.12. Most of the details of the dialog box will be discussed in Chapter 14, but for the moment if you click on the box labelled 'Show

160 *Large Models*   *Chapter 9*

Task 6 Days Per Column	Est Dur	Schd Dur	Task ID	Scheduled Start		Scheduled Finish	
Trial	2dy	2dy	054	28-05-90	8:00a	29-05-90	5:00p
Final design	3dy	3dy	055	30-05-90	8:00a	01-06-90	5:00p
Mock-up	3dy	3dy	053	23-05-90	8:00a	25-05-90	5:00p
Correct	5dy	5dy	048	10-05-90	8:00a	16-05-90	5:00p
Design	1wk	1wk	052	16-05-90	8:00a	22-05-90	5:00p
Obtain quotes	5dy	5dy	064	17-05-90	8:00a	23-05-90	5:00p
Proof	5dy	5dy	047	03-05-90	8:00a	09-05-90	5:00p

Figure 9.13
The result of the applying a filter

Only Selected' and then on the OK button only selected objects will be displayed in the current view. For example, following the selection shown in Figure 9.11, the Task Outline view of the software project becomes that shown in Figure 9.13. Clearly you can make use of selection conditions in combination with Show Only Selected as selection filters to reduce the display of the model to only those objects that you are interested in examining.

The final command in the Select menu that is worth mentioning is Find. This can be used to find any object by name, including multiple occurrences of the same name. The found object isn't selected but it is made the current object, that is, the cursor is moved to it. If there are multiple

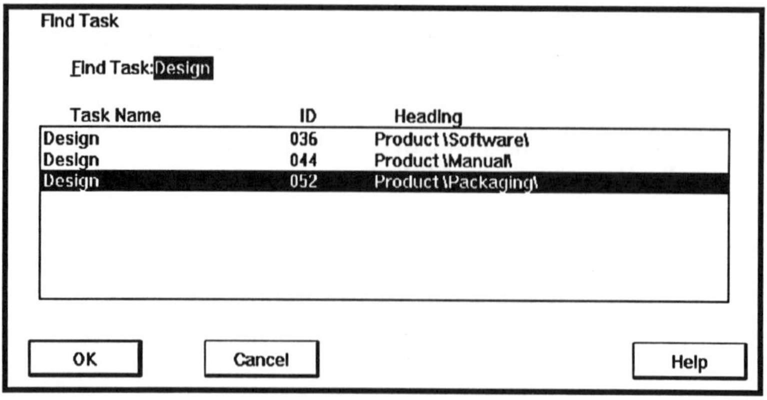

```
Find Task

    Find Task: Design

    Task Name           ID        Heading
    Design              036       Product\Software\
    Design              044       Product\Manual\
    Design              052       Product\Packaging\



    [  OK  ]      [  Cancel  ]                    [  Help  ]
```

Figure 9.14
The object selection dialog box

instances of the name then the Find dialog box, see Figure 9.14, contains a list of all of them. Double clicking on any occurrence of the name in the dialog box makes it the current object and so the cursor moves to it. Notice that you can only find objects appropriate to the current view. That is in Task Outline you can only find tasks, in Resource Outline only resources and in Account Outline (see Chapter 12) only accounts.

In Version 3 a new data field is available to help with selection. When an object is selected the Select Flag data field shows the word SEL.

Checking dependencies

When you first start linking tasks, using the Gantt chart say, it is relatively easy to keep track of what task is linked to what. As the number of links increases, however, the easy to use direct approach becomes confusing. It can also be difficult to check link type and any delay that has been specified. To make this job easier there is a variation of Task Outline view that shows the successor- predecessor relationships in a table format, see Figure 9.15. If you are using the Windows version then changing to this view is just matter of clicking on the third icon, the one that looks like a task link, in the Task Outline tool bar. Alternatively you have to select the Layout, Outline Layout command. This produces the layout dialog box shown in Figure 9.12. To change to the Predecessor/Successor display all you have to do is click on the Predecessors/Successors button. Select All Columns to return to the standard view or click on the 'table' icon to the left of the Predecessor/Successor icon.

You can browse the table to check that links are as you suppose them to be and enter any changes to link type or to lag/lead durations directly into the appropriate column.

162 Large Models — Chapter 9

Task	Predecessor Id	Predecessor Name	Typ	Lead/Lag	Successor Id	Successor Name	Typ
Packing	027	Packaging production	FS	0dy			
	026	Manual printing	FS	0dy			
	025	Disk duplication	FS	0dy			
Press pack							
Review copies							
Design					037	Coding	FS
Coding	036	Design	FS	0dy	038	Beta test	FS
Beta test	037	Coding	FS	0dy	039	Gamma test	FS
Gamma test	038	Beta test	FS	0dy			
Production disk	021	Software	FS	0dy	062	Place order	FS
	150	Production manual	FS	1mo			
	151	Production package	FS	2wk			
Design					045	Develop text	FS
Develop text	044	Design	FS	0dy	046	Layout	FS
Layout	045	Develop text	FS	0dy	047	Proof	FS
Proof	046	Layout	FS	0dy	048	Correct	FS
Correct	047	Proof	FS	0dy			

Figure 9.15
Predecessor/Successor view

Task descriptions

Task descriptions are perhaps the simplest way of adding information into a project model in an effort to help you remember detail. You can enter a task description directly in Outline view by moving to the far right-hand column and typing up to 57 characters of text. Alternatively you can view a list of all tasks and their associated descriptions by clicking on the Task Notes box in the Task Outline Layout dialog box - see Figure 9.12. If you are using the Windows version you can obtain the same view by clicking on the fourth icon in the tool bar.

You should use task descriptions to clarify any feature of the task and its relationship to the project which isn't obvious. For example, if the task's nature and purpose isn't clear from its name, make a note. If the task needs some special attention to keep the model correct, make a note. If the task is subject to some anomaly such as an apparent resource conflict which doesn't actually exist then make a note. Always remember that the details of the project may be clear to you at the time that you are constructing the model but a few days later you will wonder why you did what you did.

If you need to make notes that are longer than 57 characters then you need to make use of the task notes facility. This can be activated in any details view using Layout, View Subwindows, Note Text. This results in a text editing window being displayed where you can enter and edit up to 5000 characters of notes about each task, resource and about the project in general. These notes can be printed but it is worth keeping in mind that they use up memory when the project model is loaded. This window also supports a full range of text editing commands.

Key points

» Large project models can be difficult because of the mass of data that has to be entered, validated and controlled.

» You can either try to build an accurate model which automatically adjusts the schedule as you modify the data or manually adjust some of the tasks to keep the model's predictions accurate.

» There are a number of tools that you can use to keep the project's complexity under control and you can make use of many supplied standard layouts.

» You can select which columns to display and their order.

» Data can be sorted on up to three columns and subsets of objects which meet particular conditions can be selected.

» Filters can be used to display only selected objects.

» Successor/Predecessor dependencies can be viewed in table format.

» Task descriptions and task notes can be used to enter information as to how the project model works.

Chapter 10
Advanced Scheduling

So far our project models have produced schedules that have been determined by the logical constraints between tasks, Must dates and the availability of resources as indicated by the corresponding resource calendar. These are the obvious and 'built-in' constraints on scheduling. A slightly more sophisticated type of constraint concerns the over-commitment of resources to tasks. For example, if you have a project plan which meets the deadlines but schedules resources in an unrealistic way across tasks then it unlikely to be realisable. In simpler terms one person cannot do more than one job at a time!

SuperProject has the ability to schedule tasks to avoid resource over-commitment and this is a very powerful tool. However, there are many situations where a full and in-depth understanding of the details of the scheduling process is necessary so that manual adjustments can be made. In the rest of this chapter scheduling is examined in detail but it is assumed that you already know about the effects that linking tasks, Must dates and resource calendars have on the project schedule.

Levelling

The simplest way to describe the concept and operation of automatic resource levelling is by way of an example. If you have two tasks - Task-1 and Task-2, with no links between them and no Must dates specified then they will be scheduled to run concurrently. If you assign the same resource to each task then they will both still be scheduled to run concurrently, only now of course the resource will potentially affect the scheduled duration of both tasks. In this case it is obvious that the concurrent scheduling of the two tasks isn't realistic in that the same resource is timetabled to do a double standard day. How should this resource conflict be resolved? The most direct way is to set a Must date on the second task so that it starts after the first. The trouble with this approach is that it doesn't automatically reschedule the tasks if something changes. You have to remember to make subsequent manual changes to correct the model. In addition making a manual change isn't always this simple. For example, suppose that by moving the second task a different resource conflict is generated.

A much better solution is to allow SuperProject to automatically break the conflict by levelling resource allocation. In normal use SuperProject doesn't use levelling and to enable it you have to use the Calculation Options dialog box via the Preferences, Calculation Options command. This is available in Beginner and Expert mode but is very different in each. Figure 10.1 shows the Beginner mode box and to enable levelling in this mode click the Full box. After this recalculation not only detects resource conflicts but reschedules tasks to eliminate them, see

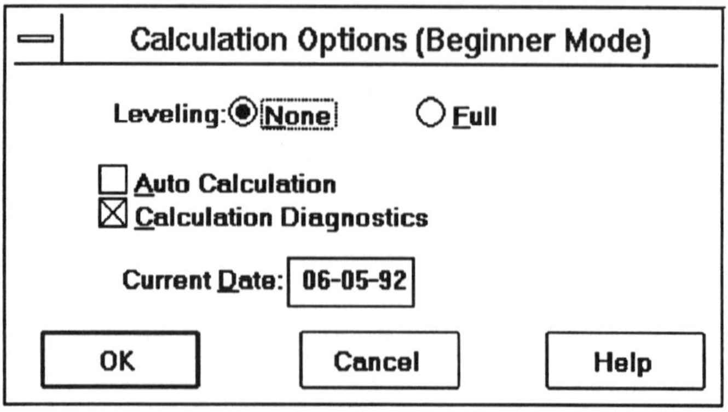

Figure 10.1
Enabling levelling in Beginner mode

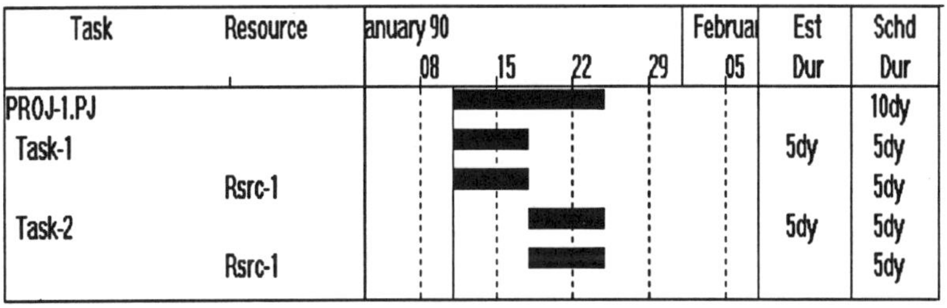

Levelling 167

Task	Resource	January 90				February	Est Dur	Schd Dur
		08	15	22	29	05		
PROJ-1.PJ								10dy
Task-1			▬▬				5dy	5dy
	Rsrc-1		▬▬					5dy
Task-2				▬▬			5dy	5dy
	Rsrc-1			▬▬				5dy

Figure 10.2
Tasks rescheduled by levelling

Figure 10.2. Notice that the pair of tasks is now scheduled to run consecutively and this isn't due to any logical constraints imposed by links.

The rescheduling will be performed so that if another resource conflict is generated by the initial rescheduling it too will be resolved and any adjustments to the project model will be made automatically. For example, if you have three tasks as shown in Figure 10.3, then Task-1 is in conflict with Task-3 over the use of Rsrc-1. If levelling is

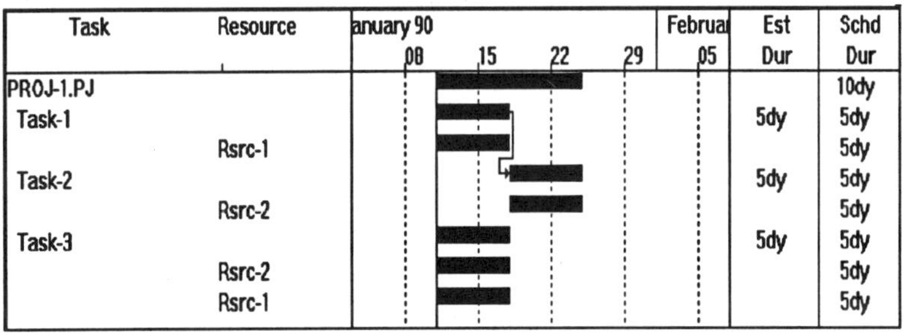

Task	Resource	January 90				February	Est Dur	Schd Dur
		08	15	22	29	05		
PROJ-1.PJ								10dy
Task-1			▬▬				5dy	5dy
	Rsrc-1		▬▬					5dy
Task-2				▬▬			5dy	5dy
	Rsrc-2			▬▬				5dy
Task-3			▬▬				5dy	5dy
	Rsrc-2		▬▬					5dy
	Rsrc-1		▬▬					5dy

Figure 10.3
Three tasks with potential resource conflicts

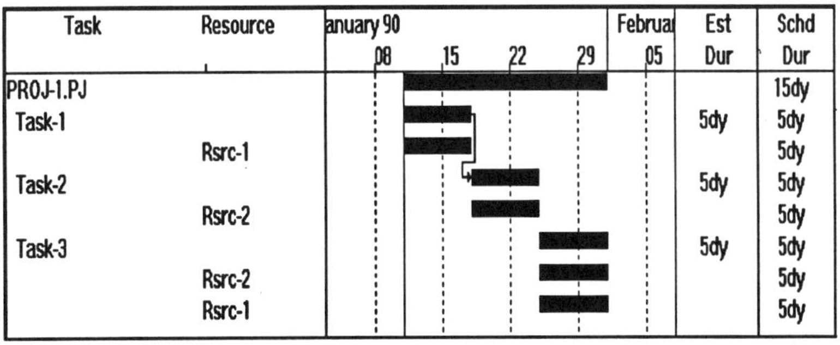

Task	Resource	January 90				February	Est Dur	Schd Dur
		08	15	22	29	05		
PROJ-1.PJ								15dy
Task-1			▬▬				5dy	5dy
	Rsrc-1		▬▬					5dy
Task-2				▬▬			5dy	5dy
	Rsrc-2			▬▬				5dy
Task-3					▬▬		5dy	5dy
	Rsrc-2				▬▬			5dy
	Rsrc-1				▬▬			5dy

Figure 10.4
After levelling

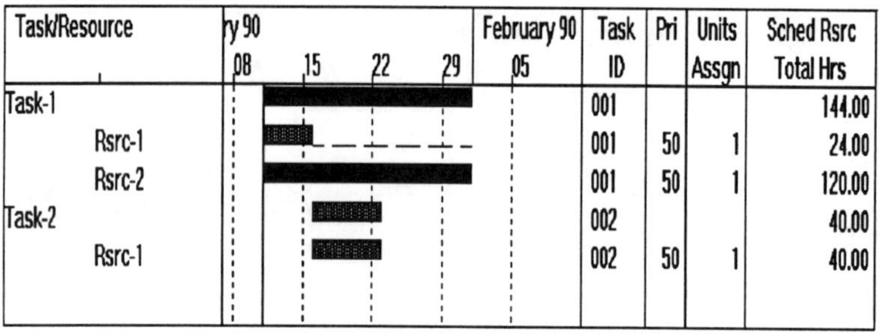

Task/Resource	ry 90 08	15	22	29	February 90 05	Task ID	Pri	Units Assgn	Sched Rsrc Total Hrs
Task-1						001			144.00
Rsrc-1						001	50	1	24.00
Rsrc-2						001	50	1	120.00
Task-2						002			40.00
Rsrc-1						002	50	1	40.00

Figure 10.5
Levelling only delays a task enough to resolve conflicts

used then Task-3 will be rescheduled to start after Task-1 but this brings it into conflict over Rsrc-2 with Task-2. SuperProject's levelling method is well up to this simple problem and so reschedules Task-3 to start after Task-2, see Figure 10.4.

It is also important to realise that tasks are only rescheduled by an amount necessary to break the resource conflict. For example, if you have two tasks with a conflict due to the assignment of Rsrc-1 which isn't allocated to Task-1 for its full duration then the second task will only be delayed until Rsrc-1's allocation to Task-1 is over, see Figure 10.5.

Controlling levelling

If you are working with a resource dependent project then levelling is a natural way of scheduling tasks without having to apply ad-hoc constraints. Its use does raise a number of additional questions. For example, why was Task-2 delayed rather than Task-1? How could you specify as part of the project model that Task-2 should be carried out before Task-1 if at all possible? In other words, levelling is a powerful scheduling tool but you need to have ways of controlling it.

Task order and priority

Currently tasks are levelled in order of their task id number. Each task is assigned an id number in order of creation starting from 1. It is this number which uniquely identifies a task and even allows you to define tasks that have the same name. When SuperProject levels resource assignments it considers tasks in order of their task id number and this means that tasks with larger id numbers will be delayed in preference to tasks with smaller id numbers. Notice that the order in which the tasks are listed in the Outline view has no effect on the order of levelling, see Figure 10.6.

You can, if you want to, renumber tasks to produce task ids in the order in which they are currently displayed or sorted. If you use the command Edit, Renumber Tasks the renumber dialog box is produced - Figure 10.7. You can select either a sorted order or the order in which the tasks are currently being displayed. After the renumber command the results of levelling may well be quite different, see Figure 10.8.

You can see that task id is acting as a sort of default task priority for levelling. In practice this may be useful for understanding why one task has been delayed instead of another but it isn't an easy way to control scheduling. Fortunately, SuperProject provides a way of assigning

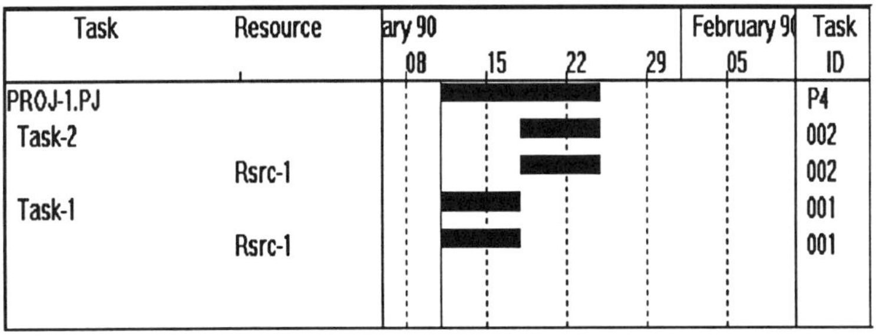

Task	Resource	ary 90 08	15	22	29	February 9(05	Task ID
PROJ-1.PJ							P4
Task-2				▬▬			002
	Rsrc-1			▬▬			002
Task-1			▬▬				001
	Rsrc-1		▬▬▬				001

Figure 10.6
Changing the order of the tasks does not affect which is delayed by levelling

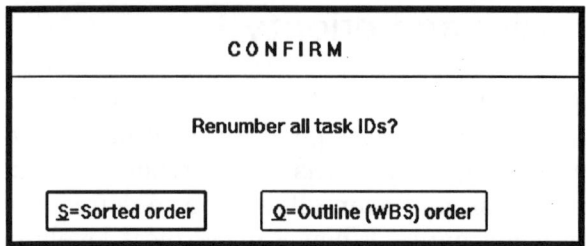

Figure 10.7
Renumbering tasks

explicit task priorities. Task priorities are entered into the column headed 'Pri'. Task priorities range from 1 to 999 with 1 being the highest priority by default. You can also enter a priority of 0 to force levelling to be switched off for the specified task. Priorities can be assigned to tasks or headings, when they apply to all the tasks and resources gathered below the heading.

If you assign a priority to a task then it will be scheduled before any task with which it is in conflict as long as it has the higher priority.

As well as assigning a priority to an overall task, you can also assign a priority to each resource assignment. Unless one task has a clear priority over another this is a much more flexible way of assigning priority because it takes the needs and characteristics of the resource into account. If you enter a task priority then all resource assignments are set to the same value. In other words, setting a task priority is the same as setting all of the resource assignments to a

Task	Resource	ary 90				February 90	Task ID
		08	15	22	29	05	
PROJ-1.PJ							P4
Task-2							001
	Rsrc-1						001
Task-1							002
	Rsrc-1						002

Figure 10.8
Re-levelling after renumbering task id

Task	Resource	ary 90 08	15	22	29	February 9 05	Task ID	Pri
PROJ-1.PJ							P4	50
Task-1				▬▬▬			001	
	Rsrc-1			▬▬▬			001	2
Task-2			▬▬▬				002	
	Rsrc-1		▬▬▬				002	1

Figure 10.9
Levelling using priorities

constant value. If you don't enter a priority then all resource assignments are set to 50 by default. You can also set a resource assignment to 0 if it isn't to be considered for levelling.

For example, in Figure 10.9 you can see that Task-2 has been scheduled before Task-1 because of the higher priority of its resource's assignment. The main problem with levelling using priorities is in assigning a consistent set of task or resource priorities that reflect the importance of each. When assigning priorities you should try to space the assigned values as much as possible to allow for new intermediate priority levels to be created. For example, if you have already rated a resource assignment as 1 how can you add a more important assignment should one occur later in the project? If you have assigned two tasks as priority 3 and 4 how can you assign a priority to a task that is more important that the first but not as important as the second? Clearly it is a good idea to use some scheme such as assigning priorities in steps of 10 or more with 500 representing a task of average importance.

If a pair of tasks are in conflict over more than one resource assignment then the resources are levelled in the order in which they were assigned to the task - i.e. the default order in which they are listed below the task. This can lead to some apparently strange behaviour. For example, if two tasks are in conflict over the same two resources and the priorities are as shown in Figure 10.9 then you might expect Task-2 to be scheduled first because Rsrc-2's assignment to it has the highest priority possible. If you look at Figure 10.10

172 *Advanced Scheduling*   *Chapter 10*

Task/Resource	90 08	15	22	29	February 90 05	1	Task ID	Pri
Task-1		▬▬					001	
Rsrc-1		▬▬					001	50
Rsrc-2		▬▬					001	20
Task-2			▬▬				002	
Rsrc-1			▬▬				002	100
Rsrc-2			▬▬				002	1

Figure 10.10
Anomalous levelling?

you can see that Task-1 is in fact scheduled first. The reason is that levelling is performed in the order in which the resources were assigned and so Rsrc-1 is levelled first. As the Task-1 assignment of Rsrc-1 is a higher priority than its Task-2 assignment, Task-2 is delayed. As this rescheduling breaks the conflict over Rsrc-2 no further levelling is performed and so the priority of Rsrc-2's assignments are irrelevant. Even so it looks as though a higher priority resource assignment has been ignored by levelling.

It also makes no difference to the results of levelling if you move the resources using (Alt) Shift and an arrow key. Such rearrangements are temporary and vanish as soon as you save and load the project file. You can think of this behaviour as if each task kept a hidden resource allocation id number.

You can see how this levelling in resource order occurs by examining Figure 10.11. In this case the first resource is

Task/Resource	90 08	15	22	29	February 90 05	1	Task ID	Pri	Units Assgn	Sched Rsrc Total Hrs
Task-1			▬▬				001			60.00
Rsrc-1			▬_ _				001	50	1	20.00
Rsrc-2			▬▬				001	20	1	40.00
Task-2		▬▬					002			80.00
Rsrc-1		▬▬					002	100	1	40.00
Rsrc-2		▬▬					002	1	1	40.00

Figure 10.11
Both resources taken into account

only allocated for 20 hours of the task's duration and so the first levelling only delays Task-2 by this much. Even after this delay there is still a resource conflict over Rsrc-2 and when this is levelled its priorities control which task is delayed. As you can see this results in Task-1 being delayed rather than Task-2.

Assigning priorities

If you do go to the trouble of assigning priorities to all resource assignments then there is no doubt that this gives you good control over levelling but it is remarkably difficult to do completely for a large project. In most cases priorities are assigned on an ad-hoc basis to resolve specific difficulties. For example, if you level a project model and are unhappy about the way a particular task has been delayed then you can correct this behaviour by assigning appropriate priorities to the tasks involved in the resource conflict.

This approach at least has the advantage that you are only troubled by priority assignment where it makes any difference to the schedule and it still ensures that changes are automatically taken care of by re-levelling. The only danger is if new tasks or resource assignments are introduced which add to an existing resource conflict. In this case you must be careful to allocate a new and appropriate priority.

Also notice that you can specify a date range to which levelling will be applied. All you have to do is enter the range for levelling in the Calculation Options box. You can use the terms BEGIN and END to refer to the start and end of the project. You can also completely remove a resource from consideration by the levelling procedure by clicking on the box labelled Levelling in the Resource Details view - see later.

Levelling by float

Although levelling by priority is a good way of resolving the question of which task or resource allocation should be delayed there are occasions when other considerations are more obvious. For example, consider the schedule produced by levelling in Figure 10.12. At first it looks reasonable, Task-1's assignment has a higher priority so it is Task-2 that is delayed. However, if you look a little closer you will see that the whole project has been lengthened by delaying Task-2 whereas delaying Task-1 would have no impact on the project's scheduled duration. Clearly it would be a very important task indeed that had to be scheduled so that the whole project was delayed as a result!

It is obvious that tasks that can be delayed without lengthening the project should be used in levelling before tasks that cannot be delayed. Further discussion of this idea is easier if we first review some fairly simple jargon.

» The **critical path** is the longest path through a project. If any task on the critical path is delayed then the whole project is delayed.
» A **critical task** is one that is on the critical path.
» **Float** is the time a task can be delayed before it delays the project. In other words it is the maximum delay before it becomes a critical task.
» **Free float** is the delay that a task can be subjected to before it delays the start of any other task.

Task/Resource	90 08	15	22	29	February 90 05	1	Est Dur	Schd Dur	Task ID	Pri
Task-1							5dy	5dy	002	
Rsrc-1								5dy	002	1
Task-2							5dy	5dy	003	
Rsrc-1								5dy	003	50
Task-3							5dy	5dy	004	

Figure 10.12
Levelling by priorities is not always best

Levelling by float 175

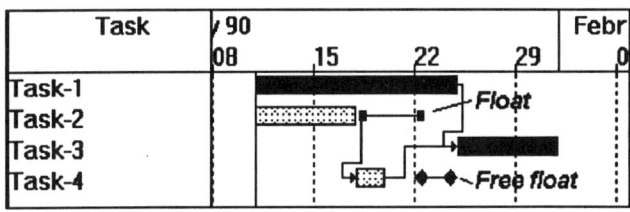

Figure 10.13
Float shown on the Gantt chart

Another definition of a critical task is one that has 0 float associated with it. In practice you may want to adopt this definition in a slightly modified form. For example, a task that has a float of 1hr relative to a 5-day duration is practically speaking a critical task. You can set the definition of a critical task using the Calculation Options dialog box in Expert mode, see Figure 10.14. All you have to do is enter the maximum length of float allowed for a critical task to the right of 'Mark Tasks Critical with Float of' at the bottom of the box.

The tasks on the critical path are always shown differently on the Gantt chart to non-critical tasks. You can also load a different Gantt chart layout which shows float and free float. All you have to do is use the command Layout,Load and select layout B20 (or GANTT2 in Version 2). For

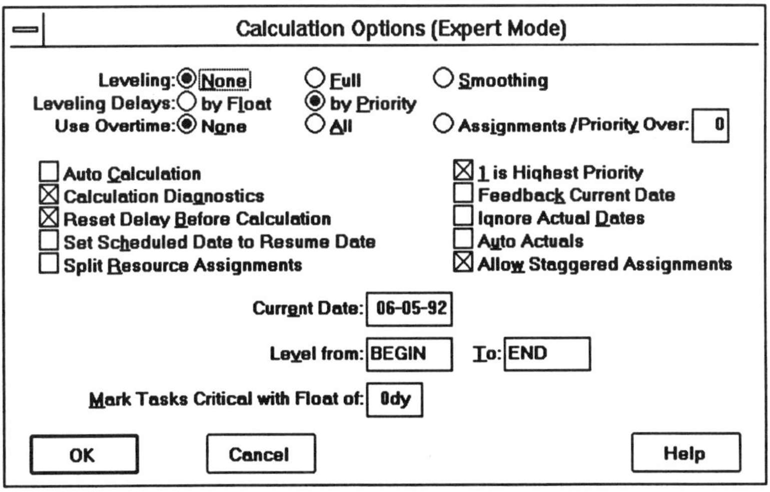

Figure 10.14
Calculation Options dialog box

example, in Figure 10.13 you can see that there is free float indicated after Task-4 because it can be delayed by this amount without delaying any other task. The reason is of course that Task-3 cannot start until Task-1 has completed. In the same way there is float shown after Task-2 because delaying it will immediately delay Task-4, i.e. it cannot be free float, but Task-2 cannot be delayed beyond the amount of free float shown without causing Task-4 to delay Task-3 and so lengthen the entire project. It can sometimes be difficult to tell by sight if float is free float or not and so it is good to be able to rely on SuperProject to work this out for you! You will also find a column headed Float and one headed Free Float which give the exact lengths of both types of float associated with tasks. Notice that in the case of Task-4 in Figure 10.13 its free float is 3 days and its float is 3 days.

The actual symbols used to represent float and free float can be customised very easily. For example, layout B20 and others which are similar use the same square line endings for float and free float and distinguish the two by colour. Obviously, this convention does not show up well in black and white and so for the remainder of this book square ends will be used to signify float and diamonds for free float.

Now it is possible to state the levelling principle implied earlier in more concise terms. Tasks with float, or even free float, should be delayed first. SuperProject's default mode of scheduling is to first delay on the grounds of priority, then free float and finally float. However, if you are in Expert mode you can set levelling to ignore priorities and level using only using float and free float. To select the type of levelling simply check the 'by Float' box in the Calculation Options dialog box - see Figure 10.14.

For example, if the project shown earlier in Figure 10.12 is levelled by float the result is as shown in Figure 10.15. You can see that now Task-1 has been delayed even though it has the higher priority because it had free float. The thin line before Task-1 indicates a delay.

Levelling by float

Task/Resource	90				February 90		Est Dur	Schd Dur	Task ID	Pri
	8	15	22	29	05	12				
Task-1			▬▬				5dy	5dy	002	
Rsrc-1			▬▬					5dy	002	1
Task-2		▬▬					5dy	5dy	003	
Rsrc-1		▬▬						5dy	003	50
Task-3		▬▬					5dy	5dy	004	

Figure 10.15
Levelling by float

» A **delay** is a period of time between when a task could start and when it is scheduled to start.

Notice that delaying a task that has float, even free float, doesn't guarantee that the delay will not lengthen the project. For example, in Figure 10.16, Task-1 is now 7 days in duration and now it lengthens the total project as indicated by the free float at the end of Task-3. Even so the alternative scheduling of Task-2 first results in a much larger overall project duration.

SuperProject always tries to be reasonable about scheduling. Even if you are using levelling by priority, two tasks or assignments that have equal priority will be scheduled according to which one has float associated with it. If neither have float then they are scheduled in order of task id number.

Task	Resource	90				February 90		Est Dur	Schd Dur
		08	15	22	29	05			
PROJ-19.PJ									12dy
Task-1			▬▬▬					7dy	7dy
	Rsrc-1		▬▬▬						7dy
Task-2			▬▬					5dy	5dy
	Rsrc-1		▬▬						5dy
Task-3				▬▬				5dy	5dy

Figure 10.16
Levelling by float sometimes delays the project

Splitting assignments

One of the more sophisticated levelling options is the ability to split an assignment so that a higher priority task can be completed. For example, in Figure 10.17 you can see that there is a resource conflict between Task-3 and Task-1. There are two possible ways of resolving this conflict:

> delay Task-1 which introduces a 10-day delay and lengthens the project by this amount

or

> delay Task-3 which introduces a 13-day delay and lengthens the project by this amount

As Task-3 has a higher priority SuperProject will accept the 10-day delay and delay Task-1.

Another alternative is to allow the higher priority task to interrupt the assignment of Rsrc-1 to the lower priority task. This lengthens the project by only 5 days and so is clearly a better schedule. However, it is only a practical schedule if it is reasonable to interrupt Task-1 in this way without making its total estimated duration longer. By default SuperProject will not split assignments in this way but all you have to do to enable this feature is click on the Split Resource Assignments box in the Calculation Options dialog box.

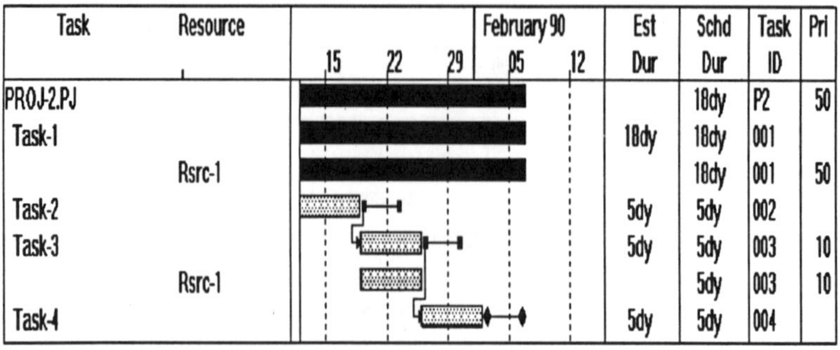

Task	Resource	15	22	29	February 90 05	12	Est Dur	Schd Dur	Task ID	Pri
PROJ-2.PJ								18dy	P2	50
Task-1							18dy	18dy	001	
	Rsrc-1							18dy	001	50
Task-2							5dy	5dy	002	
Task-3							5dy	5dy	003	10
	Rsrc-1							5dy	003	10
Task-4							5dy	5dy	004	

Figure 10.17
A difficult scheduling problem

Task	Resource	February 90				Est Dur	Schd Dur	Task ID	Prl
		15	22	29	05 12				
PROJ-2.PJ							23dy	P2	50
Task-1						18dy	23dy	001	
	Rsrc-1						5dy	001	50
	Rsrc-1						13dy	001	50
Task-2						5dy	5dy	002	
Task-3						5dy	5dy	003	10
	Rsrc-1						5dy	003	10
Task-4						5dy	5dy	004	

Figure 10.18
The result of splitting assignments.

As you can see in Figure 10.18 the result of allowing split assignments is exactly what was predicted. You can see that the split assignment is handled by assigning the same resource twice to Task-1. Notice that an assignment will not be split if the priorities are equal or if levelling by float is selected. It only works if you are levelling by priorities.

Staggering assignments

A new levelling feature introduced in Version 3 is the ability to stagger assignments. If you select Allow Staggered Assignments in the Calculation Options dialog box then levelling will be performed at the assignment, rather than the task, level. That is, if two tasks are in conflict over the use of a single resource then that resource's assignment will be delayed for one of the tasks but any other assignments will go ahead as before.

For example, in Figure 10.19 you can see a very simple resource conflict resolved in a different way. Instead of shifting the start of Task-2 forward to resolve the conflict

Task	Resource	May 92				Est Dur	Schd Dur
		04	11	18	2		
PROJ-1.PJ							10dy
Task-1						5dy	5dy
	Rsrc-1						5dy
Task-2						5dy	10dy
	Rsrc-1						5dy
	Rsrc-2						5dy

Figure 10.19
The result of staggering assignments.

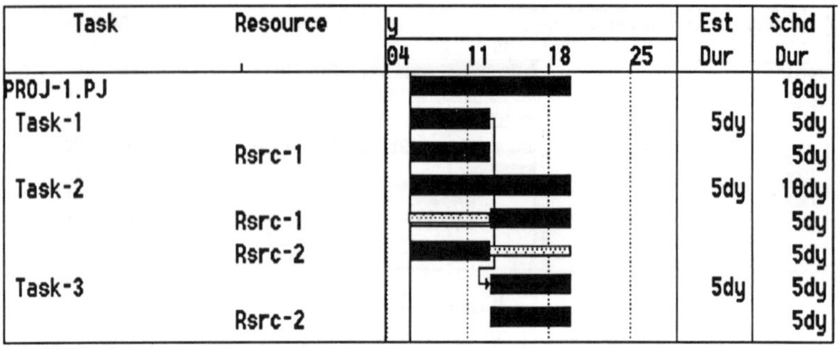

180 *Advanced Scheduling* *Chapter 10*

Task	Resource	04	11	18	25	Est Dur	Schd Dur
PROJ-1.PJ							10dy
Task-1						5dy	5dy
	Rsrc-1						5dy
Task-2						5dy	10dy
	Rsrc-1						5dy
	Rsrc-2						5dy
Task-3						5dy	5dy
	Rsrc-2						5dy

Figure 10.20
A 'staggering' improvement!

involving Rsrc-1 the starting date of Rsrc-1's assignment to Task-2 has been moved. This allows Rsrc-2 to start on the task and finish in the 5 days assigned. Of course Task-2 isn't complete at this point because Rsrc-1 still has 5 days of work to put in. Notice that staggering the assignments lengthens Task-2 but does not lengthen, or change in any way the total duration of the project. In a more complex situation it is possible that the project's total duration could be reduced by assignment staggering. If the resource that isn't delayed is needed for another task then this task could finish early as a result of staggering.

For example, in Figure 10.20 you can see that Rsrc-2 is immediately used by Task-3 while Rsrc-1 gets on with finishing Task-2. If you don't allow staggered assignments then the total project duration increases by 5 days. Of course it may be that Task-2 cannot be completed by 5 day's work from Rsrc-1 and Rsrc-2 at different times. If resources need to work concurrently on a task then do not allow staggered assignments.

Assignment status

Now that we know quite a lot more about the way a task might be scheduled it is worth looking in a little more detail at the meaning of the status column. Each assignment is categorised according to its current state of progress and it state of scheduling. The possibilities for progress are:

» Schd - Scheduled

» Prog - Work in progress

» Intr - Interrupted work

» Done - Work completed

These are described in more detail when we look at the use of a project model for tracking progress in Chapter 11.

The possibilities for an assignment's scheduling status are:

» Crit - on the critical path

» Cnf - resource conflict exists

» Neg - negative float or negative delay

After full levelling there should be no Cnf status resources. A negative float or negative delay is an indication of some serious scheduling problem. For example, negative float results if a task's finishing date is past its successor's starting date and this can only occur if an un-meetable Must date has been set. If you see Neg in the status column you should examine the schedule very carefully.

Early and late dates

Although the Gantt chart shows delays and float clearly, it is sometimes necessary to look at the way these values affect the schedule in some detail. Each task has a pair of early and late start and finish dates associated with it.

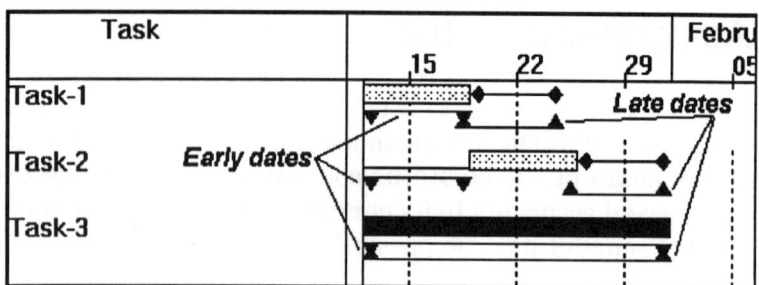

Figure 10.21
Late and early dates

A task's early start date is simply the date that it could be scheduled to start on if it wasn't for the presence of a delay. Its early finish is simply obtained by adding its scheduled duration to its early start date. In other words, the early start and early finish dates represent how the task would be scheduled in the absence of delays.

A task's late finish is the latest date it could finish without affecting the critical path. The late start is simply obtained by subtracting the task's scheduled duration from the late finish date. In other words, the late start and late finish represent how the task would be scheduled if its task type was ALAP (As Late As Possible).

The early and late dates give you some idea of the range over which the task's scheduling might be influenced. You can think of it as the 'movable range' for a task. If you look at Figure 10.21 you can see the standard symbols used for the early and late dates. To enable these all you have to do is use the command Layout,Bar Symbols and select the early and late date options in the dialog box that appears. (If you have Version 2's layout file then use layout GANTT-6.) You can also create a layout that will show early and late dates on the Gantt chart, see Chapter 14. If it helps you to interpret the diagram then think of the bars formed by the early dates and the late dates as being the extreme positions possible for the task bar within the chart.

Smoothing

Full levelling is a powerful scheduling tool but sometimes it automatically resolves resource conflicts that would be better handled some other way. In particular, it is very common for full levelling to increase the overall duration of the project by delaying tasks on the critical path. Rather than delaying the project you may prefer to allow the resource conflicts on the critical path to remain so that you can resolve them manually.

If you click on the Smoothing option in the Calculation Options dialog box SuperProject will perform levelling on all tasks that are not on the critical path but it will ignore all conflicts involving critical tasks. Not only this, it will also stop the levelling process as soon as a task has been delayed by a period that just makes it into a critical task.

In other words, levelling by smoothing cannot lengthen the overall duration of the project but equally it doesn't guarantee to resolve all resources conflicts. However, you can be sure that the conflicts that remain are the ones that are important to the overall project.

For example, in Figure 10.22 you can see that Task-1, Task-4 and Task-5 are in conflict over the assignment of Rsrc-1. If you select full levelling then Task-2 and Task-5 will be delayed sufficiently to remove all resource conflicts

Task	Resource	90 08	15	22	29	February 90 05	1	Est Dur	Schd Dur	Task ID
PROJ-2.PJ									15dy	P2
Task-1								5dy	5dy	001
	Rsrc-1								5dy	001
Task-2								5dy	5dy	002
Task-3								5dy	5dy	003
Task-4								4dy	4dy	004
	Rsrc-1								4dy	004
Task-5								12dy	12dy	005
	Rsrc-1								12dy	005

Figure 10.22
Resource conflicts on and off the critical path

Task	Resource	90 08	15	22	29	February 90 05	1	Est Dur	Schd Dur	Task ID
PROJ-2.PJ									21dy	P2
Task-1								5dy	5dy	001
	Rsrc-1								5dy	001
Task-2								5dy	5dy	002
Task-3								5dy	5dy	003
Task-4								4dy	4dy	004
	Rsrc-1								4dy	004
Task-5								12dy	12dy	005
	Rsrc-1								12dy	005

Figure 10.23
After full levelling

with a resulting increase in the overall duration of the project from 15 days to 21 days but, as you can see in Figure 10.23, all of the resource conflicts have been completely resolved. If you select smoothing, however, the result is very different. Now Task-3 and Task-5 are only delayed up to the point where they would start to lengthen the project if they were delayed any more, see Figure 10.24. The result is, of course, that after smoothing the project duration is still 15 days but resource conflicts remain between Task-1, Task-4 and Task-5. Indeed, if you examine the conflict using Resource Outline view you will discover that Rsrc-1 is scheduled to work a 24-hour day on all three tasks! The schedule is most definitely in need of some manual editing.

Task	Resource	90 08	15	22	29	February 90 05	1	Est Dur	Schd Dur	Task ID
PROJ-2.PJ									15dy	P2
Task-1								5dy	5dy	001
	Rsrc-1								5dy	001
Task-2								5dy	5dy	002
Task-3								5dy	5dy	003
Task-4								4dy	4dy	004
	Rsrc-1								4dy	004
Task-5								12dy	12dy	005
	Rsrc-1								12dy	005

Figure 10.24
After smoothing

Partial allocation

Partial allocation of resources is a useful modelling technique but it is usually slightly more complicated to understand the full implications. When it comes to levelling tasks that have been partially allocated, the behaviour is more or less what you might expect. If you allocate the same resource to two concurrent tasks then it is only over allocated if its total number of hours per day exceeds that indicated on its calendar. For example, assigning Rsrc-1 to two concurrent tasks for 4 hours each is fine and not a conflict as long as the resource's working day is 8 hours.

The situation is more interesting when the daily allocation is greater than the resource has available on its calendar. For example, if you allocate Rsrc-1 to Task-1 for 4 hours and to Task-2 for 6 hours then, assuming an 8-hour standard day there is an over allocation of 2 hours per day. If you apply full levelling to this situation the resulting schedule, see Figure 10.25, is worth studying a little more closely. Task-2 has been delayed so that Task-1 can complete in its entirety first. If you were to look at the Resource Outline view for Rsrc-1 you would see that Task-1 uses its 4 hours of time on each day and the remaining 4 hours is unallocated even though Task-2 could probably make use of it. When Task-1 is complete the leftover 4 hours is used by Task-2 which consequently finishes a little earlier than you might otherwise expect.

Task	Resource	'90 08	,15	,22	29	February 90 05		Est Dur	Schd Dur	Alloc /Day
PROJ-3.PJ									10dy	
Task-1			▨▨▨					5dy	5dy	
	Rsrc-1		▨▨▨						5dy	4hr
Task-2					▬▬▬			5dy	6dy	
	Rsrc-1				▬▬▬				6dy	6hr

Figure 10.25
A partial allocation conflict after levelling

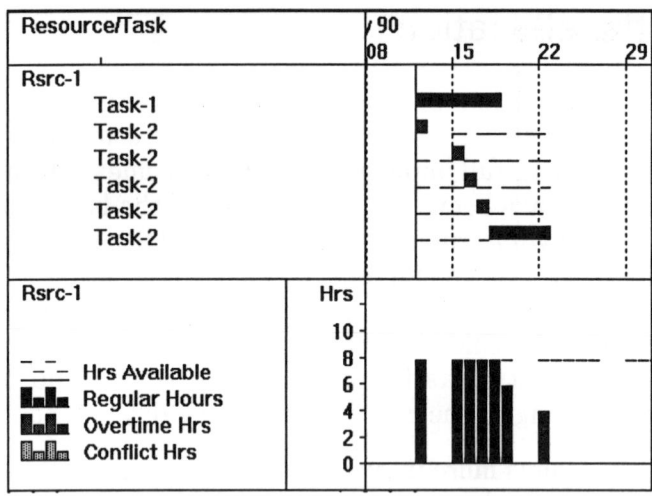

Figure 10.26
Resource outline view of the levelling

If you would like to see a slightly more intelligent levelling of the resource conflict then all you need to do is select the Split Resource Assignments option in the Calculations Options dialog box. In this case the unallocated hours on each day are used by Task-2, as can be seen in Figure 10.26. Apart from the untidy multiple allocation of Rsrc-1 to Task-2 you can see that this does actually result in a better use of Rsrc-1's time.

At this point it is worth saying that you should avoid the temptation to become too enamoured with automatic levelling as applied to partial allocation. For example, in this case a much simpler approach would have been not to over-allocate the single resource in this way in the first place!

Setting overtime

When you start to consider resource conflicts it is obvious that one way of avoiding some over-allocation is to make use of overtime working. In Expert mode you can timetable any resource to have a given number of regular hours and a given number of overtime hours available on any day.

Setting overtime **187**

Calendar For:		Rsrc-1	*Regular hours*				
1991	Sun	0.0 0	Mon	8.0 **2**	Tue	8.0 2	W
Dec Jan	29	WKND	30		31 *Overtime hours*		0

Figure 10.27
Setting regular overtime on the resource calendar

Working hours can be set using the resource's calendar. To set the number of hours of overtime available on each day of the week all you have to do is to enter the value in the top-right hand corner of the appropriate day - see Figure 10.27. This is a simple way of setting overtime hours but there is an alternative way that also allows you to specify different patterns of overtime working for different periods.

If you select the Details view of the resource and use the Layout,View Subwindows,Work Periods command then the lower portion of the form changes to display the pattern of regular and overtime hours for which the resource is available to work, see Figure 10.28. If you are using the Windows version then simply clicking on the clock icon will select the work periods display.

RsrcName:	Rsrc-1								
Type:	Labor		☒ Level		Hours Under:	2.00	Overtime Mult:	1.00	
Accrual:	Prorate		Factor:	100	Hours Avail:	82.00	Standard Day:	8.00	
Current values for	01-01-92	Sun Mon Tue Wed Thu Fri Sat					Rate:	25.00	
Start Time:	8:00a	Regular Hrs:	0.0 8.0 8.0 8.0 8.0 8.0 0.0				Allocation:	100%	
Max Units:	1	Overtime Hrs:	0.0 2.0 2.0 2.0 0.0 0.0 0.0				Default Units:	1	

Start Hour	Sun RegOvr	Mon RegOvr	Tue RegOvr	Wed RegOvr	Thu RegOvr	Fri RegOvr	Sat RegOvr	Start Date	End Date
8:00a	0.00 0	8.00 2	8.00 2	8.00 2	8.00 0	8.00 0	0.00 0	BEGIN	31-01-92
8:00a	0.00 0	8.00 0	8.00 0	8.00 0	**8.00** 0	8.00 0	0.00 0	01-02-92	END

Figure 10.28
Two patterns of work hours for Rsrc-1

The table of regular and overtime hours, roughly in the middle of the display, can be filled in and has the same effect as entering working day lengths and overtime hours on the resource's calendar. If you enter the number of regular work hours and overtime hours then these figures are transferred to the resource's calendar as if you had entered them directly.

The new element in the Resource Details form is in the window at the bottom of the screen. This can be used to set regular and overtime hours for any period specified by a start and finish date. When you first open the Resource Details form there is a single line covering the period BEGIN to END i.e. the entire project's duration. Filling in this first line alters the values in the table above. In other words, the first line of the table is just the set of working hours that you have encountered on the resource calendar and in the table of regular and overtime hours. However if you place the cursor on the End Date entry, i.e. END, and type a date the line will split into two lines. The first line sets the work hours for BEGIN to the new date and the second from the new date to END.

For example, in Figure 10.28 you can see that Rsrc-1 has two different patterns of work hours defined. The first row shows that from BEGIN to 31/1/92 Rsrc-1 is available for 2 hour overtime on the first three days of each week. This first line's worth of data is also shown in the table above which always shows the working pattern in force for the week containing the current date - i.e. the date in the box next to the label 'Current values for'. The second row indicates that Rsrc-1 isn't available for any overtime from 1/2/92 to END. You can carry on adding lines that vary the resource's working hours over any period in the same way. When a task is scheduled it will be the working hours for the relevant period that control its scheduling. Notice that the resource's calendar still controls holidays and working hour variations on a particular day.

Using overtime

Now that we know how to indicate the number of hours overtime that a resource has available, the next question is how to make use of these hours. There are some other details of overtime to discuss, in particular the important fact that overtime usually costs more, but this will be dealt with in the broader context of project costing and budgeting, see Chapter 12.

By default SuperProject ignores overtime hours and bases all of its scheduling on the use of regular working hours. You can make it take notice of the available overtime hours by simply clicking on the Use Overtime All box in the Calculation Options dialog, see Figure 10.14. After this a recalculation of the project model will produce new scheduled durations for all tasks with resources that have overtime available. This treatment of overtime is very crude and makes no attempt to minimise its use by any criterion. All overtime hours are treated as extensions to the working day and task durations are reduced accordingly.

For example, if you have a 5-day task and its one and only assigned resource has 2 hours of overtime available then then if you select Use Overtime the task's scheduled duration will be reduced to 4 days. If you look at Figure 10.29 you can see that Task-1 takes 5 days because

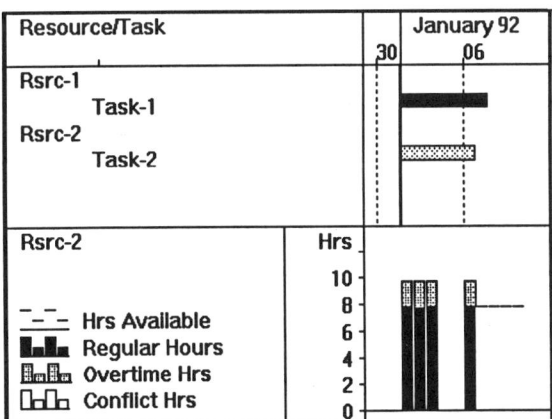

Figure 10.29
Using overtime to shorten scheduled duration

Rsrc-1 has no overtime available but Task-2 takes 4 days and the histogram actually shows the overtime being used to the full.

Overtime can be used with levelling but the only effect it has is to reduce the scheduled duration of each task that has overtime available to it. As already mentioned it is just as if the length of the working day had been increased for those resources with overtime available. The increased cost of overtime is noted, as will be explained later, but no attempt is made to minimise the use of overtime to where it is needed specifically to help with resource conflicts or any other scheduling problem for that matter. In a sense there is absolutely nothing new here apart from the differential costing of overtime hours.

What you might be looking for at this point is some way of controlling the use of overtime to just those tasks where the project benefits the most. Unfortunately this is a complex task to automate and the best that SuperProject can manage is to allow you to make use of task/resource assignment priorities to semi-manually control overtime use.

If you click on the Assignments/Priority Over box in the Calculation Options dialog box then only resource assignments with a priority over the value indicated on the right will make use of overtime. The only thing that you have to be careful of is what 'over the priority' means. By default 1 is the highest priority so if you have set a level of 50 for using overtime you will find that tasks/assignments with priorities in the range 1 to 50 will use overtime and 51 to 999 will not. You can change the way priorities are interpreted so that 999 is the highest priority by removing the check mark in the '1 is highest priority' box in the Calculation Options dialog box.

You can see a simple example of priority being used to control overtime usage in Figure 10.30. Rsrc-1 has 2 hours of overtime available on each working day but the Calculation Options dialog box has been set so that only

Task/Resource	January 92				Fe	Est Dur	Schd Dur	Pri
	30	06	13	20	27	0		
Task-1			▬▬				5dy	5dy	
Rsrc-1			▬▬					5dy	50
Task-2		▒▒					5dy	4dy	
Rsrc-1		▒▒						4dy	49

Figure 10.30
Using priority to control overtime usage

assignments with priority over 49 will use overtime. You can see that Task-1's assignment is only priority 50 and this is a lower priority than 49. However, Task-2's assignment is at a priority of 49 and this is sufficient to allow overtime to be used. You can see that this results in Task-2's scheduled duration dropping to 4 days. Notice that levelling has also been used to schedule the two tasks. In this case you can clearly see that levelling and overtime use occur independently. The only possibility for any interaction between the two is if levelling by priority and overtime by priority are both selected.

If you would like overtime to be used only to help resolve conflicts the best way to go about this is to make all assignments at priority 0. If you also set Use Overtime with a value of over 50 as having priority then this disables both levelling and overtime use for all assignments. Next look

Task/Resource	January 92			Est Dur	Schd Dur	Pri
	30	06	13			
Task-1		▒▒		5dy	5dy	
Rsrc-1		▒▒			5dy	0
Task-2		▒▒		5dy	5dy	
Rsrc-1		▒▒			5dy	0
Task-3		▒▒		5dy	4dy	
Rsrc-2		▒▒			4dy	50
Task-4			▒▒	5dy	4dy	
Rsrc-2			▒▒		4dy	50
Task-5		▬▬		5dy	5dy	
Rsrc-3		▬▬			5dy	51
Task-6			▬▬	5dy	5dy	
Rsrc-3			▬▬		5dy	51

Figure 10.31
Using priority to control overtime and levelling

through the schedule for conflicts and change the priorities of any conflicting assignments to a value in the range 1 to 50 to level using overtime and 51 to 999 to level without using overtime. Of course your third option is to leave the priority at 0 and neither level nor use overtime!

For example, if you look at Figure 10.31 you can see the three main possibilities. Each resource has 2 hours of overtime defined and Use Overtime is set at 50. In the case of Task-1 the priority is 0 and so neither levelling nor overtime is used. Task-2 has a priority of 50 and in this case you can see that overtime is used as well as levelling. Task-3 has a priority of 51 and in this case only levelling is used. Also notice that it is perfectly reasonable for one of the assignments to have a priority of 50 and the other 51. In this case levelling would be applied but overtime would be used for only one of the tasks.

Living with conflict

Finally it is important to state again that not all resource conflicts have to be resolved. In some cases the detected conflict is just a weakness of the model and doesn't occur in real life. For example, if you assign a resource to a task for 5 days and in the middle of the allocation schedule a meeting for 1 hour there generally isn't any need to modify the model to resolve such a slight conflict. In practice the resource will interrupt the first task to attend the meeting and as long as task durations haven't been estimated to an accuracy of 1 hour this lost time isn't significant.

You should examine each conflict and try to decide if it needs resolving or can be allowed to remain.

Levelling a real project

If we return for a moment to the software project introduced in the previous chapter it is worth asking if there are any resource conflicts. An easy way of concentrating on resource

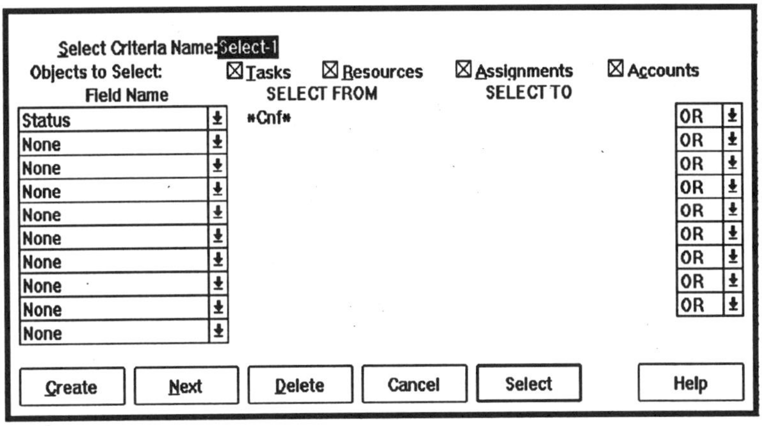

Figure 10.32
A selection filter for conflicts

conflicts is to define a selection filter like the one shown in Figure 10.32. Notice that this only selects one half of the conflicting allocations in that the first use of the resource isn't taken to be a conflict, only second and subsequent assignments of the same period. You can reduce the complexity of the display by selecting 'Show Only Selected' in the Layout, Outline Layout dialog box but in practice this isn't very useful because it also hides the first use of the resource involved in the detected conflict.

A simpler solution is to change to Resource Outline view and concentrate on resources that have conflict tasks listed under their assignments. You can see an example of this approach in Figure 10.33 - the **Design** (manual) and **Trial** tasks are both shown as in conflict and in Resource Outline view it is quite easy to see what they are in conflict with. The **Design** (manual) task is scheduled for the same period as **Coding** and the **Trial** is scheduled during **Beta test**.

The first trivial point to notice is that although it seemed reasonable to name two tasks 'Design' while they were clearly identified under their respective headings, it doesn't look like such a good idea now that the headings aren't visible. Although you can give the same name to different tasks it isn't in general a good idea and so the first correction

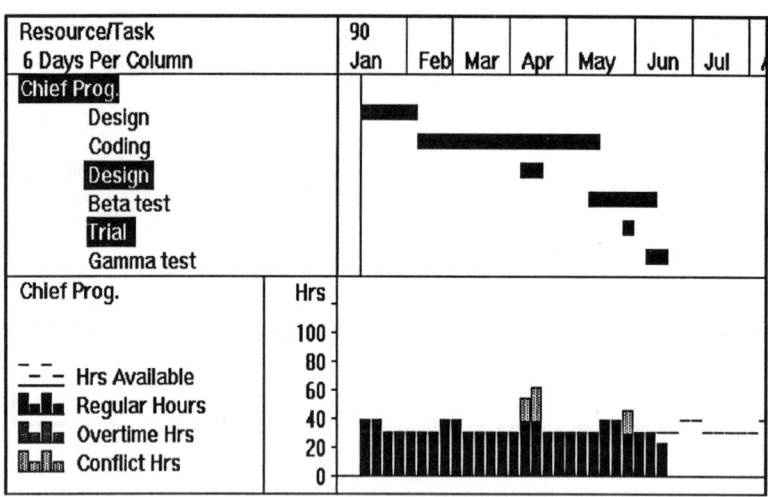

Figure 10.33
The Chief programmer's assignments

to the model is to rename these two tasks **Design prog** and **Design manual** for clarity.

Next the **Coding** and **Design manual** conflict has to be resolved. It looks at first sight as if the best way to proceed is to use levelling with split assignments and assign a higher priority to **Design manual** so that it can interrupt **Design prog**. If you try this you might be surprised at what happens, see Figure 10.34. Instead of interrupting **Coding**, the **Design manual** task has moved to first position in the schedule and the **Trial** task has interrupted the now delayed **Design prog** task. This is not only not what was expected, but also far from what is reasonable. You can try as many modifications as you like but you will not manage to make **Design manual** interrupt **Coding** by levelling. For example, increasing the priority of **Design prog** moves it back into first place but **Coding** is still delayed. The reason is that the **Design manual** task has a great deal of delay built into it because it is an ALAP task and this delay will always be used to resolve the scheduling conflict before taking drastic measures such as interrupting another task.

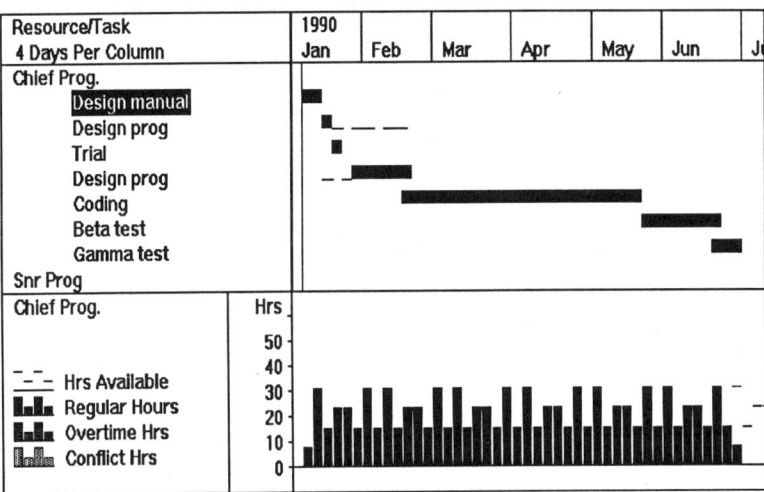

Figure 10.34
The Chief programmers assignments after levelling

So what is the solution? There are a number of ways to look at this problem. You could say that the structure of the model is wrong and this is revealed by the fact that scheduling the design of the manual before the design of the program was such an obvious mistake that it implies that there is a logical constraint between the two tasks, i.e. a Finish to Start link, that hasn't been specified. You could continue to restructure the model in this way until you fixed the **Design manual** task with respect to the **Coding** task so that interruption was the only way that SuperProject could resolve the conflict.

An alternative viewpoint is that a manual fix is all that is required. For example, if you remove the levelling and recalculate the project to schedule **Design manual** ALAP with respect to all the other conditions, you can then use this date as a Must date. All you have to do is move to the Scheduled start column and enter an = sign next to the date, and it will not be altered by SuperProject in subsequent recalculations. After this you can enable levelling with split assignments and the **Coding** task will indeed be interrupted by the **Design manual** task. You can see the result of doing this in Figure 10.35. (To make the pattern of task

196 *Advanced Scheduling* *Chapter 10*

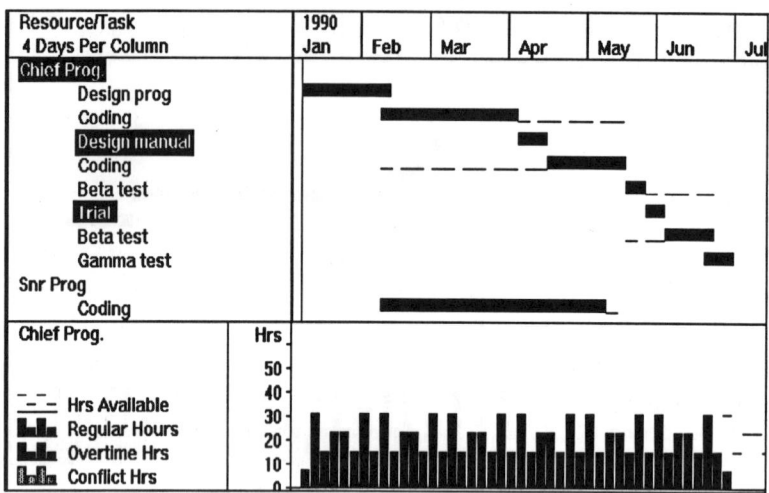

Figure 10.35
The Chief Programmer's assignments after fixing the date of the manual design and levelling

interruptions easier to see the Trials Manager has been excluded from the levelling process.) This approach has the advantage that any rescheduling of **Design manual** will be accounted for automatically.

If you look carefully you will discover that interrupting the task is probably not what the project planner actually desired. The **Coding** task has been extended by the period of the interruption but only for the Chief Programmer. This mean that the other resources are not used for the full duration of the task! It is more likely that the assignment of the Chief Programmer to the **Design Manual** task was to have little or no impact on **Coding**. This brings us to the third approach to dealing with the resource conflict - to ignore it! It is doubtful that at this stage of the plan there is any need to resolve this conflict either manually or automatically because it is reasonable to assume that the over-allocation of the Chief Programmer will not have any effect on the schedule. If you do need to take it into account for reasons other than scheduling (project costing say) then it is probably better to build an interruption in the assignment into the project model manually at a stage where the scheduling of tasks is complete.

Surprisingly, manually splitting a resource allocation is quite an involved process - simple in principle but not in practice. For example, in Figure 10.36 you can see that Rsrc-1 has a split assignment between Task-1 and Task-2. This was done by assigning Rsrc-1 to Task-1 twice and manually entering the number of resource hours allocated in each case, i.e. 5 days and 10 days. This is appropriate because the interruption occurs after 5 days of Task-1 and lasts for 5 days. This gives two resource assignments of the correct length, but both start at the beginning of the task so the next job is to move to the Scheduled start column and make the start date of the second assignment the day after Task-2's scheduled finish date. All of this is made a lot easier by altering the column layout so that it includes the resource assignments in days. There are also columns that can be added to the layout for resource assignments entered in minutes, days, weeks, months and years.

The manual split assignment works fine from the point of view of accurately reflecting the resource hours allocated to each task but it has the big disadvantage that it isn't self-adjusting in any way. For example, if the start date of Task-2 changes, then the interrupted period of Task-1 will stay the same and so move out of alignment. In short, once you have created a split assignment manually you are committed to maintaining it manually.

Task/Resource	January 90					Fe	Est Dur	Sched Rsrc Regular Dys	Schd Dur
	01	08	15	22	29				
Task-1							20dy	15.00	20dy
Rsrc-1								5.00	5dy
Rsrc-1								10.00	10dy
Task-2							5dy	5.00	5dy
Rsrc-1								5.00	5dy

Figure 10.36
Manually splitting a resource assignment

Assignment delay

You can allocate a resource for less than the total duration of a task but at the moment the unallocated period is always at the end of a task. If you want to delay an assignment at the start of a task then the only way that we currently know of doing it is to enter the Scheduled start date. In many cases this is a reasonable way of working but it has the big disadvantage that any shift in the task start date is not reflected in the allocation start date. If you really want a resource allocation to start on a fixed 'must date' then this is exactly what you get by entering a scheduled start date. However, if what you really mean is that the resource should be allocated to the task a given period after the task starts this isn't a very good method of working.

A more obvious approach is to specify an assignment delay by entering a value in the Start Delay column. If you try to do this you will see exactly what the problem is. The Start Delay column is used by SuperProject to store the delays that it calculates while scheduling a model. You might think that it would be easy for it to allow you to enter a direct override to the start delay field but unfortunately this isn't possible because the start delay is zeroed before the schedule is recalculated. The reason for this is simply that SuperProject is trying to construct a good schedule and so it starts off by removing any delays that have been introduced into the project due to resource unavailability, Must dates and levelling. This allows it to resolve all of the scheduling problems from scratch and so respond to any changes you have made since the last recalculation.

If you want to, you can turn off the resetting of the delay before each recalculation using Reset Delay Before Calculation in the Calculation Options dialog box. If you do this you will discover that you can enter task and assignment delays manually. The price for this extra power is that you now have to be on the lookout for delays that have been introduced into the model that are no longer necessary. The situation is a little more complicated than

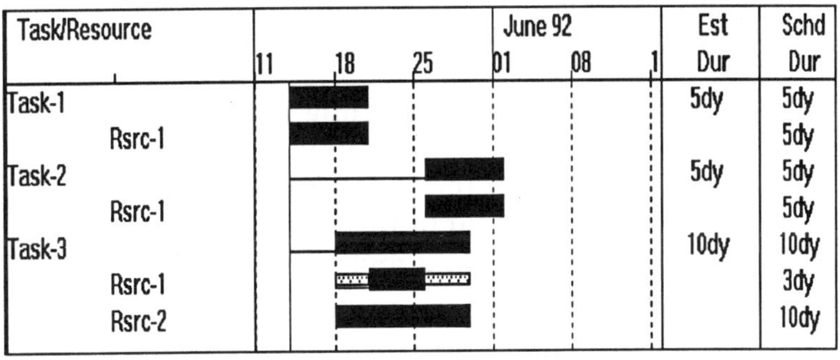

Assignment delay

Task/Resource				June 92			Est Dur	Schd Dur
	11	18	25	01	08	1		
Task-1		■■					5dy	5dy
Rsrc-1		■■						5dy
Task-2			■■				5dy	5dy
Rsrc-1			■■					5dy
Task-3			■■■■				10dy	10dy
Rsrc-1		▪▪ ▪▪						3dy
Rsrc-2			■■■■					10dy

Figure 10.37
Delaying an assignment

this because if you have levelling selected then non-entered delays are still zeroed. The only real problem that you are likely to encounter is if you turn off both Reset Delay Before Calculation and Levelling off and try to recalculate the schedule. In this case any delays introduced by the levelling will not be removed by the recalculation. In other words, if you want to enter delays manually, you also have to remove delays introduced by levelling manually. In most cases this isn't such a bad situation.

For example, in Figure 10.37 you can see that the resource assignment to Task-3 has been delayed at the start and reduced in length so that Rsrc-1 is only allocated for the middle section of the task. Also notice that Task-1 and Task-2 are correctly scheduled by the levelling method to take account of Rsrc-1's odd assignment. Reset delay is switched off and full levelling is selected. Levelling will respond to any changes made in the model. However, switching levelling off will not restore the model to its original unlevelled state unless you also turn Reset Delay Before Calculation back on. This also has the effect of erasing the manually entered delay in Rsrc-1's allocation to Task-3.

Probability fields

The basis of all accurate scheduling is good task duration estimates. In most situations supplying a single estimate seems not to be making the most of your knowledge of the project. It is very common to think in terms of how long a task might take at the worst and at the best and somehow arrive at a compromise figure for the estimate used to schedule the project.

In Chapter 9 the idea of using optimistic and pessimistic estimates to arrive at a more objective estimate of expected task duration was introduced. The basic idea was that if you can make three estimates of the task duration - an optimistic, most likely and pessimistic duration - then you can use these to arrive at an estimate of the expected duration using the following weighted average

$$\frac{\text{optimistic} + 4 \times \text{most likely} + \text{pessimistic}}{6}$$

Although this looks like a fairly ad-hoc or rule of thumb formula, it is based on a sound theory. If the actual task durations follow a Beta probability distribution and your estimates are such that there is only a 0.3% probability of the task duration being shorter than the optimistic or 0.3% longer than the pessimistic and an equal 50% chance of being longer or shorter than the most likely estimate, then expected duration is given by the formula above. You might think that the most likely duration has to be halfway between the optimistic and pessimistic estimates but this is only true if the distribution is symmetrical and this is not always the case. For example, you might feel that a task is most likely to take 1 day and it is highly unlikely to take less time but it could stretch to 2 days. In this case the most likely and the optimistic estimates are both 1 day and this is a reflection of the fact that you feel that doing better than the most likely is highly unlikely!

If you feel unhappy about trying to estimate the three durations you might find it easier to estimate a likely duration and a 68% confidence interval around it. For example, if a task is estimated to take 10 days with a 2 day deviation this means that you are 68% certain that the actual task duration will be in the range 10-2 days to 10+2 days. Once again this is assuming a Beta distribution for actual task durations. On this basis if there is a 68% chance of the actual task duration being within plus or minus one deviation there is a 95% chance of it being within plus or minus two deviations.

There is a direct connection between the two types of estimate in that:

$$\text{Deviation} = \frac{\text{Pessimistic} - \text{Optimistic}}{6}$$

Now you should be able to see that the pessimistic and optimistic estimates establish the likely spread of actual values and the value of the likely estimate determines the skewness of the task duration - either towards the optimistic or the pessimistic. If you feel both are equally likely then estimate the likely duration to be the average of (i.e. halfway between) the pessimistic and optimistic durations.

SuperProject allows you to work with probability estimates of task duration. To enable the probability fields you have to select the Show Probability fields in the Preferences, General Options dialog box. This adds four new fields - Optimum Duration, Likely Duration, Pessimistic Duration and Deviation to the project model. You can enter a value into the Deviation column and SuperProject will work out values for Pessimistic, Optimistic and Likely durations. The Likely Duration is calculated based on the assumption that the distribution isn't skewed and so it is just the average of the pessimistic and optimistic estimates.

Equally you can enter estimates of Pessimistic and Optimistic durations and SuperProject will work out the

Task	Resource	Optm Dur	Likely Dur	Pess Dur	Est Dur	Dev	Schd Dur
PAINT5.PJ		10dy	12dy	13dy		0.50dy	12dy
Prepare room		2dy	4dy	5dy		0.37dy	4dy
Clear room		1dy	1dy	2dy	1dy	0.17dy	2dy
	Bill						1dy
	Tom						1dy
Strip walls		1dy	2dy	3dy	2dy	0.33dy	2dy
	Bill						2dy
Paint room		0dy	2dy	3dy		0.33dy	2dy
Paint ceiling		1dy	1dy	2dy	1dy	0.17dy	1dy
	Bill						1dy
Paint woodwork		1dy	2dy	3dy	2dy	0.33dy	2dy
	Tom						2dy
Let paint dry		5dy	5dy	5dy	5dy	0.00dy	5dy
Paper walls		2dy	3dy	5dy	3dy	0.50dy	3dy
	Bill						3dy
Refurnish room		1dy	1dy	1dy	1dy	0.00dy	1dy
	Bill						1dy
	Tom						1dy

Figure 10.38
The paint project with probabilities

deviation. In this case it is up to you to enter a value for the likely duration.

If entering the probability estimates was all you could do there would be little point, but SuperProject will schedule the project making use of the probability estimates to derive a final project Optimistic, Pessimistic and Likely Duration.

For example, in Figure 10.38 you can see the paint project complete with probability estimates. Notice that not all tasks have a deviation associated with them - the paint has to be dry in 5 days and we don't even examine it to see if it is dry before this time and so the pessimistic, optimistic and likely time are all 5 days! You can see also that not all tasks are estimated to have symmetrical distributions. The final result is that there is only a 0.3% chance that the project will be completed faster than 10 days or take longer than 13 days. Another way of describing this information is to say that there is a 68% probability of the project taking 12 days plus or minus 0.5 of a day.

Now while probability estimates are useful and informative it is important that you do not make the mistake of thinking the project is rescheduled for the effects of the Pessimistic, Likely and Optimistic task durations. The project is only scheduled once using the estimated task durations in the usual way. The probability estimates are only used to put a confidence interval around the final scheduled project duration. For example, if a resource conflict arises if a task overruns by 1 day, this resource conflict is not taken into account in the probability estimates of the project duration. Indeed, it is possible for scheduling concerns to lengthen a project well beyond the pessimistic estimates of the project duration or shorten it well below the optimistic estimate. What you can say is that if no scheduling problems are revealed or removed by changes in task durations then the estimates of project duration are reasonable.

Probability estimates are simplistic statistical estimates and not based on the structure of the project model.

Key points

» Resource conflicts can be used to schedule tasks by automatic levelling which will delay one of the tasks enough to remove the conflict.

» Levelling can be by task/assignment priority or by float. Either method can lengthen the overall duration of the project.

» Smoothing only delays tasks by an amount that doesn't lengthen the project duration but it doesn't remove all of the resource conflicts.

» An assignment can be split by a task of a higher priority. In Version 3, assignments can also be staggered.

» Overtime can be specified and you can opt to use this for all tasks or for tasks with a priority higher than specified.

» It is very difficult to schedule a complex model by levelling and you have to be prepared to check and modify the resulting schedule manually.

» Automatic scheduling is best regarded as an aid to manual scheduling.

» Not all conflicts incorporated within a model are necessarily significant.

» You can manually enter allocation and task delays if you unselect Reset Delay Before Calculation in the Calculation Options dialog box. Notice that levelling always resets calculated delays to zero.

» Probability fields are available to allow you to work with uncertainties in estimated task duration.

Chapter 11
Tracking

The first use of a project model is in determining a feasible and acceptable schedule. Once this has been achieved the next application of the model is generally in tracking the progress of a project. The purpose of tracking can be simply to gather progress information for billing but it is usually also concerned with correcting the progress of the project to maintain the overall schedule. In this chapter we take a look at the basic ideas of project tracking and correction.

Today

So far all of the project models that we have created haven't really been concerned with the actual current date. They have been entered almost as abstract relationships between tasks, durations and resource assignments. Of course in the real world projects do have a real start date and the division into past and future is very meaningful. SuperProject automatically takes the current date from your machine's system clock and uses this to divide the Gantt chart into past and future. Tasks that are in the future can be made to appear bright and tasks (or portions of tasks) that are in the past are shown dimmer. In the normal course of things you would establish a project model with a start date some time in the future (by editing the Scheduled Start date directly or in Project Details view) and then wait for the system clock to advance naturally towards the start date. After this the tasks to the left of the current date line on the Gantt chart should either be work in progress or completed.

However, there is nothing stopping you from entering a date to be used as the current date. You can do this in the Calculations Options dialog box in either Beginner or Expert mode.

Tracking the paint project

As an example of tracking a project, let us suppose that the paint project introduced in earlier chapters is actually underway. Before tracking it, though, it is worth making one small change by deleting the **Let paint dry** task and making direct links from the **Paint room** heading to the **Paper walls** and **Refurnish room** tasks. The link to **Refurnish room** should have a lag of 5 days specified to allow for the paint to dry.

If today's date is 8/5/92 the state of the project should be as indicated by the Gantt chart shown in Figure 11.1. The tasks to the left of the vertical line should be complete or in progress. To make the distinction between past and present clear the box Bright/Dim in the dialog box that appears when you use the command Layout,Bar Symbols has been checked. You can also show future tasks as outlines. Customising the Gantt chart is discussed in full detail in Chapter 14.

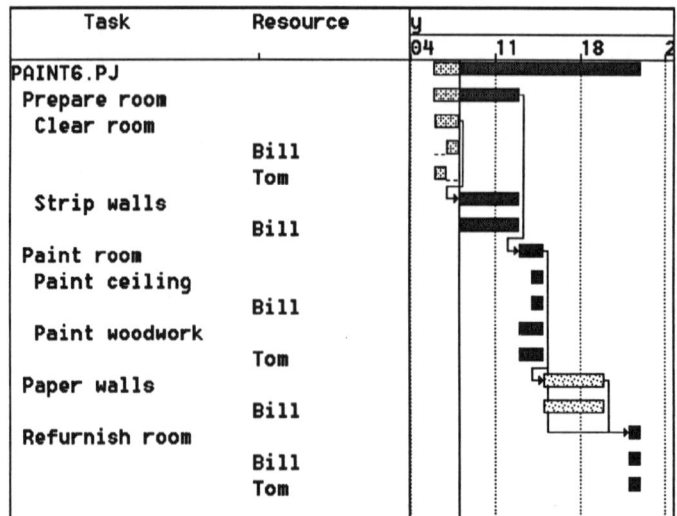

Figure 11.1
The paint project underway

This is simple enough, but what if things are already not going according to plan? You clearly cannot expect the right-hand portion of the project plan to be adhered to in the future if it has already come adrift from reality. Obviously to ensure the continued usefulness of the schedule, changes will have to be made to the model to reflect the actual start dates and durations of tasks. You could simply do this by entering the new dates but this would destroy any trace of the original model and you would have nothing with which to compare your actual progress.

The baseline model

To make sure that you have something to compare actual performance against, you can save the date from the schedule to be used as a 'baseline'. If you select Baseline Compare in the Preferences, Expert Modes menu then four additional columns of data are added to your model: Baseline Duration, Baseline Start, Baseline Finish and Baseline Resource Total Hours. Notice that when you select an expert mode it includes all of the features of the mode listed above it in the menu. This means that all of the expert features that have been described in previous chapters are still available, in addition to the extra ones, in Baseline Compare mode.

The new Baseline columns can be used to store data from the schedule that the model has produced that will not change with subsequent changes to the model. You could make entries for each task and assignment manually into each of the columns but this would be a lot of work. A simpler solution to getting data into the baseline fields is to use the command Edit, Transfer to Baseline.

When you use this command the following data transfers occur:

Scheduled Duration -> Baseline Duration
Scheduled Start -> Baseline Start
Scheduled Finish -> Baseline Finish
Scheduled Rsrc Total Hrs -> Baseline Rsrc Total Hrs

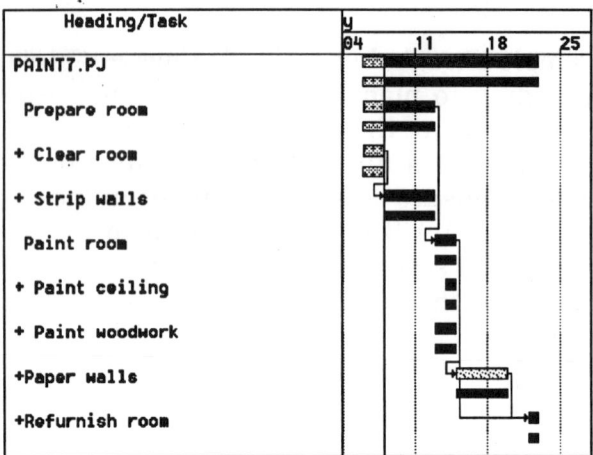

Figure 11.2
The paint project showing baseline data

You will be given a chance to change your mind because transferring this data overwrites any baseline data already stored in the fields. After this you are free to make any changes that you like to the model, safe in the knowledge that the baseline data will not change. The only way that baseline data can change is by the use of the Edit, Transfer to Baseline command.

Of course, just having the baseline data stored isn't of much use unless you can use it to compare the new model with the original. If you have the default layout loaded then the baseline data shows as a different shading of the Gantt bars but as this is difficult to see in black and white all of the figures in the rest of this book will show the baseline data as bars immediately below the scheduled bars. This layout corresponds to GANTT-3 in Version 2. You can see the baseline data for the paint project in Figure 11.2.

You can use the baseline not only to view changes that have to be made to accommodate actual progress, but to see the effect of making changes during the planning stages. For example, you can see the effect of doubling the estimated duration of the painting tasks, **Paint ceiling** and **Paint woodwork** in Figure 11.3. Notice that as well as being able to see the effect on the overall project duration you can also see the effect on each individual task.

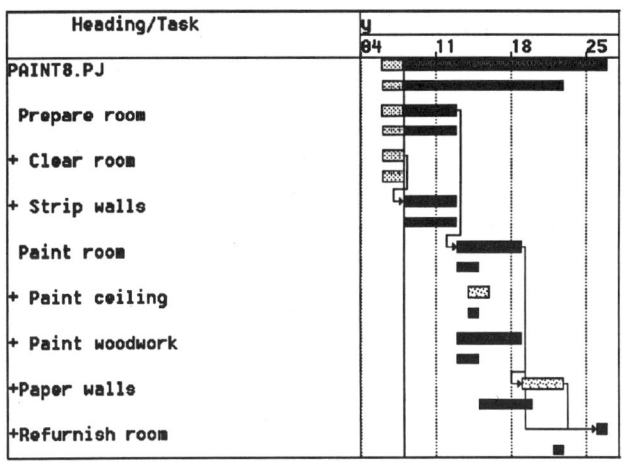

Figure 11.3
What happens if it takes twice as long to paint?

If you want to try out a number of 'what-if' comparisons it is a good idea to remember to save the project model under a different name so that you can return to it if necessary.

Actuals

Being able to set a baseline gives you a certain freedom to modify the model but it would still be an advantage to be able to record the actual start, finish and task durations as the project progresses without overwriting the original plan. If you select Expert Modes,Tracking Actuals from the Preferences menu, another set of columns are added to the familiar project model form:

>Actual Duration
>Percentage Complete
>Actual Start
>Actual Finish
>Actual Resource Total Hours
>Actual Resource Regular Hours
>Actual Resource Overtime Hours
>Actual Units
>Remaining Resource Total Hours
>Remaining Resource Regular Hours
>Remaining Resource Overtime Hours

Although this seems like a great many new data columns, it is fairly obvious how they relate to the existing data fields. All the 'Actual' columns record what actually happened to the corresponding parts of the schedule and the 'Remaining' columns show how much of the task remains to complete. To be exact:

Scheduled = Actual + Remaining

Just another baseline?

While the basic idea of recording actual data values alongside an existing project model is a simple enough idea, there are one or two complications. At its simplest the actual data could be used as a sort of auxiliary baseline to compare actual with scheduled performance. However, this doesn't address the problem of rescheduling the remaining portion of the project in the light of actual performance. Project management is usually an iterative activity where the plan has to be repeatedly revised in the light of actual performance.

SuperProject allows you considerable control over the way actual data influences the remaining schedule via the Calculation Options dialog box - see Figure 11.4.

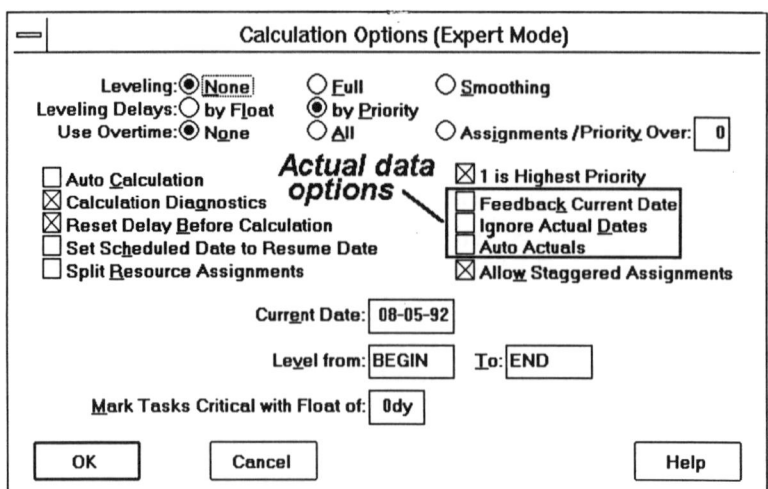

Figure 11.4
The options that control how actual data is treated

Ignoring actuals

The simplest of all uses of actual data is to record it and then use it to compare with the scheduled data or the baseline data. If you select the Ignore Actual Dates option in the Calculation Options dialog box, actual data has absolutely no effect on the schedule.

For example, in Figure 11.5 you can see a Gantt chart showing actuals and baseline data. (You can use layout GANTT-6 if you are using Version 2.). You can see that the project baseline data was saved before the project started and that the Actual Start and Finish dates for Task-1 have been entered. Notice that even though it is clear that Task-1 has been completed some days before its Scheduled Start the project schedule has not been updated to take this into account. This means that Task-2 and Task-3 will not take any advantage of the fact that Task-1 is complete. The actual data is really only being used to compare the schedule with what really happened and no attempt has been made to react to the situation. Presumably we are now waiting for the actual data for Task-2 and Task-3 to see exactly when they were done! At the completion of the project you could examine and compare the Gantt chart for the proposed and actual schedule but there is no clue as to how the planner was expecting the two to be related!

Although the example in Figure 11.5 is a little extreme, in that the obvious thing to do would have been to change the

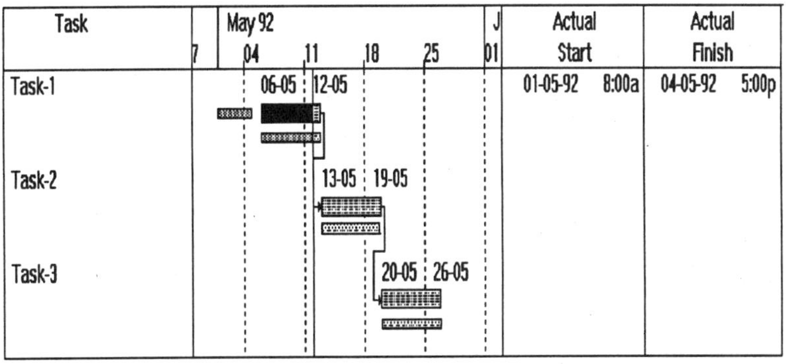

Figure 11.5
Ignoring actuals

project's start date, it does demonstrate why you would want to update the remaining schedule.

If you unselect the box 'Ignore Actual Dates' and recalculate the entire model the actual data will be moved into the scheduled data columns before the rescheduling is performed. What this means is that the entire model will be scheduled with the completed and part completed tasks using their Actual Start and Finish dates and durations. In short, while Ignore Actual Dates isn't selected each recalculation starts by transferring the actual dates for each task or resource assignment into the scheduled dates.

For example, if actuals are taken in to account in the project shown in Figure 11.5 the resulting new schedule is as shown in Figure 11.6. This is very reasonable and exactly what you would expect - but notice that Task-1's Scheduled Start and Finish dates are now equal to the Actual Start and Finish dates. There is no trace of the original schedule except in the baseline data that was saved at the start of the project for just this reason. Now you can enter actuals for Task-2 and Task-3 that can be used to examine how efficiently they have been carried out taking into account the effect of the early Actual Start and Finish on Task-1.

Unless you have selected 'Ignore Actual Dates', scheduled data is replaced by actual data when you recalculate the model. This means that when the project is complete the original model is completely replaced by a model of what actually happened.

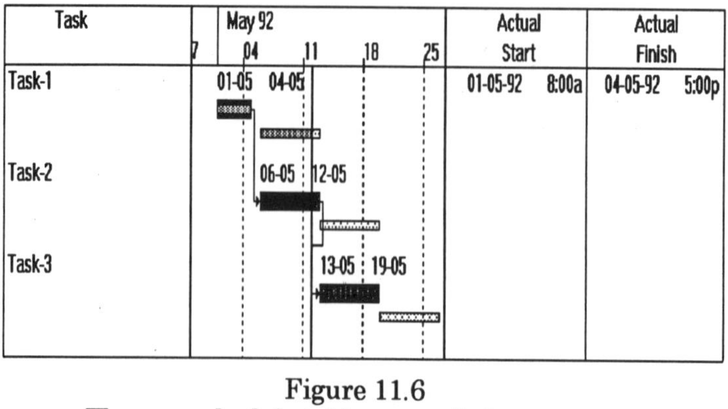

Task	May 92 04	11	18	25	Actual Start	Actual Finish
Task-1	01-05 04-05				01-05-92 8:00a	04-05-92 5:00p
Task-2		06-05 12-05				
Task-3			13-05 19-05			

Figure 11.6
The new schedule taking actuals into account

Current date feedback

There is another calculation option that has an important effect on the rescheduling of a project and, as will be explained, on the automatic gathering of actuals data. If you select the option Feedback Current Date in the Calculations Options dialog box then any task that has a Scheduled Start date earlier than the current date and no Actual Start date will be adjusted to make the current date its Scheduled Start date.

This sounds complicated but all that happens is that unstarted tasks that are in the past are rescheduled to start today. This is done in such a way that tasks constraints are honoured. What this means is that if you have a project model and none of the tasks have Actual Start and Finish dates associated with them, Feedback Current Date will result in the entire project being shifted to start on the current date. If you unselect the Feedback Current Date option then the project will return to its original start date. The reason for this is that the Must Start date for the project isn't altered by the shift. Indeed the recalculation doesn't alter any of the Must dates and you will probably see calculation diagnostic messages about Must dates that have been ignored in the shift to the new starting date.

For example, in the project model shown in Figure 11.7 you can see that all three tasks should be underway, if not actually complete. As no Actual Start or Finish dates have been entered, selecting Feedback Current Date will change the start date of Task-1 and Task-3 to the current date and

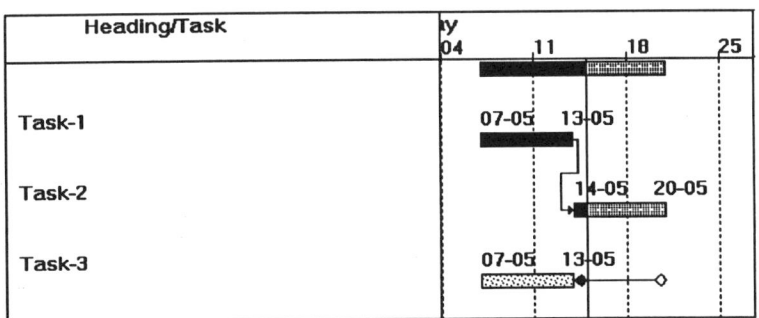

Figure 11.7
A project that is past its 'start by date'

214 *Tracking*   *Chapter 11*

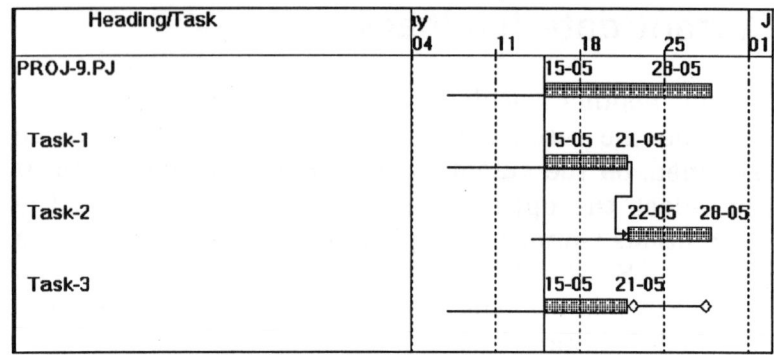

Figure 11.8
The effect of current date feedback

adjust the starting date of Task-2 accordingly. You can see the result of doing this in Figure 11.8. Notice that each of the tasks has a delay indicated. This is caused by the fact that the project Must Start date is still set at 07-05-92>, that is, after the 7th. If you move to the Must Start column and edit this date to be the same as the project's Scheduled Start date then the delays will vanish and there will be no trace left that the project was ever intended to start after the 7th.

Notice that this doesn't give you an easy automatic way of moving a project from one date to another unless you are also prepared to edit any Must dates manually.

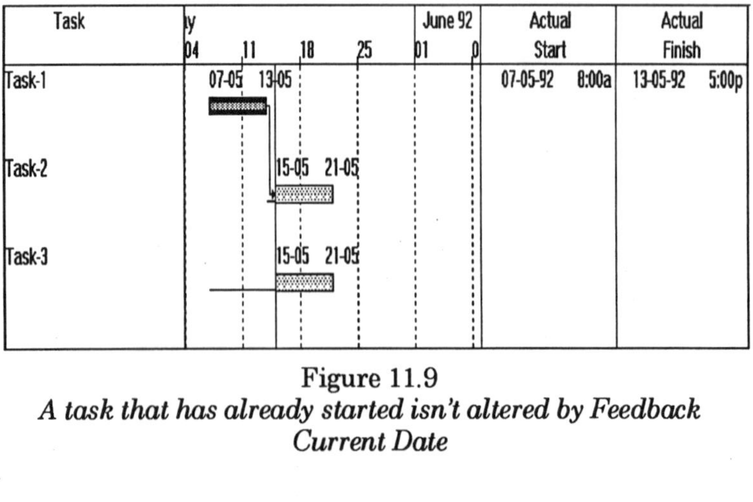

Figure 11.9
A task that has already started isn't altered by Feedback Current Date

What is interesting about Feedback Current Date is the way that it differentiates between tasks that are complete or in progress from tasks that haven't started. The Feedback Current Date option will only move tasks forward that haven't an Actual Starting date specified. For example, in Figure 11.9, you can see the same project as in Figures 11.7 and 11.8 but in this case Task-1 has Actual Start and Finish dates associated with it. As a result only Task-2 and Task-3 are moved to start on the current date. Notice that now Task-2 is moved because it falls into the category of a task that could have started but hasn't.

Done and to-be-done

You can see the scope for using Feedback Current Date to correct a project that has a number of tasks that should have started but haven't, but this is not its major use. It is worth looking at its behaviour just a little more closely in the case of a task that has an Actual Start date recorded but not an Actual Finish date. In this case the start date isn't moved forward but the task now has three dates associated with it:

Actual Start ->   current date   -> Scheduled Finish

The task is thus split into two portions - from the Actual Start date to the current date and from the current date to the Scheduled Finish date. You can see that this divides the task into 'done' and 'to-be-done'.

For example, in Figure 11.10, Task-1 has a 20-day duration and an Actual Start has been entered. When the project is

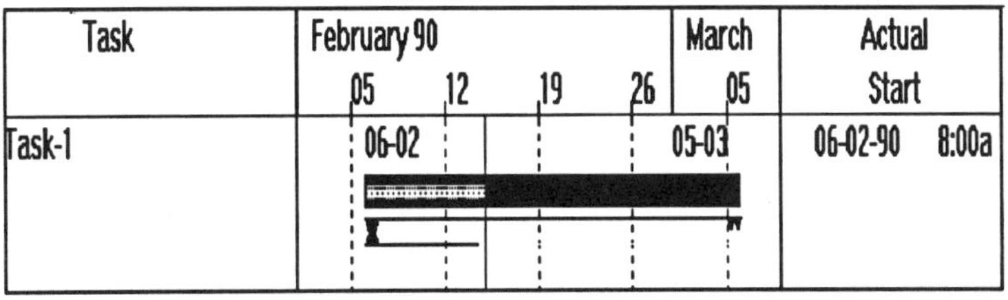

Task	February 90 05 12 19 26	March 05	Actual Start
Task-1	06-02	05-03	06-02-90 8:00a

Figure 11.10
A task that has an Actual Start but not an Actual Finish is split into done and to-be-done

recalculated with Feedback Current Date selected, the portion of the task that is completed is shown on the Gantt chart. If you switch off Feedback Current Date then this division isn't displayed. You can see that with Feedback Current Date selected the current date acts as if it was a temporary entry for Actual Finish.

In other words, Feedback Current Date has two effects on the schedule. Firstly, it updates to the current date any Scheduled Start dates that are earlier than the current date. These are then overwritten by any Actual Start dates that have been specified. Secondly, it makes SuperProject treat the current date as a temporary entry for Actual Finish.

Notice that you can enter an Actual Start date after you have recalculated with Feedback Current Date selected. In this case the model will first be converted into something of a mess due to all of the tasks with Scheduled Start dates earlier than the current date being shifted forward. However, this mess slowly clears up as you enter Actual Start dates and the tasks move back to their correct places on the Gantt chart. Of course, any tasks that really haven't started will have their Scheduled Start dates moved forward to the current date. After you have entered all the actual dates, recalculating the model will give you a true picture of what remains to be done.

Percentage complete

As well as producing a display of the portion of any task complete or remaining to be done on the Gantt chart, the Feedback Current Date option also allows various measures of work remaining to be calculated. The most obvious of these are the Percentage Complete and Actual Duration fields. Both of these measures are worked out using the current date to show the amount of the task done. If you don't have Feedback Current Date selected then neither will be calculated. If you type in an entry in one of them it will be used to calculate the other and it will be used to display the amount of the task complete on the Gantt chart correctly. In other words, selecting Feedback Current Date is a way of ensuring that actual duration and percentage complete are automatically filled in.

Auto Actuals

If you want to enter all of the actual data concerning a project by hand, then Ignore Actual Dates and Feedback Current Date is really all you need to know about. However, entering actual data can be a very time-consuming activity and very frustrating if the project is running to schedule and most of the actual data duplicates the scheduled data already entered or calculated.

SuperProject provides a way of automatically transferring scheduled data to the the actuals column when the current date has passed the necessary points. This facility is referred to as Auto Actuals and to activate it you have to select the box of the same name in the Calculation Options dialog box. If you do this you will quickly discover that you need to have the Feedback Current Date selected as well. In fact you must select Feedback Current Date before you select Auto Actuals if you want to avoid generating an error message! With Auto Actuals selected the actual data columns are filled in as the current date passes the Scheduled Start and Finish dates of each task.

For example, in Figure 11.11 the Actual Start date was filled in for Task-2 as soon as the current date passed 20-2. Its Actual Finish date was filled also filled in as soon as it passed 26-2. The Actual Finish date for Task-1 will not be filled in until the current date passes its Scheduled Finish date.

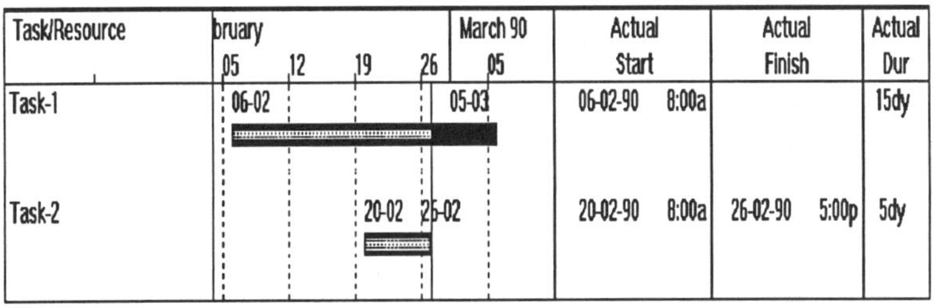

Task/Resource	bruary 05 12 19 26	March 90 05	Actual Start	Actual Finish	Actual Dur
Task-1	06-02	05-03	06-02-90 8:00a		15dy
Task-2		20-02 26-02	20-02-90 8:00a	26-02-90 5:00p	5dy

Figure 11.11
Using Auto Actuals to enter data

If at this point you are thinking that there is very little good in just transferring the scheduled data into the actuals column, then it is worth pointing out that it means that the data can be safely edited. Once there is an entry in an actual, SuperProject will not overwrite it with calculated data. Also notice that any actual data that has been entered by Auto Actuals is subsequently treated as if it had been entered manually, i.e. it will not be changed by a subsequent recalculation. This also means that turning off Auto Actuals will not remove the entries or return the project model to its earlier state. This makes it a good idea to save a project model before recalculating with Auto Actuals.

Using Auto Actuals you can reduce the amount of data that has to be entered to only those tasks and assignments which deviate from the schedule.

Notice that for Auto Actuals to work you must select Feedback Current Date and you must not select Ignore Actual Dates. If you do select Ignore Actual Dates the Auto Actuals mechanism will work but the task will be repeatedly rescheduled to start on the current day. This can result in a 100% complete task with a Scheduled Start on the current date!

Editing actuals

You can edit Auto Actuals and indeed actuals that you have entered manually but you do need to keep in mind that Auto Actuals overwrite the Scheduled Start and Finish dates on each recalculation. How can this cause problems? Suppose you have a 10-day task starting on the 1st and you use Auto Actuals to enter its Start and Finish date. If you later discover that the task did not start on time, editing the Actual Start date will not alter the Actual or Scheduled Finish date - with the result that the scheduled task duration will change. However, if you edit the Actual Start date before the task is completed the Scheduled Finish date will be recalculated using the scheduled duration. Always remember that actual dates override scheduled dates.

Another potential trap is that editing an Auto Actual Start date will not cause the Actual Start date of a task that is in progress to change even if it is linked so that it cannot start until the first task finishes. The reason for this is again due to the way that Auto Actuals overwrite scheduled dates and the way that Auto Actuals will not overwrite existing actuals entries. For example, in Figure 11.12 the current date has moved on sufficiently for Task-1 to have completed and Task-2 to have started. The Auto Actuals entered were believed to be perfectly correct but then it was discovered that Task-1 started 2 days late. When Task-1's actual dates were modified to reflect this and the project recalculated the Actual Start data of Task-2 was not updated and so it is now showing as having started before Task-1 finished. The only solution to this problem is either to enter the Actual Start date of Task-2 manually or to delete the entry made by Auto Actuals and recalculate the project.

In general the best method of correcting Auto Actuals data is to delete the actual data relevant to the change, then enter the correct Start and Finish dates and finally recalculate the project. There is one situation in which this doesn't work, however. If you want to change the actual data for a task that is grouped below a sub-heading that has its actual start and finish data entered then you will find that the heading's actual finish data cannot be deleted and will keep on overriding any changes you try to make. The only solution to this problem is to delete all of the relevant actual data, turn off Auto Actuals in the Calculations Options dialog box and recalculate. This will clear the Auto Actuals on the heading and allow you to continue as normal.

Task	June 92				Actual Start		Actual Finish		Est Dur
	18	25	01	08					
Task-1					21-05-92	8:00a	27-05-92	5:00p	5dy
Task-2					26-05-92	8:00a			5dy

Figure 11.12
Editing Actual Start dates can cause problems

Actuals and resources

So far we have only considered the actual data associated with tasks but you can also enter or allow Auto Actuals to calculate similar work data for resource allocations. In fact if you enter actual data for a task SuperProject will ask if you want the corresponding data entered for each of its tasks. You will also discover that there are actual duration, percentage complete and remaining hours calculations for each resource based on the current date calculated in the same way as the corresponding task data. For example, in Figure 11.13 you can see that the column Actual Rsrc Total Hrs shows the number of hours that each resource should have worked given the current state of completion of the task.

As long as the resources worked according to schedule this is little different, but what if a resource works fewer hours than scheduled? If you enter a smaller number of hours into a resource's Actual Rsrc Total Hrs than it should have worked, what happens depends on the state of the task. If the task is complete then nothing happens! The Actual Start, Finish and Actual Duration remain the same, as does the shorter number of Actual Rsrc Total Hrs that you have entered. This can produce a situation in which the task is 100% complete but with the number of hours that a resource worked less than scheduled. However, if the task is still in progress, entering a different actual number of hours worked has a major effect on the task's scheduling.

Task/Resource	11	18	25	June 01	Est Dur	Schd Dur	Actual Dur	Actual Rsrc Total Hrs
Task-1					5dy	5dy	5dy	40.00
Rsrc-1						5dy		40.00
Task-2					5dy	5dy	2dy	32.00
Rsrc-1						5dy		16.00
Rsrc-2						5dy		16.00
Task-3					5dy	5dy	0dy	0.00
Rsrc-2						5dy		0.00

Figure 11.13
Using Auto Actuals to enter data

Task/Resource				June	Est Dur	Schd Dur	Actual Dur	Actual Rsrc Total Hrs	Pct Comp
	11	18	25	01					
Task-1	▓▓▓▓▓				5dy	5dy	5dy	40.00	100
Rsrc-1	▓▓▓▓▓					5dy		40.00	100
Task-2		▓▓▓▓▓			5dy	7dy	3dy	32.00	40
Rsrc-1		▓▓▓▓▓▓▓				5dy		24.00	60
Rsrc-2		▓▓▓				7dy		8.00	20
Task-3			▓▓▓		5dy	5dy	0dy	0.00	0
Rsrc-2			▓▓▓			5dy		0.00	0

Figure 11.14
Altering allocation actual hours

Reducing the Actual Rsrc Total Hrs increases the resource's remaining hours to be worked and this automatically increases the task's duration. The Scheduled Finish date is pushed back accordingly. For example, in Figure 11.14 you can see that the Actual Rsrc Total Hrs for Rsrc-2 as assigned to Task-2 has been reduced to 8 hours from the expected 24 hours. As a result the Gantt chart shows that it hasn't worked its full allocation up to the current date and the task's Finish date has been pushed back by 2 days. Also notice that Rsrc-1's allocation hasn't been increased and that the percentage complete is shown correctly in each case.

If all of the resources have worked for fewer hours than expected then the task is said to be 'interrupted'. For example, in Figure 11.15 you can see that Rsrc-1 and Rsrc-2 only worked 8 hours of a scheduled 24 hours and so the task has had to be increased by 2 days. The 2 day non-work period is shown as interruption of the task on the Gantt chart. As long as the task really is resource driven, this is an appropriate adjustment. You can see that work is supposed to have occurred at the start of the task and that the new schedule shows that it will re-commence on the current date. If you want to, you can opt for the Scheduled Start of an interrupted or an in-progress task to be shown as the current date. All you have to to is select the Set Scheduled Date to Resume Date in the Calculation Options box.

Task/Resource	June 92 11 18 25 01	Est Dur	Schd Dur	Actual Dur	Actual Rsrc Total Hrs	Pct Comp
Task-1	▓▓▓▓▓▓▓	5dy	5dy	5dy	40.00	100
Rsrc-1	▓▓▓▓▓▓▓		5dy		40.00	100
Task-2	▄▄ ▄▄	5dy	7dy	3dy	16.00	20
Rsrc-1	▄		7dy		8.00	20
Rsrc-2	▄		7dy		8.00	20
Task-3	▄▄	5dy	5dy	0dy	0.00	0
Rsrc-2	▄▄		5dy		0.00	0

Figure 11.15
An interrupted task

Notice also that a task can be shown as interrupted if you enter an actual duration that is shorter than the time interval between the Actual Start and the current date.

If you alter the number of hours that a resource has actually worked on an assignment before the assignment is complete then it is vitally important that you remember to go back and change the entry as the task progresses. You cannot rely on Auto Actuals once you have made manual entries.

Task status

Task status was discussed in the previous chapter in connection with resource allocation conflicts but it is also relevant once a project is under way. A task's progress is indicated as:

» **Schd** - if it is scheduled but not yet underway, i.e. there is no Actual Start date.
» **Prog** - if the task is underway, i.e. an Actual Start date has been entered but no Actual Finish date.
» **Intr** - if the task is interrupted either because resources haven't worked the hours possible or if the actual duration has been reduced.
» **Done** - if the task is complete and an Actual Start and Actual Finish date have been entered. Notice that if you don't enter these dates or use Auto Actuals to enter them for you then the task will not show as Done even though it might show 100% complete.

Tracking the paint project

The task's status can be used within a selection criteria filter to show only tasks that have started, not started or are complete.

Tracking the paint project

Tracking a large project is very much a matter of trying to keep control of the quantity of actual data that has to be entered and, of course, trying to find ways of putting the project back on schedule. The by now familiar paint project is too small to illustrate these difficulties in a realistic way but it does serve to highlight some of the pitfalls.

With Auto Actuals turned on and baseline data gathered before the project started, the situation on the 19th can be seen in Figure 11.16. Later on in the day the news arrives that the **Paint woodwork** task did not start until after the weekend - i.e. the Actual Start date was the 18th not the 13th. Changing this by editing and re-calculating the project produces the schedule in Figure 11.17. Of course, the fact that **Paint woodwork** didn't start until the 18th caused the **Paper walls** task not to start on time, but notice that the Auto Actuals procedure doesn't reschedule this task. If you examine Figure 11.17 you can see that the project model is still incorrect and either the Actual Start

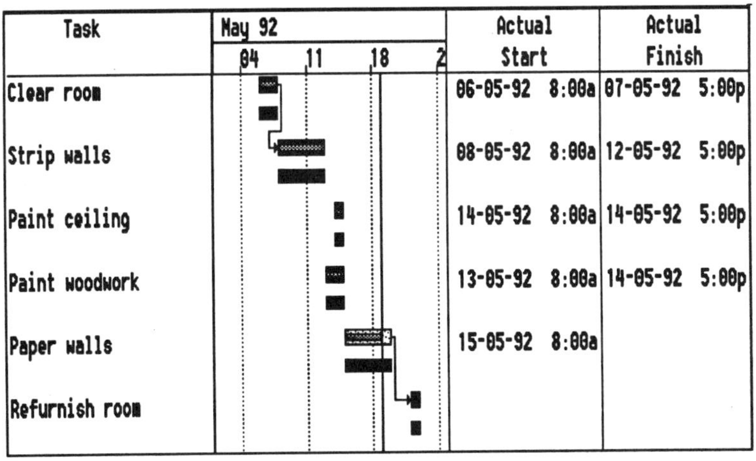

Task	May 92			Actual Start	Actual Finish
	04	11	18		
Clear room	▬			06-05-92 8:00a	07-05-92 5:00p
Strip walls	▬▬			08-05-92 8:00a	12-05-92 5:00p
Paint ceiling		▪		14-05-92 8:00a	14-05-92 5:00p
Paint woodwork		▬		13-05-92 8:00a	14-05-92 5:00p
Paper walls			▬▬	15-05-92 8:00a	
Refurnish room			▪		

Figure 11.16
The paint project on the 19th

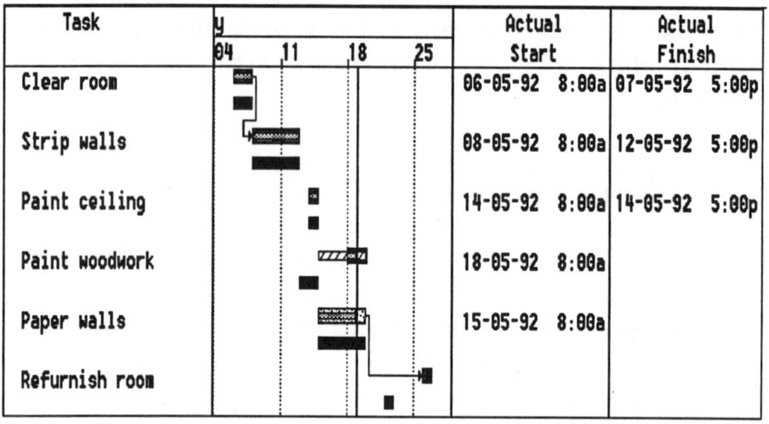

224 Tracking   Chapter 11

Task		Actual Start	Actual Finish
Clear room		06-05-92 8:00a	07-05-92 5:00p
Strip walls		08-05-92 8:00a	12-05-92 5:00p
Paint ceiling		14-05-92 8:00a	14-05-92 5:00p
Paint woodwork		18-05-92 8:00a	
Paper walls		15-05-92 8:00a	
Refurnish room			

Figure 11.17
The updated but incorrect paint project

date of the **Paper walls** task has to be entered manually or the Auto Actual date has to be deleted and the project recalculated again. In fact the project model contains a rather more subtle error than this. If you examine the Scheduled Duration for the **Paint woodwork** task you will discover that it is 1 day and that Tom is allocated for a single 16-hour day! The reason is that the Auto Actual calculation entered 16 as the Actual Rsrc Total Hrs and while the Actual Start date has been corrected the Scheduled Finish date is also wrong. To correct the model not only do you need

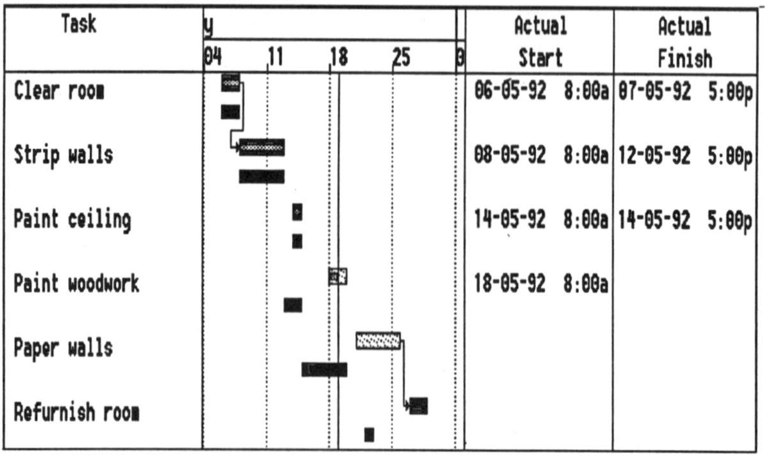

Task		Actual Start	Actual Finish
Clear room		06-05-92 8:00a	07-05-92 5:00p
Strip walls		08-05-92 8:00a	12-05-92 5:00p
Paint ceiling		14-05-92 8:00a	14-05-92 5:00p
Paint woodwork		18-05-92 8:00a	
Paper walls			
Refurnish room			

Figure 11.18
The corrected paint project model

to correct the start date for the **Paper walls** task but you also need to change the actual hours worked to be correct. In this case both can be achieved by simply deleting the entries of the Actual Start date of **Paper walls** and the Actual Rsrc Total Hrs for Tom and recalculating the project. If you examine Figure 11.18 you can see that now everything appears correct. You can see how the delay has affected the project by comparing the current bars with the baseline data saved at the start of the project.

If you have to go back and edit the actual data then you do run a very real risk of failing to change all of the data necessary to correct the model. Remember that you may need to change Actual Start dates, Actual Finish dates and Actual Rsrc Total Hrs.

Sometimes it can appear that the model has become a complete mess due to incomplete editing. In such cases it is sometimes easier to discard the edited model and return to the original and start again. For this reason it is worth saving the model under a new name before starting to edit actual data.

Key points

» Baseline data can be saved and displayed on the Gantt chart so that you can compare any changes with the original plan.

» Baseline data is transferred to the baseline fields each time you select the Edit,Transfer to Baseline option, and overwrites any existing data.

» You can also enter actual data into special actuals fields. If you select Ignore Actuals this acts just like a second baseline to compare scheduled and actual data.

» Actuals can also be used to update the remaining schedule in the light of the actual data.

» Actual data is transferred to the corresponding scheduled data fields before each recalculation of the model. This means that tasks that have not started will automatically be rescheduled to take account of the actual starting and finishing dates of tasks in progress and completed.

» Auto Actuals will transfer appropriate scheduled data to actuals fields automatically when the current date has passed the Scheduled Start and Finish dates.

» Auto Actuals will not overwrite any data already present in the actuals fields and this allows you to edit the actuals data to enter exceptions from the schedule.

» If you enter a shorter actual duration, or reduce the hours a resource worked on a task, it will be shown as interrupted.

Chapter 12
Costing

As well as as means of scheduling, a project model can be a convenient way of recording resource costs and calculating total project costs. If you enter costing information for resources then an estimated cost for each assignment of the resource can be calculated. These estimates can be updated as the project progresses using associated 'actuals' fields in much the same way that task start, finish and duration actuals can be entered. Using these and other facilities you can track project costs in a dynamic way as opposed to a simple static cost estimate.

The cost fields

If you select Show Cost Fields in the General Preferences dialog box yet another set of fields is added to the project model. These fields are added to those already on display according to the particular Expert mode in force. That is, if you have already selected Tracking/Actuals then not only will scheduled cost field columns be added, but actual costs columns will also be included in the model. Notice that the cost fields can not be displayed in Beginner mode.

At this stage in using SuperProject it is likely that the table of data has so many columns that it is vital that you know how to use the commands to move to a given column and to create custom layouts to reduce the number of columns on display just those in which you are interested.

Scheduled costs

The first set of new fields to examine are the Scheduled Cost fields. These are:

» **Scheduled Variable Cost**
This is the cost associated with using a labour resource for the total number of hours, regular and overtime, for which it is assigned to the task.
Scheduled Variable Cost= Scheduled Regular Cost + Scheduled Overtime Cost

» **Scheduled Regular Cost**
This is the cost of the number of regular hours for which a labour resource has been assigned to a task. The cost per hour is set in a new field called Rate - which defaults to £25 per hour. The default rate can be set for any resource and it can also be made to vary according to the date.
Scheduled Regular Cost=Scheduled Regular Hours x Rate

» **Scheduled Overtime Cost**
The cost of the overtime hours for which the resource has been assigned. The differential for overtime hours can be set for each resource in a field called Overtime Mult. How to do this will be explained later, but notice that while Rate can be varied according to the assignment the overtime multiplier cannot.
Scheduled Overtime Cost=Scheduled Overtime Hours x Rate x Overtime Mult

» **Scheduled Fixed Cost**
This is simply any fixed one-time cost associated with the assignment. Obviously this cannot be calculated so it is up to you to enter an appropriate value. It defaults to £0.

» **Scheduled Overhead Cost**
This is a fixed proportion of the assignment's variable cost. The proportion is set on a per-project basis in a field called Overhead Mult. This field is to be found in the Project Details window, see later. You can see that overhead cost is simply a premium charged on the

hourly use of a resource.
Scheduled Overhead Cost=Scheduled Variable Cost x
Overhead Mult

» **Scheduled Total Cost**
This is simply the total of the assignment costs, i.e. the sum of variable, fixed and overhead costs.

Costs are calculated or entered for each assignment and then aggregated to give task, and eventually project, costs. That is, the task cost is simply the sum of each of the individual assignment costs of each type and the project cost is the sum of each task's costs. In the case of hourly rates, recorded in the Rate column, assignment rates are entered but in the case of tasks and the project as a whole an average hourly rate is calculated. This can be used to gain some idea of the cost efficiency of each task.

Costing the paint project

As a simple example of entering costing data Figure 12.1 shows the paint a room project model (starting again from PAINT6.PJ) with variable and fixed costs included. In this case the default rate of £25 per hour has been left unaltered in the variable cost calculation and no overtime has been scheduled. How to change the default rate will be discussed later.

Notice the way that fixed costs have been used to enter data on the consumables used to perform each task. For example, the fixed costs involved in the two painting tasks are for a given number of gallons of paint. Modelling consumables as fixed costs is often the simplest way of building such costs into a project model but it does have its limitations. For example, it is all too easy to fall into the trap of recording a variable cost as a fixed cost simply because you fail to notice that the charge has a time-dependent factor.

For example, in the case of the **Strip walls** task the fixed cost is for the hire of a wallpaper stripper. This £15 charge is itself made up of a large fixed component and a smaller

Task	Resource	Scheduled Regular Cost	Scheduled Overtime Cost	Scheduled Fixed Cost	Scheduled Overhead Cost	Scheduled Total Cost
PAINT12.PJ		2400.00	0.00	115.00	0.00	2515.00
Prepare room		800.00	0.00	15.00	0.00	815.00
Clear room		400.00	0.00	0.00	0.00	400.00
	Bill	200.00	0.00	0.00	0.00	200.00
	Tom	200.00	0.00	0.00	0.00	200.00
Strip walls		400.00	0.00	15.00	0.00	415.00
	Bill	400.00	0.00	15.00	0.00	415.00
Paint room		600.00	0.00	50.00	0.00	650.00
Paint ceiling		200.00	0.00	30.00	0.00	230.00
	Bill	200.00	0.00	30.00	0.00	230.00
Paint woodwork		400.00	0.00	20.00	0.00	420.00
	Tom	400.00	0.00	20.00	0.00	420.00
Paper walls		600.00	0.00	50.00	0.00	650.00
	Bill	600.00	0.00	50.00	0.00	650.00
Refurnish room		400.00	0.00	0.00	0.00	400.00
	Bill	200.00	0.00	0.00	0.00	200.00
	Tom	200.00	0.00	0.00	0.00	200.00

Figure 12.1
Cost data for the paint project

daily rate. To create an accurate project model the wallpaper stripper should be included as a separate resource, allocated to the task and charged at a hourly rate and fixed cost. However, as long as the task duration doesn't alter too much, this simpler model should suffice. In all cases you must balance the tendency to make the model accurate but perhaps complex against that to make it simple but not entirely accurate.

Viewing costs

SuperProject has a range of different ways of viewing and analysing cost data. In particular it can show you graphs of cumulative cost over time in either Resource or Task Details View.

If you select Resource Details view and then use the command Layout,Histogram Symbols you will see the Histogram dialog box. You can use this to add a customised histogram in any view. To see the cumulative cost simply select Total Cost as the variable and choose the histogram

Viewing costs 231

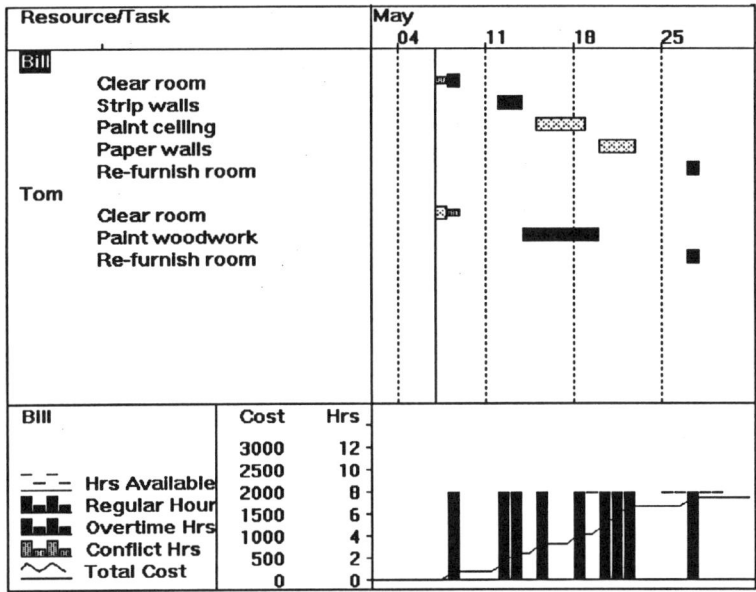

Figure 12.2
Viewing cost data in Resource View

symbol to use. If you are using Version 2 then layout HISTOGRAM-5 will automatically produce a graph of cumulative cost on top of the usual resource hours histogram, see Figure 12.2.

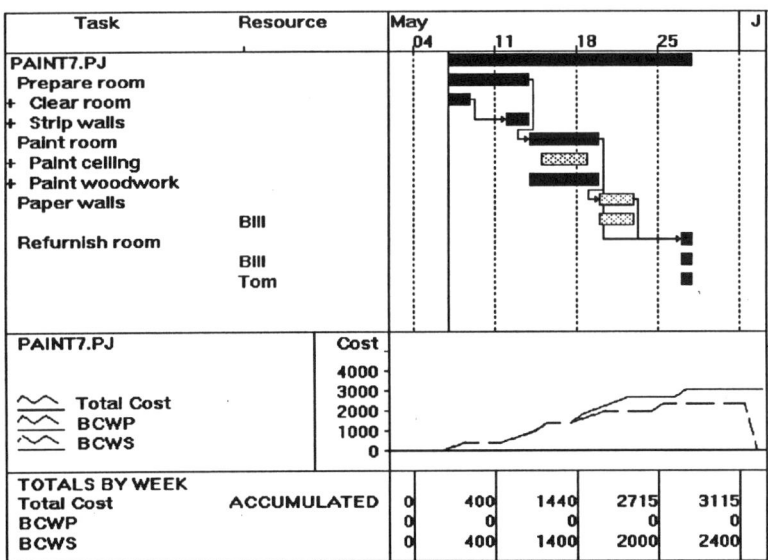

Figure 12.3
Viewing cost data in Task View

If you select Layout, Gantt Window Commands, Cost/Rsrc by Resource then you will see a cost graph for all of a resource's assignments. However, if you select Layout, Gantt Window Commands, All Cost/Rsrc then the graph will only show the cumulative cost for the assignment or resource that you have selected.

To view cost data in Task Details view simply load layout D07 (GANTT-7 in Version 2), see Figure 12.3. Notice that in this case the graph also shows details of quantities that have yet to be discussed.

Resource Details view

As already discussed in earlier chapters, you can look at data specific to any task, resource or even to the whole project gathered together in a single on-screen form. The Resource Details screen was introduced in the previous chapter as a way of setting available overtime hours but there is much more of interest on a details screen than just this.

The Resource Details screen can shows the basic resource data in its top half and in its bottom half details of the resource's assignments, its work periods or its rates. Which type of data fills the lower half can be set by using the command Layout, View Subwindows and then selecting

RsrcName:	Bill								
Type:	Labor		☒ Level		Hours Under Scheduled:	8.00			
Accrual:	Prorate		Factor: 100	Max Units:	1 Hours Available:	72.00			

Task Name	Schd Dur	Res ID	Scheduled Start	Scheduled Finish	Pri	Alloc /Day	Units Assgn	
Clear room	1dy	001	07-05-92 8:00a	07-05-92 5:00p	50	100%	1	
Strip walls	2dy	002	08-05-92 8:00a	12-05-92 5:00p	50	100%	1	
Paint ceiling	1dy	003	14-05-92 8:00a	14-05-92 5:00p	50	100%	1	
Paper walls	3dy	006	15-05-92 8:00a	19-05-92 5:00p	50	100%	1	
TOTAL								

Figure 12.4
Resource detail's view with assignments

Assignments, Work Periods or Rates. If you are using the Windows version you can swap between these different displays by simply clicking on the table, clock or dollar sign icons respectively.

The basic Resource Details, see Figure 12.4, are easy to understand and should be familiar from other contexts - apart that is from Accrual which is discussed later. You can edit any of the fields with the exception of Hours Underscheduled and Hours Available which are worked out to be consistent with the other data you provide.

If you select Work Periods or Rates/Units then you will see additional resource data. The use of the Work Periods subwindow to set regular and overtime hours has already been described in Chapter 10. In this chapter the emphasis falls onto the Rates/Units display, see Figure 12.5. You can see that you can set an hourly rate for the resource and an overtime multiplier. Bill has been assigned an hourly rate of £5.00 and an overtime multiplier of 1.5 (i.e. time and a half). You can also set a basic rate that varies according to the date. This works in exactly the same way as setting variable overtime hours as described in Chapter 10. All you have to do is edit END to be the date that the next period begins and then enter the appropriate rates. In Figure 12.5 Bill has been awarded a pay rise of £1 starting on the 1-6-92. You can enter as many rate changes as needed using this method. Notice that you can also set the number of Units to change automatically in the same way. This could be used

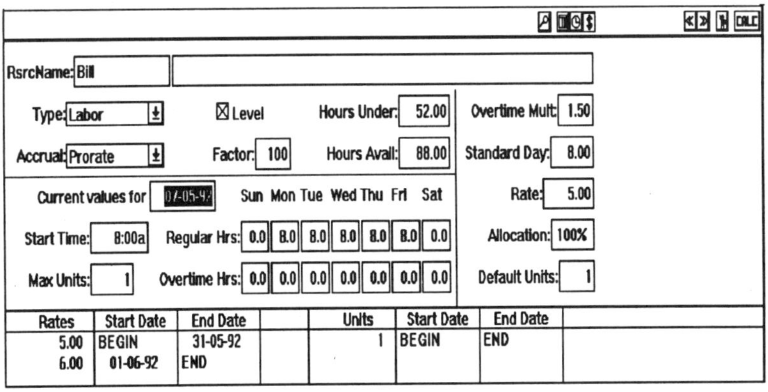

Figure 12.5
Resource details view with rates and units

Painting with overtime

With the correct rates entered for Bill, £5 per hour to the end of May and then the same rate as Tom, £6 per hour, and with the correct overtime rate, 1.5, entered for both of them it now becomes possible to arrive at an accurate costing for the project, see Figure 12.6. You can see that the total cost of the project is £627.

The duration of the project is 12 days and the obvious question is how much could the project's duration be shortened by using overtime. Both Bill and Tom are available for 2 hours overtime Monday through Friday and their calendars have been updated to reflect this fact. So to recalculate the project using overtime all we have to do is

Task	Resource	Scheduled Regular Cost	Scheduled Overtime Cost	Scheduled Fixed Cost	Scheduled Overhead Cost	Scheduled Total Cost
PAINT13.PJ		512.00	0.00	115.00	0.00	627.00
Prepare room		168.00	0.00	15.00	0.00	183.00
Clear room		88.00	0.00	0.00	0.00	88.00
	Bill	40.00	0.00	0.00	0.00	40.00
	Tom	48.00	0.00	0.00	0.00	48.00
Strip walls		80.00	0.00	15.00	0.00	95.00
	Bill	80.00	0.00	15.00	0.00	95.00
Paint room		136.00	0.00	50.00	0.00	186.00
Paint ceiling		40.00	0.00	30.00	0.00	70.00
	Bill	40.00	0.00	30.00	0.00	70.00
Paint woodwork		96.00	0.00	20.00	0.00	116.00
	Tom	96.00	0.00	20.00	0.00	116.00
Paper walls		120.00	0.00	50.00	0.00	170.00
	Bill	120.00	0.00	50.00	0.00	170.00
Refurnish room		88.00	0.00	0.00	0.00	88.00
	Bill	40.00	0.00	0.00	0.00	40.00
	Tom	48.00	0.00	0.00	0.00	48.00

Figure 12.6
An accurate costing of the project without using overtime

Task	Resource	4	11	18	Est Dur	Schd Dur	Scheduled Start	Scheduled Finish
PAINT13.PJ					11dy		06-05-92 8:00a	21-05-92 7:00p
Prepare room					4dy		06-05-92 8:00a	12-05-92 1:00p
+ Clear room					1dy	2dy	06-05-92 8:00a	07-05-92 5:00p
+ Strip walls					2dy	2dy	07-05-92 5:00p	12-05-92 1:00p
Paint room						3dy	12-05-92 1:00p	14-05-92 10:00a
+ Paint ceiling					1dy	3dy	12-05-92 1:00p	14-05-92 10:00a
+ Paint woodwork					2dy	2dy	12-05-92 1:00p	13-05-92 7:00p
+Paper walls					3dy	3dy	14-05-92 10:00a	18-05-92 3:00p
+Refurnish room					1dy	1dy	21-05-92 10:00a	21-05-92 7:00p

Figure 12.7
The project using overtime

select Use Overtime All in the Calculations Options box and press F9 to recalculate. Using overtime the project takes one day less and costs £675, i.e. an increase in cost of £48. You can see the new plan and compare it with the old in Figure 12.7. Notice that Transfer to Baseline was used to keep the original schedule. You can see that the improved performance is due mainly to the earlier start on painting the room.

If you also examine the way overtime has been allocated using Resource Details view you will discover that this has resulted in tasks being completed before the end of the working day and other tasks started on the same working day. The oddest feature is the way that the **Refurnish room** task starts at 10:00am. The reason is that this is exactly 5 days after the end of the **Paint room** task has finished and so the paint must be dry! Such precise scheduling is in this case an artefact of the model rather than anything to be enforced in the real world!

The next stage in the analysis of the project would be to allocate priorities to tasks to restrict the use of overtime in an effort to see if the project duration can be shortened while reducing the total cost.

Account outline view

The use of the hierarchy as a way of controlling the complexity of a project model was introduced in Chapter 9 and has been used many times. The question now arises of how to organise costing data into useful hierarchies? Many project costs are organised so that particular costs should be charged to particular accounts. The accounts also often have a hierarchical structure, either organised by function, activity or department. The only problem is that the accounts hierarchy is unlikely to correspond to the project's natural hierarchy. This makes it necessary to define and store along with the project model a completely separate hierarchy that reflects the account structure.

To do this you have to select Account Outline View. Notice that this is only available in Expert mode. When you first see your project data in this view all you will see is a complete list of tasks with a single, default, accounting code at the head of the list - see Figure 12.8. This is the start of our new hierarchy and at this stage there is one single account defined by one single account code.

To create new account codes all you have to do is to select Edit,Create or press F3 in the usual way. Each account code that is created automatically increments by one to make it unique. Once created you can demote or promote an account

Account	Task	Resource	Schd Dur	Acct ID	Scheduled Start	Scheduled Finish
01.00.00.00.0000				001		
	Clear room	Bill	1dy	001	07-05-92 8:00a	07-05-92 5:00p
	Clear room	Tom	1dy	001	06-05-92 8:00a	06-05-92 5:00p
	Strip walls	Bill	3dy	002	07-05-92 5:00p	12-05-92 1:00p
	Paint ceiling	Bill	2dy	003	12-05-92 1:00p	14-05-92 10:00a
	Paper walls	Bill	3dy	006	14-05-92 10:00a	18-05-92 3:00p
	Refurnish room	Bill	1dy	007	21-05-92 10:00a	21-05-92 7:00p
	Refurnish room	Tom	1dy	007	21-05-92 10:00a	21-05-92 7:00p
	Paint woodwork	Tom	2dy	004	12-05-92 1:00p	13-05-92 7:00p

Figure 12.8
Account Outline View

Account	Task	Resource	Account Name	Acct ID	Scheduled Total Cost
01.00.00.00.0000				001	675.00
01.01.00.00.0000				002	488.00
01.01.01.00.0000			Decorators	003	285.00
	Strip walls	Bill		002	105.00
	Paper walls	Bill		006	180.00
01.01.02.00.0000			Painters	005	203.00
	Paint ceiling	Bill		003	75.00
	Paint woodwork	Tom		004	128.00
01.02.00.00.0000			Site gang	004	187.00
	Clear room	Tom		001	48.00
	Clear room	Bill		001	40.00
	Refurnish room	Tom		007	54.00
	Refurnish room	Bill		007	45.00

Figure 12.9
Account Outline View after building a hierarchy

code in the usual way - i.e. (Alt)-Shift followed by a left or right arrow. Unfortunately you cannot move account codes to the tasks that they include so tasks have to be assigned to accounts by moving them to the correct position. The easiest way of working is to create the majority of accounting levels and then move tasks under the appropriate codes. This can take some time for a large project. In Figure 12.9 the paint project model has been classified into appropriate accounting groups.

Notice that the account codes are structured to reflect their position in the hierarchy. By default the code uses the first two digits to specify the first level, then two for the second level, third and fourth. Finally four digits are used to record the position in the fifth level. Thus an account code such as

01.02.03.01.0100

is sufficient for you to deduce its place in the hierarchy i.e. (reading from the right of the number) the 100th account in the fifth level, of the first account in the fourth and so on.. Also notice SuperProject adjusts the account number as you promote or demote it - see Figure 12.9.

Once you have an account hierarchy set up it will be saved along with the project model. You can subsequently use the

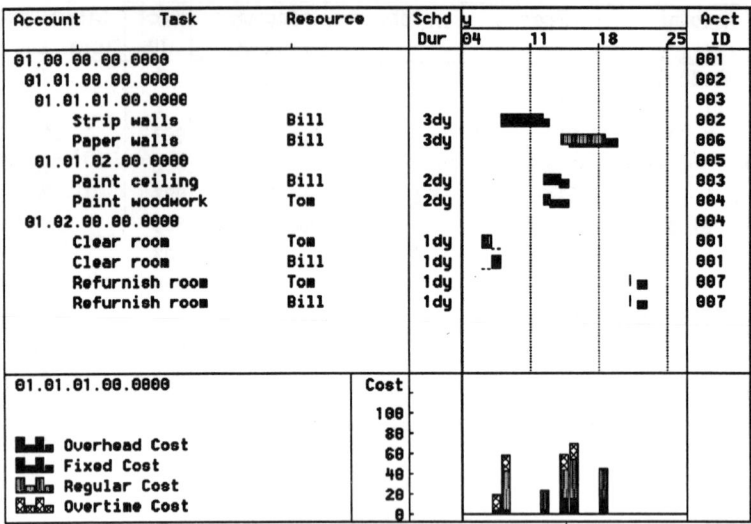

Figure 12.10
Viewing costs by account

account hierarchy to produce reports and graphs showing the cost breakdown of the project. For example, in Figure 12.10 you can see a graph of the cost breakdown for any account category. You can discover how to do this in Chapter 14.

Custom account codes

The default pattern used for the assignment of accounts codes can be changed to almost any regular numbering system you want to use. To specify the account code pattern you have to create a template or mask that acts like a picture of what a typical account code should look like. You can use a number of different types of symbol in a template. The digits 1,2, 3, 4 and 5 signify that the level number is to be used. That is, when an account code is created the digits are replaced by a number that signifies the position in that level. The number of digits that you use specify the number of digits that will be used to number that level. For example, the default account code mask is 11.22.33.44.5555 and this

Custom account codes

specifies two digits giving the position in the first level, two digits for the second level and so on until the fifth level, where four digits are used. This produces an account code something like - 01.02.00.00.0000, i.e. position 1 in level 1, position 2 in level 2. Notice that the number of digits used in the mask gives you a picture of what the account code will look like.

Any text that you place in the mask appears exactly as you type it and in particular so do the separators . (dot), -, and /. For example, the mask MAN-11-2/333 will produce account codes something like MAN-01-5/012, i.e. 1st in level 1, 5th in level 2 and 12th in level 3. Again you can see that the mask does a good job of representing what a typical account code will look like.

If you leave blanks in the mask then you can enter text into the space in the account code after it has been allocated. For example, the mask 1-22- -333 produces account codes like 3-32- -057. You can then edit the account code to introduce any text you want into the spaces. For example, you might want to enter a four character resource code as in 3-32-TOM1-057.

Finally, if you use ???? as part of the mask this is replaced by the task's id number. For example, the mask MAN-11-???? produces account codes like MAN-05-0012 i.e. 5th in level 1 and task number 12. Because of the typical structure of an accounts hierarchy it isn't often useful to include the task id number.

It is important to note that an account code mask cannot have more than 16 characters in total. This means that including too much punctuation or fixed text can limit the number of levels of the hierarchy that can be specified.

When cost fields are displayed, the account code for each task is displayed in a column of its own. This enables you to select tasks on the basis of account code.

Entering the account mask

The only remaining question is, how exactly you can enter an account code mask? The answer is in the Project Details view. Most of the entries in this dialog box determine the defaults that are used in the project. For example, the field Dflt Dur sets the default task duration - 5 days in this case. You will also find entries for project-wide data. For example, Overhead Mult, and of course the account code mask, see Figure 12.11.

The account mask is entered into the field of the same name roughly towards the middle of the account details. Notice that you can change the account mask at any time and new account codes will be generated using the new mask. If the mask shown in Figure 12.11 is used to generate account codes for the paint project account hierarchy originally shown in Figure 12.9 the result can be seen in Figure 12.12.

ID: P1		Dir: D:\SPJWIN3\DISK\PAINT\			
Author:		Lead:	WBSMask: 11.22.33.44.????		Std Day: 8.00
Revised: 16-03-90	Rev #: 0	Account Mask: PP-1-U22-3333			Days/Week: 5
Start: 06-05-92 > 8:00a	Pri: 50	☐Freeze	Dflt Dur: 5dy		Days/Month: 22
Finish: 21-05-92	7:00p	Dur: 11dy	Dev: 0.41		Overhead Mult: 0.00
PessFin: 22-05-92	4:00p	Task Option: Resource	↕	Task: 9	Rsrc: 2

Workday	Start	Finish	Hrs	12 1 2 3 4 5 6 a 7 8 9 10 11 12 1 2 3 4 5 6 p 7 8 9 10 11
Sunday	8:00a	8:00a	0.00	
Monday	8:00a	5:00p	8.00	
Tuesday	8:00a	5:00p	8.00	
Wednesday	8:00a	5:00p	8.00	
Thursday	8:00a	5:00p	8.00	
Friday	8:00a	5:00p	8.00	
Saturday	8:00a	8:00a	0.00	

Figure 12.11
Project details

```
Account         Task            Resource
PP-1-U00-0000
 PP-1-U01-0000
  PP-1-U01-0001
    Strip walls               Bill
    Paper walls               Bill
  PP-1-U01-0002
    Paint ceiling             Bill
    Paint woodwork            Tom
 PP-1-U02-0000
    Clear room                Tom
    Clear room                Bill
    Refurnish room            Bill
    Refurnish room            Tom
```

Figure 12.12
A custom account code mask in use

WBS codes

The Work Breakdown Structure has already been discussed in Chapter 6. The WBS is nothing more than the standard project model hierarchy and it is important to realise that it isn't a separate structure like the accounts hierarchy. However, like the accounts hierarchy, codes can be assigned to tasks according to their position in the hierarchy. WBS codes are always assigned to tasks but to see them you have to select Expert Mode, Earned Value Analysis. You can also opt to display them in WBS outline view (see Chapter 6).

WBS codes are controlled by a mask entered in the Project Details. The WBS mask works in exactly the same way as the accounts code mask works. The main difference is that it is more likely that you would want to include the task id number in the assigned code. The default WBS code is 11.22.33.44.???? which uses the task id as the last four digits but you are free to use any system of WBS numbering that suits your purpose. For example, in Figure 12.13 you can see WBS codes generated using the mask WU-1.2.3-J????. Notice that only bottom level tasks have WBS codes which include task id numbers. Headings all have a WBS code that ends in 0000.

Task	Resource	Est Dur	Work Breakdown Code
PAINT11.PJ			WU-1.0.0-J0000
Prepare room			WU-1.1.0-J0000
Clear room		1dy	WU-1.1.1-J0001
	Bill		
	Tom		
Strip walls		2dy	WU-1.1.2-J0002
	Bill		
Paint room			WU-1.2.0-J0000
Paint ceiling		2dy	WU-1.2.1-J0003
	Bill		
Paint woodwork		3dy	WU-1.2.2-J0004
	Tom		
Paper walls		3dy	WU-1.3.0-J0006
	Bill		
Refurnish room		1dy	WU-1.4.0-J0007
	Bill		
	Tom		

Figure 12.13
Custom WBS codes

Tracking costs - actuals

If you have selected Expert Mode, Tracking/Actuals then you will discover that there are a complete set of additional columns that allow you to record details of actual as opposed to scheduled costs. For each of the scheduled cost fields, that is Regular, Overtime, Variable, Fixed, Overhead and Total, there is a corresponding Actual field and a corresponding Remaining field. The relationships between these fields are such that each remaining cost field is the difference between scheduled and actual cost. It is important to realise that these fields are calculated from the actual hours and remaining hours fields already discussed. What this means is that while in some cases you can directly enter new values for the actual and remaining costs, you should really only modify actual dates, hours worked etc. and allow SuperProject to calculate the new actual and remaining cost fields. For example, if a task is in progress and you reduce the actual number of regular hours for an allocation, then the actual regular cost will be reduced accordingly. However, if you enter a lower actual regular cost then the actual regular hours will not be reduced automatically. In this sense the actuals relating to hours worked are more fundamental to the project than the costing data. However, if for some reason you do need to override the calculated values you can, as long as you are aware that your model is no longer consistent.

You can, of course, make use of Auto Actuals to enter actual and remaining cost data for you. Notice that fixed costs are only transferred to the Actual Fixed Cost column when a task finishes. Again although you can override actual cost data entered by Auto Actuals it is preferable to alter the actual resource hours and/or the actual start and finish dates.

As well as actual cost fields there is also a set of baseline cost fields - Baseline Variable, Fixed and Total Cost. As with the other baseline fields, data is transferred to them when you use the command Edit,Transfer to Baseline. Any existing data in the baseline cost fields is overwritten.

Notice that as in the case of the other actual fields the actual cost data overwrites the scheduled cost data as the project progresses. In the case of Actual Start and Finish dates this seemed entirely reasonable in that it allowed the project to be rescheduled in the light of what has actually happened. However, for the cost data it seems a disadvantage to lose the original detail in the scheduled data. You can of course always keep the original scheduled costs in the baseline fields but this doesn't give as much detail as the original scheduled costs. In other words, the scheduled and actual costs are always identical for a completed task and this makes it difficult to perform an accurate analysis of how the project is progressing from the point of view of cost.

The cost of painting

The simplest use of baseline data is to compare the way modifications to the plan affect costs. For example, in the case of the paint project, baseline cost data could be stored before recalculating with overtime use allowed. If you want to make this sort of comparison then you also need to load the Compare Costs layout. The result of doing this for the paint project with and without overtime can be seen in Figure 12.14. Notice that there are sub-totals for each heading. In Chapter 14 you will discover how to create your own custom reports that summarise data in this way.

As an example of the use of cost actuals, consider the painting project as shown in Figure 12.14. The scheduled and actual variable costs are shown in the two columns to the right of the Gantt chart. The actual costs were entered using Auto Actuals and you can see that there are entries only for those tasks that are either completed or in progress. In the case of tasks that are in progress the actual cost data shows the percentage of the cost that has been incurred. Notice that if you change the actual costs associated with finished tasks then the corresponding scheduled quantity will be updated to show the same. For example, if the paint cost more and you enter a new value in actual fixed cost then the scheduled fixed cost would be updated to show the same cost. It is worth repeating again that the rationale behind this is that the scheduled data of the part of the

Task Resource	Scheduled Total Cost	Actual Total Cost	Baseline Total Cost
PAINT15.PJ			
Prepare room			
+ Clear room	88.00	0.00	88.00
+ Strip walls	105.00	0.00	95.00
Subtotal Prepare room	193.00	0.00	183.00
Paint room			
+ Paint ceiling	75.00	0.00	70.00
+ Paint woodwork	128.00	0.00	116.00
Subtotal Paint room	203.00	0.00	186.00
+Paper walls	180.00	0.00	170.00
+Refurnish room	99.00	0.00	88.00
TOTAL	£ 675.00	£ 0.00	£ 627.00

Figure 12.14
Comparing costs

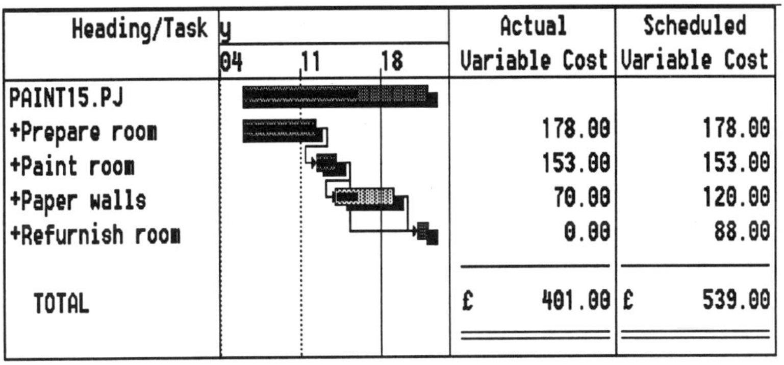

Heading/Task	04	11	18	Actual Variable Cost	Scheduled Variable Cost
PAINT15.PJ					
+Prepare room				178.00	178.00
+Paint room				153.00	153.00
+Paper walls				70.00	120.00
+Refurnish room				0.00	88.00
TOTAL				£ 401.00	£ 539.00

Figure 12.15
Tracking the variable costs

model that is completed or in progress should be updated to the actual values, so that the scheduled data for tasks in the future can be adjusted to take account of what has actually happened. This means that you cannot make a meaningful comparison of scheduled and actual data, apart from seeing what percentage of the project plan is completed. Only the baseline data can be used to make an eventual comparison between a predicted project cost and and actual project cost and this brings us to the subject of earned value analysis.

Earned value analysis

Earned value analysis has a reputation for being less than obvious. Partly this is due to a misunderstanding of the way that actual and scheduled data values interact as the model progresses, and partly it is due to the rather sketchy explanations to be found in the SuperProject manuals. In practice earned value analysis is very simple and corresponds more or less to the common sense procedures that you would apply to evaluate the efficiency of a project plan.

To illustrate the principles of earned value analysis it is best to first consider the simplest project possible - a single task and a single resource. As a full earned value analysis is simply an aggregation of the same method applied to each task and allocation in the entire project, understanding how a single task behaves tells you all you need to know.

Earned value analysis makes use of the baseline costs and other data to compare the actual performance of the project with what was planned on the basis of the model. So, before you can perform any earned value analysis you have to save the baseline data using the command Edit,Transfer to Baseline.

Of course it is vital that the baseline data represents your final plan, i.e. the one that you are going to use to run the real project. Failure to secure good baseline data simply means that you are comparing the actual performance of the project with a plan that has little or nothing to do with that performance. Also notice that if you fail to transfer any data at all to the baseline fields then the earned value analysis calculations will fail and generate a large number of error messages along the way. In short, you must transfer some data to the baseline before trying to calculate or plot the earned value analysis data.

If you use the command Preferences,Expert Mode,Earned Value Analysis, several new columns of data will be added to your model. The most important are BCWP - Budgeted Cost of Work Performed, and BCWS - Budgeted Cost of Work Scheduled. You can see that the only difference in the two quantities is that one is for work performed and the other for work scheduled - the meaning of this difference will become clear as we progress. The only other complication is that BCWP is also often referred to as the Earned Value.

The definition of BCWP for an allocation is:

Baseline Total Cost x Percentage Complete

This is just the percentage of the total cost appropriate to the current state of completion of the allocation. If the task/allocation hasn't started then BCWP is zero, if it is 50%

complete then BCWP is half the baseline cost and when the task is finished BCWP is equal to the baseline cost. What is slightly more subtle here is that BCWP depends on the baseline total cost which, as long as you don't accidentally update it, has nothing at all to do with the scheduled or actual costs. In other words, even if the plan deviates from the baseline, BCWP is still just the percentage of the predicted total cost appropriate to the amount of the project that has been completed by the current date.

The definition of BCWS for an allocation is:

$$\frac{\text{current date} - \text{baseline start date}}{\text{baseline duration}} \times \text{baseline total cost}$$

This looks complicated but the first part is simply the fraction of a task/allocation that should have been completed, according to the baseline data, by the current date. Multiplying this by the baseline total cost gives you the proportion of the baseline cost that is appropriate if the task started on its baseline start date.

You should now be able to see that BCWP gives the percentage of total baseline cost according to how much of the task has been completed irrespective of its starting date and BCWS gives the percentage of baseline total cost assuming the task started on its baseline start date. The first measures the state of completion of the actual project and the second measures how much should have been completed. If they are both equal then the project is exactly on time and budget.

To make this explanation a little more practical consider a project with a single 5-day task assigned a resource for 40 hours at £25 per hour. The first step is to save the baseline data and this must not be changed during the course of tracking the project. As you can see in Figure 12.16, before the project has begun both BCWP and BCWS are zero. This is perfectly reasonable as in the case of BCWP the percentage of the task completed is 0% and in the case of

Task/Resource	January 92 30 06 1	BCWP	BCWS	Est Dur	Schd Dur
Task-1	▬▬	0.00	0.00	5dy	5dy
Rsrc-1	▬▬	0.00	0.00		5dy

Figure 12.16
The project and the baseline

BCWS the percentage of the task that should have been completed is also 0%.

On the third day of the project's schedule the values of BCWP and BCWS can be seen in Figure 12.17. BCWS shows a value of £400 because this is the cost of the proportion of the task that should have been completed by now (based on the baseline starting date). The reason that BCWP is zero is simply that no actual start date has been entered and so the percentage complete for the task is also zero. If the task hasn't actually started yet then its BCWP, i.e. its earned value, is zero.

If the task did start on schedule then its actuals can be filled in automatically using Auto Actuals. The result can be seen in Figure 12.18. Now both BCWP and BCWS are £400 because the actual percentage of the task completed is 40% and the percentage that should be completed is 40%.

Task/Resource	January 92 30 06	BCWP	BCWS	Pct Comp
Task-1	▬▬	0.00	400.00	0
Rsrc-1	▬▬	0.00	400.00	0

Figure 12.17
On the third day

Task/Resource	January 92 30 06	BCWP	BCWS	Pct Comp
Task-1		400.00	400.00	40
Rsrc-1		400.00	400.00	40

Figure 12.18
After setting the actual start date

Rsrc-1 should have spent 16 regular hours on the task. Suppose that instead only 8 regular hours were actually worked, how would this affect BCWP and BCWS. You can see the result of changing the actual hours worked to 8 in Figure 12.19. As the resulting Percentage Complete is now only half what it should be, the value of BCWP is only half the value of BCWS.

Notice that the difference between BCWP and BCWS is only due to the change in the value of Percentage Complete. If you increase the actual costs, for example, by directly entering an actual fixed cost value, then BCWP and BCWS will be unchanged. As already discussed, they are insensitive to any changes in actual cost as they are both percentages of baseline total cost.

Task/Resource	January 92 30 06	BCWP	BCWS	Pct Comp
Task-1		200.00	400.00	20
Rsrc-1		200.00	400.00	20

Figure 12.19
The task is running late

Schedule performance

This behaviour of BCWP and BCWS suggests using them to form more direct measures of project performance. In fact there are two types of measure that can be calculated - schedule and budget performance.

A measure of schedule performance should only be used to reflect the degree to which costs are different from those planned due to variations in the schedule and not direct increases or decreases in costs. For example, a measure of schedule performance should not be affected by an increase in actual hourly rate or actual fixed costs. Measures of schedule performance simply tell you how much of the work, using cost as its measure, has been completed as compared to how much should have been completed. Notice that this implies that such measures are only useful while the project is in progress, because once the project is completed the ratio of work done to work planned should eventually settle down to 1:1.

On the other hand, measures of budget performance should not be influenced by variations from the schedule, only by variations in costs. Measures of budget performance are discussed in the next section.

SuperProject automatically works out three measures of schedule performance:

» **Schedule Variance**
The difference between BCWP and BCWS. That is, the cost difference between the stage the project is at and the stage it should be at according to the baseline data. A positive value indicates that the project is ahead of schedule, a negative value that it is behind schedule.

» **Schedule Variance Percent (SV%)**
The difference between BCWP and BCWS as a percentage of BCWS. That is Schedule Variance %= $\frac{\text{schedule variance}}{\text{BCWS}} \times 100$

The value can be interpreted as follows

-100% -------------------- 0 -------------------- +100%
behind schedule   on schedule   ahead of schedule

Notice that a value of -100% corresponds to a task actual percentage completion of 0%, i.e. if the task hasn't started and it should have then Scheduled Variance Percent is -100%. Also notice that values greater than 100% are possible if the task is completed before it should have started.

» **Scheduled Performance Index Percent (SPI)**
The ratio of BCWP to BCWS as a percentage. An SPI of 100% indicates that the project is on schedule, more than 100% indicates ahead of schedule and less than 100% indicates behind schedule.

As well as these indicators involving BCWS and BCWP it it also worth mentioning two other indicators of how on-target a project is:

» **Remaining Duration/Baseline Duration %**
This is simply the remaining duration of an allocation or task as a percentage of the baseline duration. This indicates what percentage of a task or allocation is yet to be completed.

» **Actual Duration/Baseline Duration %**
This is simply the percentage of the baseline duration that has been completed.

Notice that these two quantities can be considered to be measures of work to be done and work done respectively. The only time these quantities will not add up to 100% is if the total number of hours allocated to a task changes from the baseline value.

As an example of all of these performance indicators consider the project details shown in Figure 12.20. The task should be 60% complete but Rsrc-2 has only completed 40% of its allocated hours. If you examine the performance indicators you should be able to see how this shortfall affects

252 Costing   Chapter 12

Task/Resource	BCWP	BCWS	Schedule Variance	SV (%)	RemDurfBase (%)	ActDurfBase (%)	SPI (%)	Pct Comp
Task-1	1000.00	1200.00	-200.00	-17	50	50	83	50
Rsrc-1	600.00	600.00	0.00	0	40	60	100	60
Rsrc-2	400.00	600.00	-200.00	-33	60	40	67	40

Figure 12.20
Performance indicators

each one. Notice that Rsrc-1 is on schedule but Task-1 is still behind schedule.

You can also view BCWP and BCWS in graph form if you load layout D06 (or GANTT-6 in Version 2) - see Figure 12.21. Notice that the BCWS graph shows how the total cost increases over the predicted life of the project. The BCWP graph, on the other hand, is only meaningful up to the current date.

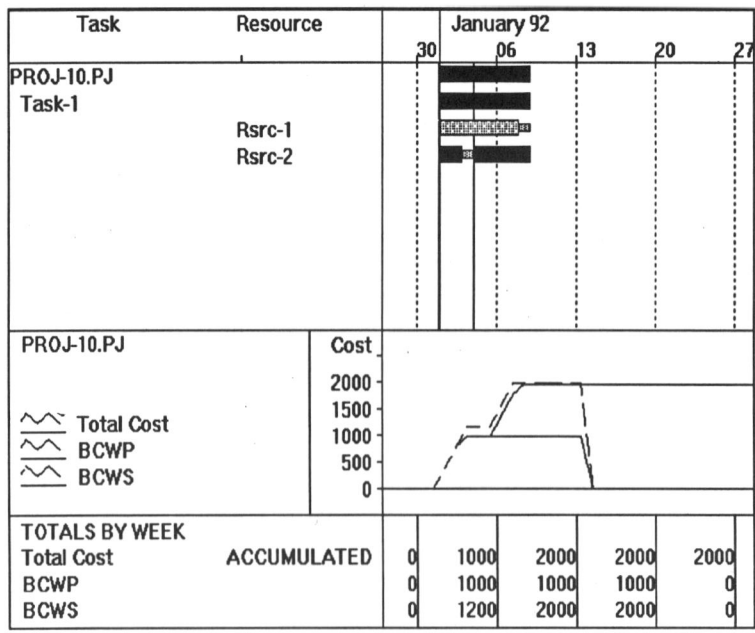

Figure 12.21
A chart of performance indicators

Budget performance

All of the measures so far do not take into account any cost increases or decreases. They only reflect the rate of progress of the project as compared to the baseline data. For example, if you enter a higher or lower actual fixed cost this makes no difference to any of the measures described so far. However, as the actual costs are available it is possible to construct measures of actual versus baseline costs.

SuperProject calculates three measures of budget performance:

» **Cost Variance**
This is just the BCWP minus the actual costs. As the BCWP is the cost of as much of the project as has been completed to date according to the baseline data, Cost Variance is just the amount the project is over or under budget on the current date. If Cost Variance is negative the project is over budget. If it is positive then the project is under budget, and of course zero indicates exactly on budget. Notice that Cost Variance doesn't reflect any deviation of the project from its schedule.

» **Cost Variance Percent (CV%)**
This is the Cost Variance expressed as a percentage of the BCWP. It indicates the percentage the project is over or under budget on the current date.

» **Cost Performance Index Percent (CPI)**
This is the ratio of BCWP to actual total cost. If this is 100% then the costs are exactly on budget. If it is less than 100% then the actual costs are under budget and over 100% indicates actual costs over budget.

You should be able to see that each of these measures is similar to one of the measures of schedule performance introduced in the previous section. To make this relationship clear the following table lists the corresponding measures.

Schedule Performance	Budget Performance
Schedule Variance	Cost Variance
Schedule Variance Percent (SV%)	Cost Variance Percent (CV%)
Scheduled Performance Index Percent (SPI)	Cost Performance Index Percent (CPI)

The best way to make sure that you understand the way that these indicators work is to examine a small example. In Figure 12.22 you can see the six indicators along with BCWS, BCWP and Percentage Complete (Pct Comp). Rsrc-1 has failed to complete the number of hours allocated to the task. It has only completed 24 of the 32 regular hours allocated and so its measures of schedule performance - Schedule Variance, SV% and SPI - all show values that indicate that it is behind schedule. However, as its failure to keep to schedule doesn't affect the cost of the project none of the budget indicators - Cost Variance, CV% and CPI - show anything other than perfect performance.

Now consider Rsrc-2. It has managed to complete its necessary number of hours, 32 regular hours, on Task-1, but only by working 24 regular hours and 8 overtime hours. This means that Rsrc-2 is on schedule but over budget. As a consequence the three indicators of schedule performance - Schedule Variance, SV% and SPI - all show that it is on schedule but the three measures of budget performance -

Task/Resource	BCWP	BCWS	Schedule Variance	SV (%)	SPI (%)	Cost Variance	CV (%)	CPI (%)	Pct Comp
Task-1	1400.00	1600.00	-200.00	-13	88	-100.00	-7	93	70
Rsrc-1	600.00	800.00	-200.00	-25	75	0.00	0	100	60
Rsrc-2	800.00	800.00	0.00	0	100	-100.00	-13	89	80

Figure 12.22
Schedule and budget performance indicators

Cost Variance, CV% and CPI - all show that it is over budget. Of course it is quite possible for an assignment to be behind schedule and over budget and in this case the problem would show in both sets of indicators! Indeed, if you look at the values shown for Task-1 you can see that it is quite clearly both running late and over budget.

A combined measure

This brings us to the question of a measure that reflects both schedule and budget performance in one. SuperProject calculates a single combined measure:

» **Actual Performance Index Percent (API)**
Actual Total Cost expressed as a percentage of BCWS. This is simply a ratio of actual cost to what it should be if it was on schedule and budget. A value of 100% indicates that the project is on schedule and on budget. A value less than 100 indicates that it either late or under budget - both reduce the actual cost on the current date. A value larger than 100 indicates that the project is either early or over budget - both increase the actual cost on the current date.

You can see the API for the example described above in Figure 12.23. Notice that in the case of Rsrc-1 the 75% simply means it is late and in the case of Rsrc-2 the 113% simply means that it is over budget. To fully interpret the API you have to look at other indicators.

Task/Resource	API (%)	Schedule Variance	Cost Variance	Baseline Total Cost	Variance at Completion	Calculated EAC
Task-1	94	-200.00	-100.00	2000.00	-100.00	2150.54
Rsrc-1	75	-200.00	0.00	1000.00	0.00	1000.00
Rsrc-2	113	0.00	-100.00	1000.00	-100.00	1123.50

Figure 12.23
Estimated variance and cost at completion

Predicting the final costs

Using the measures of budget performance available on the current date it seems reasonable to try to estimate the final budget performance. SuperProject calculates two such estimates:

» **Variance at Completion (VAC)**
This is the total baseline cost minus the scheduled total cost. As the scheduled total costs are updated using any actuals that are available this is a prediction based on the actuals of the amount the project will be under or over budget on completion. Any actuals that deviate from the scheduled values entered later in the life of the project will, of course, alter this estimate.

» **Calculated EAC - Estimate at Completion**
Using the cost performance index (CPI) it is possible to estimate the final total cost of the project. For example, if the CPI is 110% then this tells you by how much the actual costs are above BCWP. That is:

$$\text{actual cost} = \frac{\text{BCWP}}{\text{CPI}} \times 100$$

If you assume the same degree of over or under budgeting will continue to the end of the project, the same equation can be used to estimate the final total project cost by substituting the baseline total cost for BCWP. That is:

$$\text{Calculated EAC} = \frac{\text{baseline total cost}}{\text{CPI}} \times 100$$

Notice that both of these estimates are based on the current performance of the project and so are liable to change as the project progresses.

You can see the Variance at Completion and the Calculated EAC for the previous example in Figure 12.23. Notice that for the assignment that is simply running late, the Variance at Completion is 0 and the Calculated EAC is the same as the Baseline Total Cost. This is exactly how things should be because a delay in the schedule, in theory at any rate, should have no effect on the final budget totals. On the other hand Rsrc-2 is over budget and this affects both the Variance at Completion and the Calculated EAC. You can make use of the Calculated EAC and the Baseline Total Cost to manually compute an estimated percentage over or under budget using the formula:

$$\frac{(\text{Baseline total cost} - \text{Calculated EAC})}{\text{Baseline total cost}} \times 100\%$$

Accrual methods

So far it has been implicitly assumed that the cost of a resource's assignment is directly proportional to the percentage completed. This is certainly true where most labour resources are concerned, and for any resource that charges on unit time. However, some resource costs are incurred in full at the actual start of an assignment and others are are deferred in full until the completion of the assignment. For example, if you hire equipment you may have to pay in full at the start of the loan period. You can include both of these behaviours in your project model by altering the Accrual field in a resource's Details view. The choices are Prorate, Start or End. If you select Prorate (the default) then all of the earned value analysis measures are calculated exactly as described. However, if you select Start or End then the BCWP is zero until the actual start or actual end of the assignment when it becomes the full baseline total cost. In the case of the BCWS the same all-or-nothing behaviour occurs except that it is the baseline start and end dates that are used as the dates on which the value changes.

Reporting earned value

There are a great many possible on-screen and printed reports that you can construct. Many of the most useful involve the use of the account code and/or the WBS code. Instead of describing some typical cost performance reports here, discussion of all reports is postponed until Chapter 14.

Key points

» You can optionally show costing fields in any of the Expert modes. These include Scheduled Regular, Overtime, Total Variable, Fixed, Overhead and Total Costs.

» A resource's hourly rate and an overtime multiplier can be set in the Resource Details view. Variable costs are automatically calculated using these values and the scheduled regular and overtime hours.

» Corresponding to each scheduled cost field there is one for actual and one for remaining data.

» The Edit,Transfer to Baseline command saves baseline variable, fixed and total costs.

» Auto Actuals transfers scheduled cost data to actual cost data when an assignment's start and finish dates pass.

» Actual cost data is also transferred to the scheduled data fields to keep the portion of the project model that lies in the future up-to-date.

» Account Outline view allows you to build a hierarchy of accounts that is independent of the task hierarchy.

» The account and WBS mask, stored in the Project Details view, control the format of account and WBS codes.

» Earned value analysis provides a range of indicators that are sensitive to scheduling and budget performance.

Chapter 13
Material Resources and User Fields

The types of project that we have looked at so far have concentrated on the use of labour or hourly charged resources. However, SuperProject can also model material resources and consumer/producer relationships. While this type of modelling isn't particularly sophisticated it is very usable as long as you recognise its limitations.

In addition to material fields SuperProject Version 3 has a set of 90 user-defined fields and these are described at the end of this chapter. As their name suggests, these can be used for storing ad-hoc data that isn't included in the range of standard project fields. As well as being able to store data in user-defined fields, you can also define formulas that calculate values from any other fields in the model.

Resource type

To set a resource's type to something other than the default - labour resource - you need to view its Details and select one of the possible types - Labor, Material or Other. Labor resources have been the main topic of earlier chapters and Other resources are treated like Labor resources but they do not shorten effort driven tasks. That is, an Other resource is charged hourly and is necessary for the task but it doesn't motivate the task in the same way that a Labor resource does. You can use the Other resource type to model equipment and other plant.

You cannot select the third type of resource, Material, unless you have first selected the Show Material Fields option in the Preferences,General Options dialog box. This adds a new field and enables the calculation mechanisms necessary to deal with material production and consumption.

Material fields

Although selecting Show Material Fields only adds one new field to the data table - Material Allocation - it alters how some of the existing fields behave with respect to a material resource. Notice that you have to be in one of the Expert modes for Material fields to actually show.

When you assign a material resource to a task you can specify the nature of the use of the material within the task. The material can be produced or consumed. It can also be produced or consumed at a regular rate or in one go at the start or end of the task. Of course, in practice you may opt to model a task that actually consumes or produces a resource at a steady rate by one that consumes or produces all of the material at the start or end of the task. For example, if a material is used at a steady rate but a delivery is made only once at the start of the task then as far as the producer tasks are concerned it consumes all of its resources at the start.

The rate of material production or consumption can be specified by entering a value into the Material Allocation field as indicated in the table shown opposite. For example, entering 10h means that 10 units are consumed per hour, 14 bp means that 14 units are produced at the start of the task.

Consumer	Producer	Meaning
n h	n hp	n units per hour
n d	n dp	n units per day
n b	n bp	n units at the start
n e	n ep	n units at the end

Material allocation

The Material Allocation field works in combination with the Allocation per Day field to determine how many units are produced over the duration of the task. If you specify the production rate per day it is first converted into a rate per hour by dividing by the length of the standard day, usually 8 hours. Similarly, the Allocation per day is converted to hours per day if it is expressed as a percentage of the working day. Once the hourly rate and allocation are known the number of units produced is calculated using:

Material Allocation per hour x
 Allocation per Day in hours x
  Scheduled Duration in days

This value is stored in the Units Assigned field which now represents the total number of units produced or consumed by the task. Notice that material resources obey the dictates of the project and their own resource calendar.

For example, in Figure 13.1 you can see that Rsrc-1 has been set as a material resource. Its Material Allocation has been set to 10 units per hour produced. With a 50% Allocation per day only half of the standard working day is used for production. Assuming that the standard working day is 8 hours this means a total of 4 x 10, i.e. 40, units will be produced per working day. As the task's estimated

Task	Resource	Est Dur	Schd Dur	Alloc /Day	Mat Allc	Units Assgn
PROJ-3.PJ			5dy			
Task-1		5dy	5dy			
	Rsrc-1		5dy	50%	10 hp	200

Figure 13.1
Material allocation

duration is 5 days this gives Units Assigned a value of 40x5, i.e. 200.

If you allow SuperProject to calculate the Units Assigned from Material Allocation and Allocation per Day then the scheduled duration of the task will equal the estimated duration of the task, unless the project or resource calendar indicates that the resource is unavailable on particular days. However, you can opt to enter a value in the Units Assigned field directly, so overriding the calculated value. If you do this SuperProject will calculate the scheduled duration of the task so that it is long enough for the specified number of units to be produced.

For example, in Figure 13.2 you can see that the Units assigned has been set to 400. Given that only 40 units can be produced in a day, this implies that 10 days are needed for the task.

You should recognise the way that SuperProject handles material allocation as being the same basic mechanism used for labour resources. If you don't specify the resource's allocated hours they are calculated from the estimated duration and if you do they are used to calculate scheduled duration.

Task	Resource	Est Dur	Schd Dur	Alloc /Day	Mat Allc	Units Assgn
PROJ-3.PJ			10dy			
Task-1		5dy	10dy			
	Rsrc-1		10dy	50%	10 hp	400

Figure 13.2
Materials allocation determining scheduled duration

Inventory and costs

When you create a material resource SuperProject automatically adds a data field to keep a count of the inventory for that resource. The Inventory field simply keeps a count of the number of units of the resource that are available, i.e. it is a cumulative sum of units produced and units consumed.

Although there is no direct access to the inventory data, in the sense that it isn't available as a column in the data table, you can view it as a graph at the bottom of the Resource Outline view. (In fact you can also view it as a graph at the bottom of the Task Outline view but, as will become apparent, Resource Outline view is particularly appropriate for a material resource.) If you select Resource Outline view and then load layout B08 (INVENTORY in Version 2) then you will see a chart of inventory and units used for each resource.

For example, in Figure 13.3 you can see the inventory graph for a single producer, Task-1, and a single consumer, Task-2. The total number of units produced and consumed in each case was manually set to be the same. The production and consumption rates were different and you can see how the tasks have been scheduled for different durations. However, this scheduling is fairly simple and based purely on the time needed to produce or consume the total number of units. For example, there is nothing stopping the inventory from going negative if the rate of consumption was higher than the rate of production - which would not be reasonable.

You can also include costing information for material resources. The details of the calculation are the same as for labour resources only in this case the Rate is cost per unit consumed. That is:

Scheduled regular cost = Rate x Number of units consumed

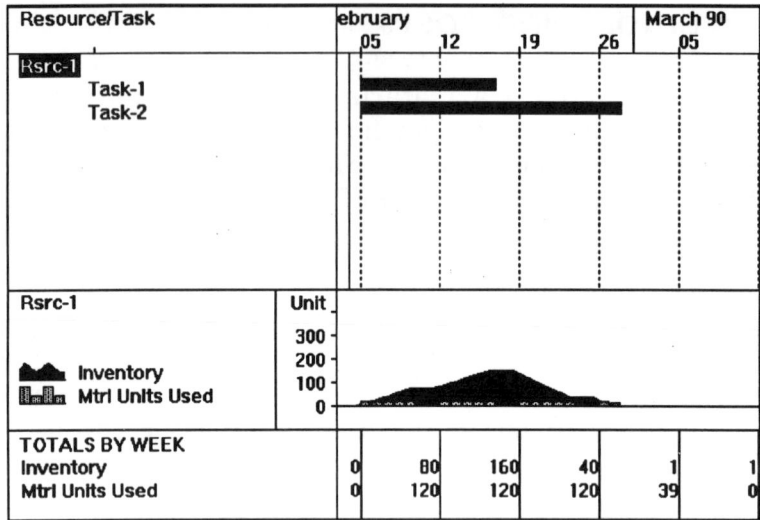

Figure 13.3
Examining inventory

Notice that Overtime cost is meaningless for a material resource but both Fixed and Overhead cost can be used.

By default the rate for a producing task is set to zero, no matter what rate is indicated for the resource. If you want to override this setting then you can simply type the correct value in the Rate column. Similarly, if you want to allocate a fixed cost to the material production or consumption simply set the rate to zero and and enter the fixed cost.

Beyond this material costs are handled in exactly the same way as other costs and you can use baseline and actual fields to track the progress of the project.

Levelling

The availability of material resources allows us to construct consumer/producer models, but so far the automatic scheduling of such models is very unsophisticated. All that happens is that the production rates are used to derive totals or task durations. If you set up a situation in which the schedule results in the inventory for the resource going negative there is nothing to stop it.

For example, in Figure 13.4 you can see that the producer task, Task-1, simply isn't keeping pace with the consumer task, Task-2. You can see that the inventory goes increasingly negative until the consumer task finishes and only then does the inventory slowly climb back up to a positive value.

You could deal with this situation manually by moving Task-2's start date until a sufficient stock of Rsrc-1 had been built up, but you would have to do this either using trial and error or by examining the inventory graph for the producer resource on its own. This is relatively easy in the case of a single producer and a single consumer but quickly becomes difficult when more tasks are involved.

As you might guess, the allocation of the same resource to two concurrent tasks such that it results in a negative inventory is an example of a resource allocation conflict. SuperProject will level this conflict by automatically shifting the start of the consumer task so that the producer has time to build up sufficient stock of material.

You can select automatic levelling for materials simply by selecting the Levelling Full option in the Calculation

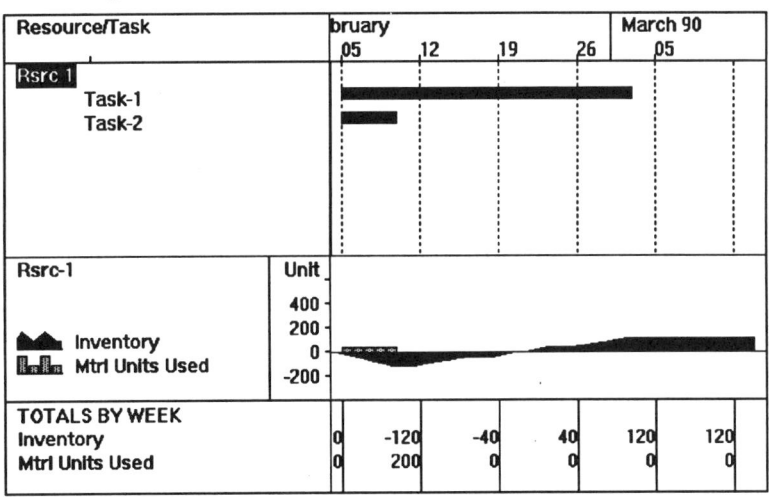

Figure 13.4
The producer cannot keep up with the consumer

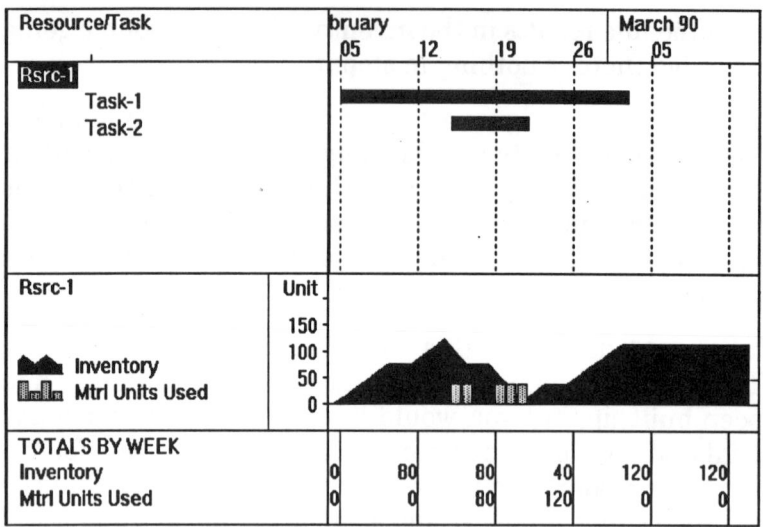

Figure 13.5
After levelling

Options dialog box. The same rules apply to levelling irrespective of resource type. If you look at Figure 13.5 you can see the way that Task-2 has been shifted so that the Inventory never actually goes negative.

SuperProject's levelling method for materials is rather simple and it is difficult to build into a model considerations other than production/consumption rates. For example, if you are scheduling two tasks which consume a resource at different rates then the task with the smaller rate of consumption will start first, irrespective of priorities. The reason is that SuperProject starts a task as soon there is enough inventory and so the one that makes the smaller demands starts first. This makes it difficult to schedule tasks according to priority. If you want to make sure that one material-consuming task follows another, then really the only way of doing this is to impose a logical constraint between the tasks. Notice that this stops tasks from starting until the logically prior tasks have completed.

Building blocks - an exercise in material scheduling

As an example of how SuperProject's material resources can be used to construct a model, consider the problem of the supply of concrete blocks from a single producer to a number of projects. In this case the single block making machine can manage to produce 200 blocks per day and there is enough raw material to make a total of 5000 blocks. Because of the limited size of the Material Allocation field it is necessary to work in units of 100 blocks. It is very important to choose sensible units when you are building a model because there is an upper limit on the size of Material Allocation and you cannot specify fractional units.

In the model in Figure 13.6 you can see that the **Block Making** task has been specified as a daily producer of 200 blocks and the three other tasks are consumers at daily rates of 100, 200 and 100 blocks. You can also see that the totals number of blocks that can be used per day has also been entered. This data immediately tells you that it will be 25 days before the block making material runs out, 8 days to block the garage, 5 to block the garden wall and 20 for the house.

The next stage is to use SuperProject's levelling to schedule the three projects so that the inventory of blocks never goes negative. The result of levelling can be seen in Figure 13.7 in Resource Outline View. The house building task starts first simply because it has the lowest rate of block consumption.

Task	Resource	Est Dur	Schd Dur	Alloc /Day	Mat Allc	Units Assgn
BLOCKS.PJ			25dy			
Block making		5dy	25dy			
	Blocks		25dy	100%	2 dp	50
Garage		5dy	8dy			
	Blocks		8dy	100%	1 dy	8
Garden wall		5dy	5dy			
	Blocks		5dy	100%	2 dy	10
House		5dy	20dy			
	Blocks		20dy	100%	1 dy	20

Figure 13.6
Block production/consumption data

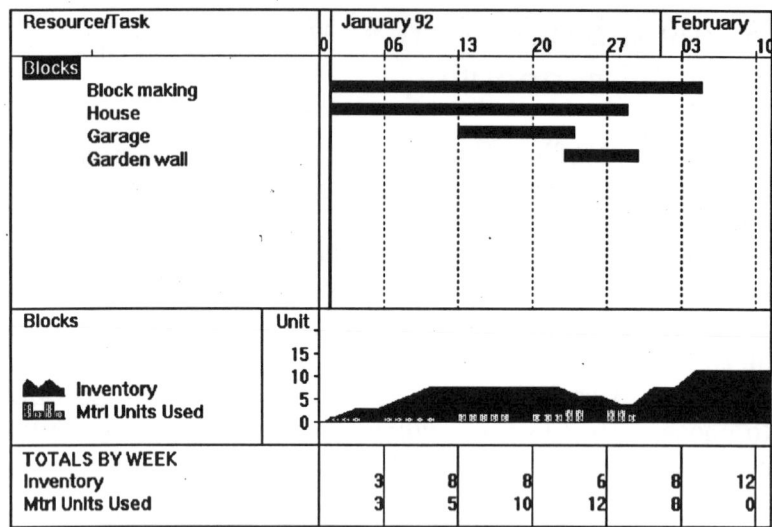

Figure 13.7
Block production/consumption data

This plan is reasonable, but it misses the important fact that blocks are delivered to the site of each task in lorry loads. If we can assume that the whole quantity of blocks needed is delivered at the start of the task then it is easy enough to alter the model to take this into account. All that has to be done is to change the Material Allocation to the total number of blocks needed at the beginning of each task, that is: 8b, 10b and 20b in each case. You can see the result of this change on the schedule in Figure 13.8. As you might have anticipated, each task now has to wait until sufficient blocks are available for it to start. Also notice that the tasks are scheduled in order of size of block consumption.

Of course this 'everything delivered at the start' model isn't particularly realistic either. It is much more likely that the blocks would be delivered in more than one consignment. To model this you would have to break each task down into smaller units corresponding to the phases of the project that depended on each delivery. These phases would then have to be linked together to form a single project. The only danger with this approach is that a task with a smaller demand might delay one of the phases.

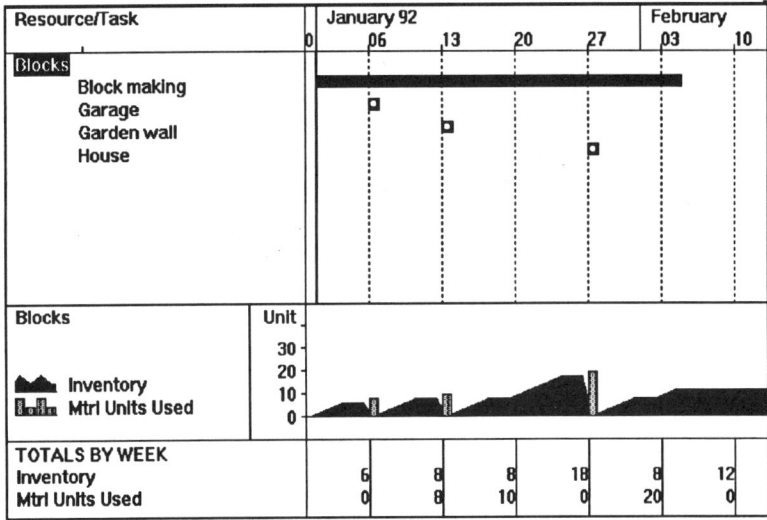

Figure 13.8
Block consumption at start of task

For simple producer/consumer models SuperProject's material resources work well. If you discover that you are spending a lot of time trying to make a scheduling model for materials work properly then the chances are that you need a more specific scheduling package.

Also notice that you can use a material resource within a project model that is predominantly a labour resource model. Each type of resource scheduling and costing will be handled correctly.

User-defined fields

A powerful feature introduced in Version 3 of SuperProject are the 90 user-defined fields. There are a group of 30 fields for tasks, resources and assignments. Although any or all of the user-defined fields can be included in the usual display via the Column Layout dialog box, the easiest way of examining them and entering data is to use the pop-up editor. If you double click on a task the pop-up editor window will appear and clicking on the User button takes you to the Task - User Defined Fields editor, see Figure 13.9.

There is a similar pop-up editing window for assignments which appears when you double click on a task in Task Outline view and one for resources which appears when you double click on a resource in Resource Outline view.

The pattern of data fields is the same in each case and their fieldnames tell you the type of data that can be stored. There are six types of field: Text, Integer, Currency, Flag, Start date and Finish date. The Flag fields can accept a Yes/No type of entry. Each type of object, Task, Resource and Assignment has five of each type. For example, each task has Task Text 1 to Task Text 5, Task Integer 1 to Task Integer 5 and so on. Notice that the full fieldname includes the name of the object so for example, Resource Text 1 is a different user-defined field to Task Text 1.

You can store whatever you like in the user-defined fields as long as the data is of the correct type for the field. SuperProject will treat the data appropriately for the type of object. For example, if you enter data into Task Integer 1 it will be shown totalled for any sub-heading that Task may be under. In addition you can draw bars on the Gantt chart corresponding to the values in Start 1 and Finish 1. Simply use the command Layout,Bar Symbols and select the box User Defined Start/Finish.

What makes the user-defined fields even more valuable is that it is possible to define formulas that SuperProject will

```
┌─────────────────────────────────────────────────────────────────┐
│  ─ │              Task - User Defined Fields                    │
├─────────────────────────────────────────────────────────────────┤
│ Task Name:Task-1            ID:        WBS:01.01.00.00.0001    │
│     Text 1:                                                     │
│     Text 2:                                                     │
│     Text 3:                                                     │
│     Text 4:                                                     │
│     Text 5:                                                     │
│     Integer 1:   0          Currency 1:    0.00                 │
│     Integer 2:   0          Currency 2:    0.00     ┌────────┐  │
│     Integer 3:   0          Currency 3:    0.00     │ Close  │  │
│     Integer 4:   0          Currency 4:    0.00     ├────────┤  │
│     Integer 5:   0          Currency 5:    0.00     │ Short  │  │
│     Start 1:                Finish 1:               ├────────┤  │
│     Start 2:                Finish 2:               │ Effort │  │
│     Start 3:                Finish 3:               ├────────┤  │
│     Start 4:                Finish 4:               │ Costs  │  │
│     Start 5:                Finish 5:               └────────┘  │
│     Flag 1:No               Flag 2:No     Flag 3:No             │
│     Flag 4:No               Flag 5:No                           │
└─────────────────────────────────────────────────────────────────┘
```

Figure 13.9
The pop-up editor showing the Task user fields

work out as part of a recalculation to give them values. If you have used a spreadsheet you will be familiar with this idea but you may not be familiar with the way the formulas are constructed. Every data field used in SuperProject has unique fieldname that can be used to identify it. A full list of these names can be found at the back of the SuperProject manual but the naming scheme is obvious and anyway when building a formula you can select the fieldname from a list.

To build a formula you first use the command Edit,Project Formulas. The produces a dialog box that you use to enter the formula, see Figure 13.10. You can type directly into the relevant sections of the dialog box but it is much easier to use the scroll bar and menu list to find fieldnames. The large scroll bar at the left allows you to scroll through the full list of user-defined fields. You can see in Figure 13.10 that Assignment Integer 1 has been selected and any formula that is entered into the box labelled Formula will be used to work out a value for Assignment Integer 1.

You can type a formula directly into the User Defined Formulas box but if you press F6 or click on the arrow to the left of the box a list of variables appears as shown in Figure 13.10. This list of variables takes the form of a hierarchical list. You first select which type of variable you want to use in the formula - account, assignment, general and so on. You are then presented with another list that narrows down your choice even more and perhaps even a third list for the final choice. You can repeat the process to enter other fieldnames and join them together with the usual mathematical symbols +. -, * , / and brackets. You can also make use of comparisons such as < and > which return a 1 if the result is true and 0 if it is false. Perhaps the best way of making all this clear is by way of a simple example.

As an aid to project tracking it would be nice to have a field that supplies the number of days late a task is in starting. The simplest way of doing this is to add an integer user-defined field to the model, Task Integer 1 say. To add it to the model all you have to do is use the command Layout,

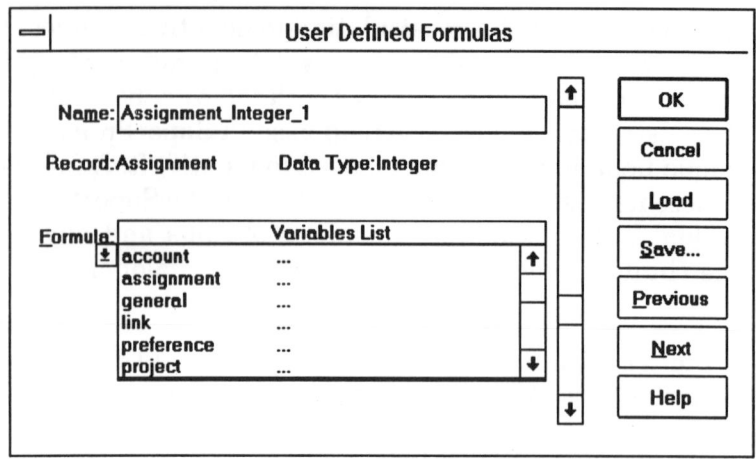

Figure 13.10
The User Defined Formulas dialog box

Column Layout and fill in the dialog box that appears as shown in Figure 13.11. You can see that the new data field is in position 3 and its column heading is 'Days late'. It is usable in this form because you could simply enter the number of days each task starts late manually. However, it is quite easy to get SuperProject to do the whole job for you. If you use the Edit, Project Formulas command and fill in the dialog box that results as shown in Figure 13.12 then SuperProject will indeed do the subtraction of the baseline value from the scheduled value each time you recalculate, as can be seen in Figure 13.13.

Once you get used to the field naming method it is quite simple. There is one final subtlety in that you can include

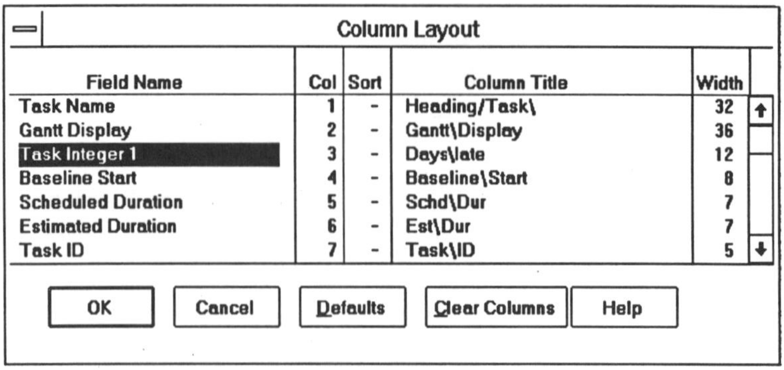

Figure 13.11
The Column Layout dialog box

User-defined fields 273

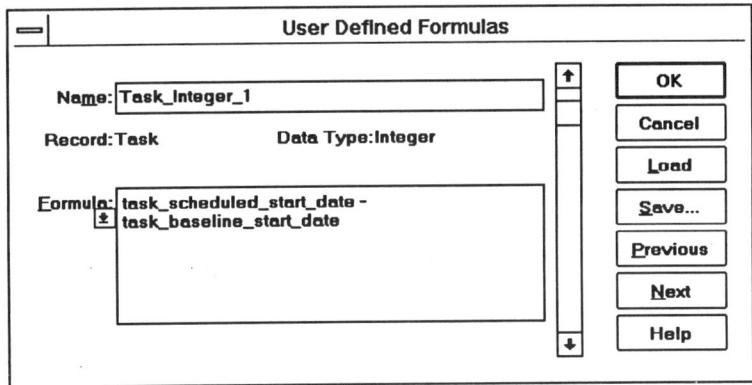

Figure 13.12
Entering a user-defined formula

an object identity number to pick out the value of a particular object. For example, task{0}scheduled_total_cost is the scheduled total cost of the whole project because task{0} is the task identify for the project heading.

User-defined fields and formulas are a powerful new feature and there is no end of potential applications. The biggest problem that you will encounter in using custom formulas is the way that sometimes values will be summed to form heading values or will be subtotalled when this isn't meaningful.

Task	Resource	4	11	18	25	Days late	Scheduled Start	Baseline Start
PAINT16.PJ							06-05-92> 8:00a	06-05-92 8:00a
Prepare room							06-05-92 8:00a	06-05-92 8:00a
Clear room						0	06-05-92 8:00a	06-05-92 8:00a
	Bill						07-05-92 8:00a	07-05-92 8:00a
	Tom						06-05-92 8:00a	06-05-92 8:00a
Strip walls						0	08-05-92 8:00a	08-05-92 8:00a
	Bill						08-05-92 8:00a	08-05-92 8:00a
Paint room							14-05-92 8:00a	13-05-92 8:00a
Paint ceiling						0	14-05-92 8:00a	14-05-92 8:00a
	Bill						14-05-92 8:00a	14-05-92 8:00a
Paint woodwork						4	18-05-92 8:00a	13-05-92 8:00a
	Tom						18-05-92 8:00a	13-05-92 8:00a
Paper walls						4	21-05-92 8:00a	15-05-92 8:00a
	Bill						21-05-92 8:00a	15-05-92 8:00a
Refurnish room						3	27-05-92 8:00a	22-05-92 8:00a
	Bill						28-05-92 8:00a	22-05-92 8:00a
	Tom						27-05-92 8:00a	22-05-92 8:00a

Figure 13.13
The user-defined field and formula in use

Key points

» A material resource has a new field associated with it and a new way of calculating its assignment.

» The number of units produced or consumed is calculated using:
Material Allocation per hour x
  Allocation per Day in hours x
    Scheduled Duration in days

» If you enter the number of units then SuperProject will calculate the task duration.

» An inventory field is kept for each material resource to keep track of the stock level, i.e. the cumulative effect of production and consumption.

» You can view the inventory field in Resource Outline view by loading layout B08/INVENTORY.

» Material resource conflicts, i.e. a negative inventory, can be automatically resolved using full levelling. Tasks are delayed to avoid a negative inventory.

» Costing, actuals and baseline data all work normally for material resources with only obvious and natural modifications.

» Version 3 added user-defined fields and formulas which can be used to extend the range of information that can be included in a model.

Chapter 14
Presentation

Unlike many applications programs, SuperProject makes it very easy to produce customised displays and reports. Almost every aspect of the standard graphs, charts and tables can be customised. Although you do not have absolute control over every detail of display, its flexibility means it is very easy to use. In most cases you should be able to produce a close approximation to what you need by customising SuperProject's general presentation. If you want to gain more control than this then you have no choice but to export the project data to another package. However, before you even contemplate this you should consider if the, usually very great, effort is worthwhile.

WYSIWYG

SuperProject is tries to be a What You See Is What You Get (WYSIWYG) package in the sense that it attempts to print what you can see on the screen as accurately as possible on the printer. Of course any printer will have different characteristics to the screen and how closely the printout corresponds will depend on the printer. For example, if you are using a colour display and a black and white printer then there will be an obvious difference between the two! In practice more subtle differences are usually more troublesome because they are often unexpected. For example, if a printer doesn't support a full range of fonts it may not be possible to print a layout exactly as it appears on the screen. Another common problem stems from the fact that even if a printer supports the printing of graphics, it may not have enough memory fitted to print a whole A4 page.

However, for all these difficulties, SuperProject's approach to generating output has many advantages. Essentially you don't have to worry too much about creating layouts specifically for the screen and for the printer. In most cases you can compose what you want to print out on the screen and then print it. SuperProject even has a print preview facility that allows you to see an even closer representation of what will appear on paper. Mostly this allows you to see how a large report will be cut up to fit onto sheets of paper.

If you want to get the best out of SuperProject then it is a good idea to make use of a laser printer. Personally I would prefer a full PostScript printer but an HP LaserJet is a good alternative. A laser printer of this sort will allow you to print a full range of graphics in a range of typestyles and sizes. If your budget doesn't run to a laser printer then an inkjet, perhaps even a colour inkjet, is a good alternative.

Layouts

We have already discovered that SuperProject maintains a list of standard layouts that can be used in each view. As well as simply making use of the standard layouts you can construct your own and save them for use with any project model. All you have to do is modify the existing layout and, when you are satisfied with it, save it as a named layout.

Named layouts aren't valuable only as a way of viewing data or getting it ready to be printed. Having a good range of layouts customised to show particular views of the project data can be an excellent way of making data entry and editing easy. You can quickly load a layout that shows you just the data columns with which you want to work and in an order that is meaningful and helpful to the task in hand. A new set of standard layouts designed to facilitate data entry and the examination of particular aspects of the

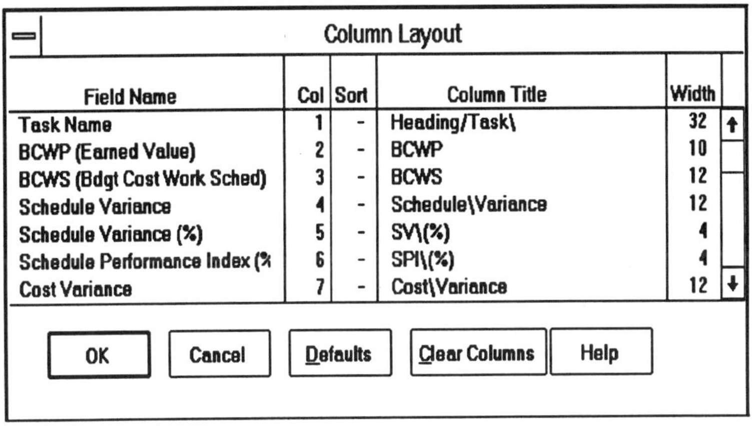

Column Layout				
Field Name	Col	Sort	Column Title	Width
Task Name	1	-	Heading/Task\	32
BCWP (Earned Value)	2	-	BCWP	10
BCWS (Bdgt Cost Work Sched)	3	-	BCWS	12
Schedule Variance	4	-	Schedule\Variance	12
Schedule Variance (%)	5	-	SV\(%)	4
Schedule Performance Index (%	6	-	SPI\(%)	4
Cost Variance	7	-	Cost\Variance	12

[OK] [Cancel] [Defaults] [Clear Columns] [Help]

Figure 14.1
Column Layout dialog box

model is available in Version 3. It is important that you familiarise yourself with them.

For example, if you are working with the earned value fields it makes sense to define a layout that brings the earned values fields to the far left of the data table. (Layout D06 is close to this column ordering.) You can select which columns appear and in what order using the Layout,Column Layout dialog box - see Figure 14.1. All you have to do is enter numbers which indicate the position in which the column should be listed in the table. A '-' dash indicates that the column should not be listed. A suitable ordering of columns for examining earned value analysis indicators can be seen in Figure 14.1. When you save a layout nearly every aspect of the current display format is saved and can be restored by simply loading the layout. For example, you might opt to display only assignments rather than headings, tasks and assignments and this selection would also be saved as part of the layout.

To save a layout all you have to do is use the command Layout,Save and fill in the dialog box that appears - see Figure 14.2. You can specify a layout name and a brief description to characterise the layout.

The most common mistake to make is not to realise that nearly all of the current settings of the display are saved

```
┌─────────────────────────────────────────────────────┐
│ ─                      Layout Save                  │
│                                       Layout:earn1  │
│                                                     │
│      Preference File Name:C:\SPJWIN\REPORTS.SPJ     │
│                                                     │
│         Layout Name:earn1                           │
│                                                     │
│      Layout Description:Earned Value Analysis       │
│                                                     │
│            ☐ Compress User-Defined Column Layouts   │
│                                                     │
│     ┌──────┐  ┌────────┐                ┌──────┐    │
│     │ Save │  │ Cancel │                │ Help │    │
│     └──────┘  └────────┘                └──────┘    │
└─────────────────────────────────────────────────────┘
```

Figure 14.2
The Layout,Save dialog box

and loaded as part of the layout. For example, if you have just spent half an hour customising the look of a Gantt chart - see later - it can be a little disheartening to load a layout that defines a completely different Gantt chart layout without first remembering to save the current layout.

Outline layout

Using the Column Layout dialog box you can restrict and reorder the columns of data that actually appear in the data table. By using the Outline Layout dialog box you can go even further and create reports on specific types of data that include totals, subtotals and even a breakdown by other categories.

The Task Outline Layout dialog box can be seen in Figure 14.3. There is actually an outline layout dialog box for each of the outline views but this one is a good starting point and contains all of the major options. Starting from the top of the box:

» The View Options are simply repeats of those in the View menu and control what is listed in the rows of the table.

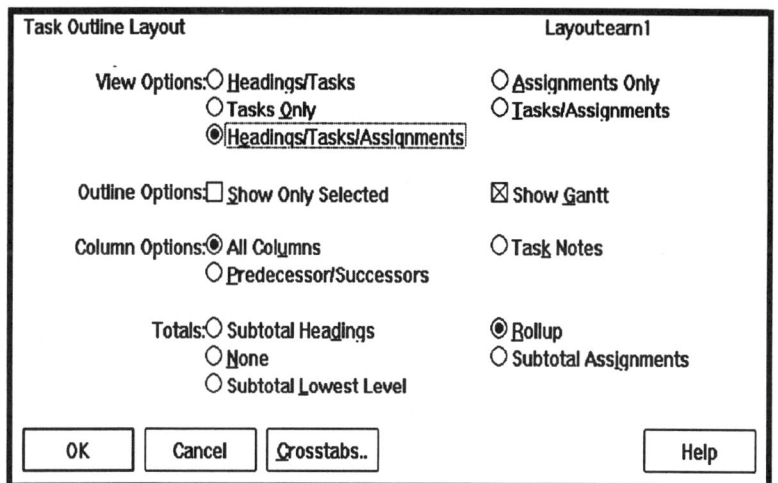

Figure 14.3
The Task Outline Layout dialog box

» The Show Only Selected option has already been discussed in connection with selection operations and filters in Chapter 9.
» The Show Gantt option is an alternative way of showing or removing the Gantt chart display. If this isn't checked then the Gantt chart isn't offered as a possible column.
» Column Options allows you to show Task Notes or Predecessor/Successors along with the columns that you have selected. Notice that both of these can be selected by clicking on icons in the Windows version.
» The Totals options govern how values are aggregated and are the subject of the next section.

Totals

There are four totals options, not counting None. According to which one you select, the values shown in summable columns will be sub-totalled for various groupings. The most common selection, and the one that is the default in most of the supplied layouts is Rollup, which forms totals going up the project hierarchy. That is, assignment values are totalled to give task values, task values are totalled to give heading values, and heading values are totalled to give project values. This is so standard an option that selecting None to remove rollup results in an outline view that looks distinctly odd.

If you select Subtotal Headings a separate subtotal is formed for tasks grouped by heading for each summable field, see Figure 14.4. This has obvious uses in preparing cost breakdowns by project phase. (Notice that you can select the currency symbol using Preferences,Date & International Formats.)

To see the difference between Subtotal Headings and Subtotal Lowest Level you need to look at a hierarchy with more than a single level of headings. Subtotal Lowest Level will only form subtotals for the first grouping of tasks whereas Subtotal Headings continues the aggregation for each grouping all the way to the project level. In Figure 14.5 you can see that Task-2 and Task-3 are subtotalled but Task-1 is not. If you were to select Subtotal Headings then a separate total for Task-1 would be shown. Also notice that the project total is always shown.

The final subtotal option is Subtotal Assignments which shows subtotals for each assignment group. Essentially, this subtotals each task.

Heading/Task	Scheduled Overtime Cost	Scheduled Fixed Cost	Scheduled Overhead Cost	Scheduled Total Cost
PAINT14.PJ				
Prepare room				
+ Clear room	0.00	0.00	0.00	88.00
+ Strip walls	30.00	15.00	0.00	105.00
Subtotal Prepare room	30.00	15.00	0.00	193.00
Paint room				
+ Paint ceiling	15.00	30.00	0.00	75.00
+ Paint woodwork	36.00	20.00	0.00	128.00
Subtotal Paint room	51.00	50.00	0.00	203.00
+Paper walls	30.00	50.00	0.00	180.00
+Refurnish room	33.00	0.00	0.00	99.00
TOTAL	£ 144.00	£ 115.00	£ 0.00	£ 675.00

Figure 14.4
Subtotal headings

PROJ-7.PJ			
Task-1			
Task-2			
+ Task-4	1000.00	1000.00	0.00
+ Task-5	1000.00	0.00	1000.00
Subtotal Task-2	2000.00	1000.00	1000.00
Task-3			
+ Task-6	1000.00	0.00	1000.00
+ Task-7	1000.00	0.00	1000.00
Subtotal Task-3	2000.00	0.00	2000.00
TOTAL	£ 4000.00	£ 1000.00	£ 3000.00

Figure 14.5
Subtotals at the lowest level

Notice that subtotals do not work if a filter is used and only selected tasks are displayed. This limits the usefulness of the subtotals facility slightly.

Crosstabs

The crosstabulation facility in SuperProject is very useful as long as you are entirely clear about exactly what it is doing. If you select the Crosstabs button in the Task Outline Layout dialog box another dialog box appears, see Figure 14.6.

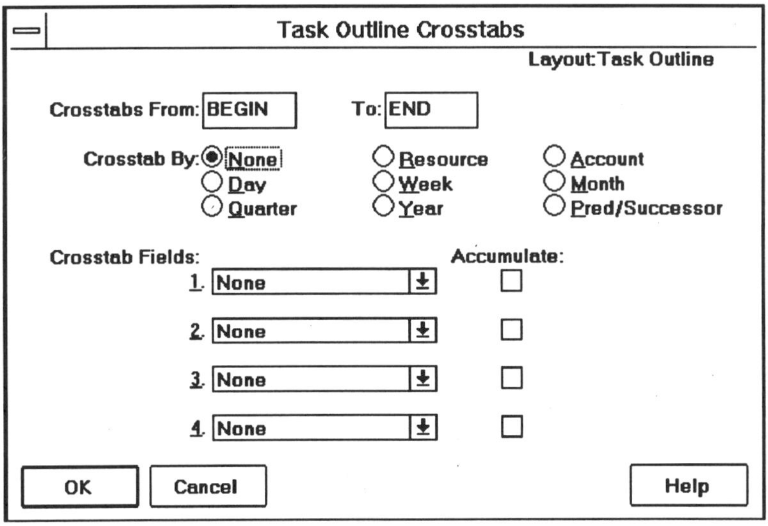

Figure 14.6
Crosstabs dialog box

Task/Resource		Week of 01-01-90 Total Hours	Week of 08-01-90 Total Hours	Week of 15-01-90 Total Hours	Week of 22-01-90 Total Hours
	Rsrc-1	40.00	0.00	0.00	0.00
Task-5		0.00	40.00	0.00	0.00
	Rsrc-1	0.00	40.00	0.00	0.00
Task-6		0.00	0.00	40.00	0.00
	Rsrc-1	0.00	0.00	40.00	0.00
Task-7		0.00	0.00	0.00	40.00
	Rsrc-1	0.00	0.00	0.00	40.00

Figure 14.7
Crosstabs of Total Hours by Weeks

You can select four crosstab fields using the four drop-down lists. Each crosstab field that you select is added to the display at the far right, beyond the Description field. There is a separate crosstab field for each value of the Crosstab By quantity that you select. For example, if you select Total Hours as the Crosstab Field and Week as the Crosstab By quantity there will be a Total Hours field for each week for which there is valid data.

For example, in Figure 14.7 you can see the additional columns added by crosstabulating Total Hours by Weeks. There is one extra column for each of the weeks that the project covers. If you check the Accumulate box then the values shown in the additional columns are summed to show the total to date. The same principle applies to all of the Crosstab Fields and selecting all four to be crosstabulated by a quantity that has many values can result in a very large number of additional columns.

As well as being able to crosstabulate by time periods - weeks, months etc.- you can also crosstabulate by resource, account and predecessor/successor. Notice that it doesn't make sense to crosstabulate every type of data by predecessor/successor.

Customising the Gantt chart

So far we have only used the Layout,Load command to customise what the Gantt chart is showing and the way that it shows it. In fact it is possible to customise the chart on a feature-by-feature basis. There are two dialog boxes concerned with this. The first is the Layout,Gantt Layout dialog box, which controls general features, and the second is the Layout Bar Symbols dialog box which controls what will be displayed and exactly how.

The Gantt Layout dialog box can be seen in Figure 14.8. Most of the options are entirely obvious and really you only need your attention drawn to the fact that they exist. The Benchmark Fixed Milestones is worthy of comment. If selected, any milestones (i.e. tasks with zero duration) that are associated with Must dates cause a vertical line to be drawn marking that date.

The final three options are also of particular interest. Using the Start, Finish and Side Label pull-down menus you can select almost any field to label the start, finish or side of the task bar on the Gantt chart. For example, in Figure 14.9 you can see a custom Gantt chart with Scheduled Start and Finish dates used for the start and finish labels and

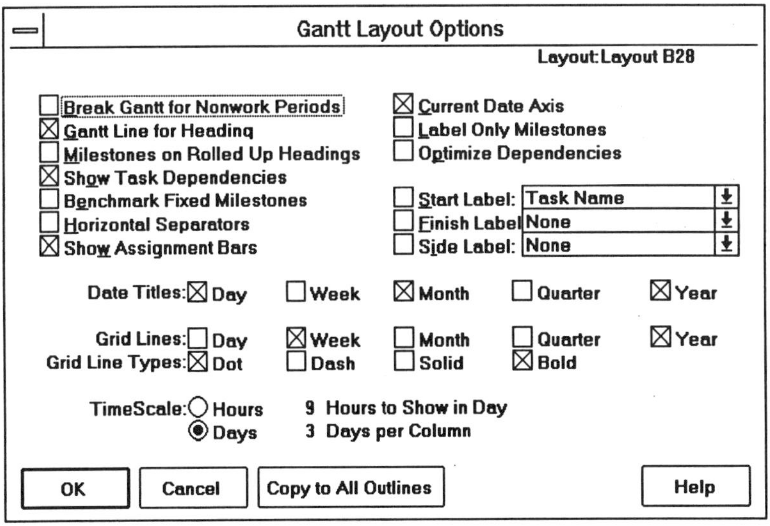

Figure 14.8
The Gantt Layout dialog box

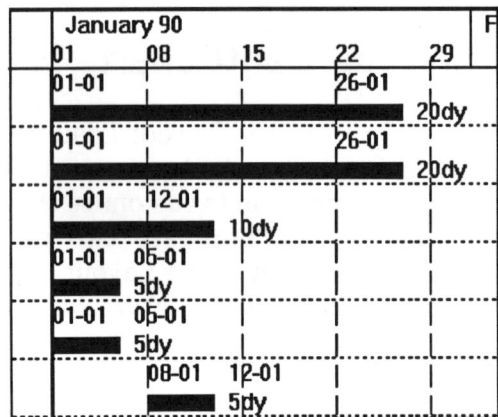

Figure 14.9
Gantt chart with labels

Scheduled Duration for the side label. Also notice that horizontal dividing lines have been selected in an attempt to make the chart easier to read. One of the problems with including any extra information on a Gantt chart is that it very quickly becomes difficult to read.

The Bar Symbols dialog box is equally obvious in its use, see Figure 14.10. You can select any of the quantities in the list at the left to be shown on the Gantt chart. The Size column controls the size of the corresponding bar expressed as a percentage of the height of a single character. Clearly this only works if it is possible to display fractions of a character and so this option will not be available in some of the DOS versions' display modes. Which of the Top, Mid or Bot buttons you select determines where the bar will display in the character row. You can select three quantities to display in a single character row by making one occupy the top, one the middle, and one the bottom of the row. The Symbol column shows the symbol that will be used to represent the quantity. You can modify the symbol used by clicking on the Symbols button. This produces yet another dialog box - the Gantt Symbols selector, see Figure 14.11. Using this you can select the quantity and its current symbol on the left-hand side and then select its colour and symbol style. Notice that you may want to select a symbol as much for the way that it prints out as for the way it looks

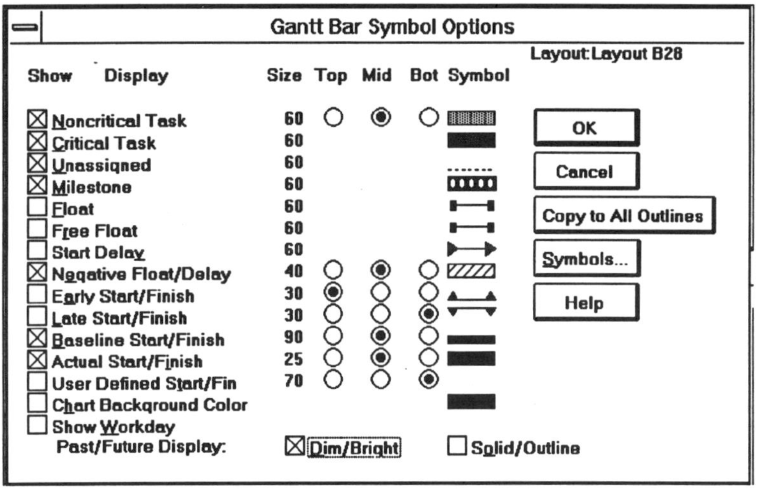

Customising the Gantt chart

Figure 14.10
The Symbols Options dialog box

on the screen. Indeed it is a good idea to develop standard layouts that you can use for screen display and for printout. For example, if you have a black and white only printer then selecting symbols based on the percentage fill symbols and hatches at the top of the dialog box will produce identifiable shades of grey. Notice that you can also select the chart background colour. If you do this remember that you will also have to select the colour of all of the symbols to be contrasting.

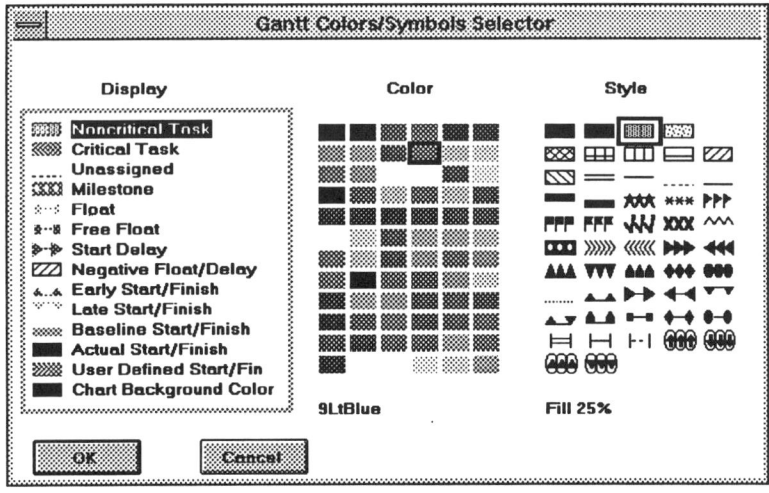

Figure 14.11
The Gantt Symbols Selector dialog box

The final options on the main Bar Symbols dialog box are slightly different. The Show Workday option adds dots, one per workday below the bars. The Dim/Bright and Solid/Outline options control how the bar is drawn to show the difference between the past and the future. If you select Dim/Bright then the part of the bar that corresponds to the future is shown bright or if Solid/Outline is selected it will be shown as an outline. In Version 3 you can also opt to show the dates entered into User Defined Task and Assignment Start 1 and Finish 1. Of course it is entirely up to you what these are used to record!

Adding histograms

You can add a graph or histogram of a combination of quantities to the bottom of the task or resource outline view. The command Layout,Histogram Symbols produces a dialog box which controls which quantities, if any, are graphed and how they are displayed - see Figure 14.12. This is one of the few cases where the DOS and Windows versions are slightly different.

You can select up to seven quantities to graph but in most cases you would be advised to restrict yourself to two or, at most, three quantities. The graphs are drawn in order from top to bottom of the list of quantities. This means that a later graph can completely obscure an earlier graph. Notice that you can select Material Units Used and Inventory Level even though these are not listed in the main project table. If you want the graphs to be cumulative check the box labelled Accum and to show a total for the quantity check the Total box.

In the case of the Windows version the type of graph used for each quantity is determined by another dialog box - the Colors/symbols selector which appears when you click on the Graphs button, see Figure 14.13. This dialog box allows you to select the colour, fill style and the actual type of graph. Using the Graph option you can select a simple bar chart. The total type of chart aggregates together all of the

Adding histograms

```
┌─────────────────────────────── Spj ───────────────────────────▼─┐
│ Task Outline          SuperProject                    PROJ-1.PJ │
│ File Edit View Layout Select Output Preferences Help            │
│ ┌─Cost/Resource Charts────────────────── Layout:Task Outline ─┐ │
│    Field         Graph        Style         Color     Accum Total│
│ 1. [Total Cost ]↓ [Bar  ]↓ [Fill 100%█]↓ [1Blue    ]↓ [ ] [ ]   │
│ 2. [None       ]↓ [Bar  ]↓ [Fill 50% █]↓ [10LtGreen]↓ [ ] [ ]   │
│ 3. [None       ]↓ [Bar  ]↓ [Fill 25% ▓]↓ [11LtCyan ]↓ [ ] [ ]   │
│ 4. [None       ]↓ [Bar  ]↓ [Hatch-1 XXX]↓[12LtRed  ]↓ [ ] [ ]   │
│ 5. [None       ]↓ [Bar  ]↓ [Hatch-2 ###]↓[13LtMagen]↓ [ ] [ ]   │
│ 6. [None       ]↓ [Bar  ]↓ [Hatch-3 ===]↓[14Yellow ]↓ [ ] [ ]   │
│ 7. [None       ]↓ [Bar  ]↓ [Hatch-4 |||]↓[9LtBlue  ]↓ [ ] [ ]   │
│                                                                 │
│         [ ] Show graph                                          │
│         [X] Stack bars for total hour or cost components        │
│                                                                 │
│   Scaling:( ) Use calculated min/max values for project.        │
│           (■) Use calculated min/max values for each view.      │
│           ( ) Use:                                              │
│               Min-Hours:   0 Units:    0 Costs:   0.00 Percent: 0│
│               Max-Hours:   8 Units:    1 Costs: 200.00 Percent:100│
│                                                                 │
│ (Enter=Confirm)   (Esc=Cancel)                       (F1=Help)  │
│                                                                 │
│ <Ins> to expand list, <Arrows> to select, <Enter> to accept. NUM│
├─────────────────────────────────────────────────────────────────┤
│ ─                    Cost/Resource - Histogram Charts           │
│                                                   Layout:Layout B28│
│         Field              Accum   Total    Graph               │
│    1. [Total Cost    ]↓     [X]     [ ]     ▪▪▪                 │
│                                                                 │
│    2. [None          ]↓     [ ]     [ ]     ▪▪▪     ┌────────┐  │
│                                                     │   OK   │  │
│    3. [None          ]↓     [ ]     [ ]     ▪▪▪     └────────┘  │
│                                                     ┌────────┐  │
│    4. [None          ]↓     [ ]     [ ]     ▪▪▪     │ Cancel │  │
│                                                     └────────┘  │
│    5. [None          ]↓     [ ]     [ ]     ▫▫▫     ┌────────┐  │
│                                                     │Graphs...│ │
│    6. [None          ]↓     [ ]     [ ]     ▫▫▫     └────────┘  │
│                                                     ┌────────┐  │
│    7. [None          ]↓     [ ]     [ ]     ▫▫▫     │  Help  │  │
│                                                     └────────┘  │
│   Options: [ ] Show graph       [X] Stack bars    Height:[MIN]  │
│   Scaling: ( ) Use calculated min/max values for project.       │
│            (●) Use calculated min/max values for each view.     │
│            ( ) Use:  Min-Hours:  0 Units:   0 Costs:   0.00 Percent:  0│
│                      Max-Hours:  8 Units:   1 Costs: 200.00 Percent:100│
└─────────────────────────────────────────────────────────────────┘
```

Figure 14.12
*The Histogram dialog box
(DOS version above, Windows version below)*

data in a particular time period. The time period used depends on the scale of the Gantt chart - usually weekly or monthly. The line chart shows the data points connected by a line and if you select a solid fill style then the area under the line will be shaded in. To produce an unshaded line graph you have to select solid line or one of the dotted line fill styles. The step graph type joins the data points with

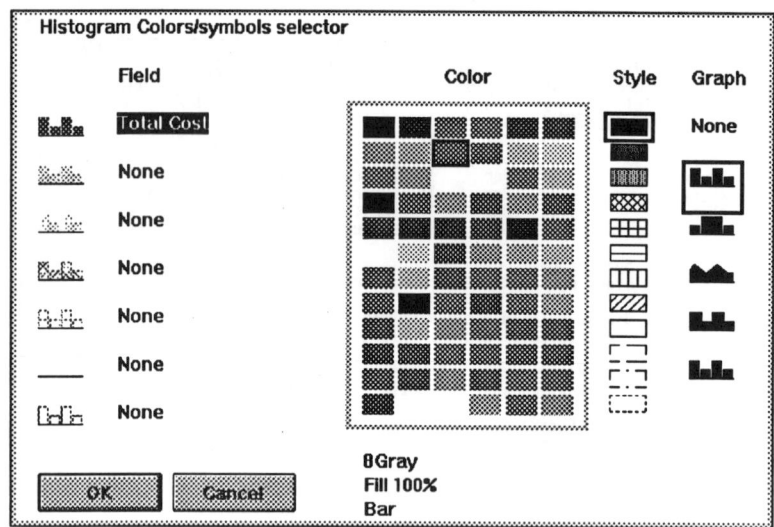

Figure 14.13
The Colors/symbols selector dialog box

horizontal and vertical lines which gives the impression of the outline of a histogram. Finally, the level chart just shows the lines that would be the tops of the bars in a histogram.

To make the graphs that you have selected actually appear you have to check the Show Graphs box in the Histogram dialog box. You can use manual scaling by setting the maximum and minimum values but in most cases it is better to leave SuperProject to determine the appropriate scale factors.

If you select the Stack bars option then, where it makes sense, fields will be stacked together. There are two groups of fields that can be stacked. The group labelled S1 are hours fields - Regular, Overtime and Conflict and the group labelled S2 are costing fields - Regular, Overtime, Fixed and Overhead. It makes sense to stack each of these two groups because when added together the total is a meaningful quantity, i.e. total hours and total cost. Stacking the bars shows how the total is made up.

One of the most difficult aspects of using the graphing facilities to show more than one graph at a time is making

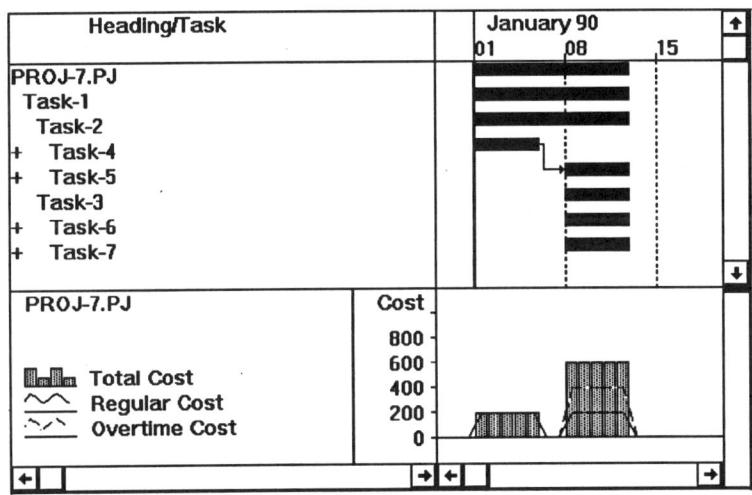

Figure 14.14
A histogram of more than one quantity

sure that one graph doesn't obscure another. The simplest rule to follow is to make sure that the first graph, or set of stacked graphs, that you define is solid but to specify subsequent graphs as line graphs without shading.

For example, in Figure 14.14 you can see that Total Cost is the first to be charted with Regular Cost and Overtime Cost as line graphs defined later. If you want to see detailed numerical values then all you have to do is check the Total box for each quantity that you are interested in. Similarly to see a cumulative graph put checks in the Accum column.

If you are using the Windows version you can turn the histogram on and off by simply clicking of the graph icon just below the menu.

Other views

The Layout menu has similar options in other views to those in Task Outline View. Of course some of the options will make no sense in a particular view, in which case they are generally left out of the menu or dialog box. For example, the Gantt layout dialog box doesn't have a Show

Dependencies option in Resource Outline View because task dependencies cannot be shown on the Gantt chart in Resource Outline View.

Notice that you can use sub-totals and crosstabs in Resource and Account Outline views.

PERT and WBS layout

The layout of both types of 'box' chart - the PERT and WBS chart - can be controlled in very similar ways. In the PERT view selecting Layout,PERT Layout produces the PERT Layout dialog box - see Figure 14.15. Most of these layout options are self-explanatory but notice that Arrange Tasks inside Pages and Show Page Breaks on Screen are particularly applicable if you are going to print the PERT chart. If you select Arrange Task Inside Pages no task box will be split between pages. Also notice that Show Only Selected Tasks can be used in conjunction with a suitable filter, see Chapter 9, to view or print a subset of the full PERT chart. If you don't like the standard arrangement produced by SuperProject you can unselect Auto Positioning and Auto Arrange After Edit and manually position PERT boxes. To move a PERT box simply double

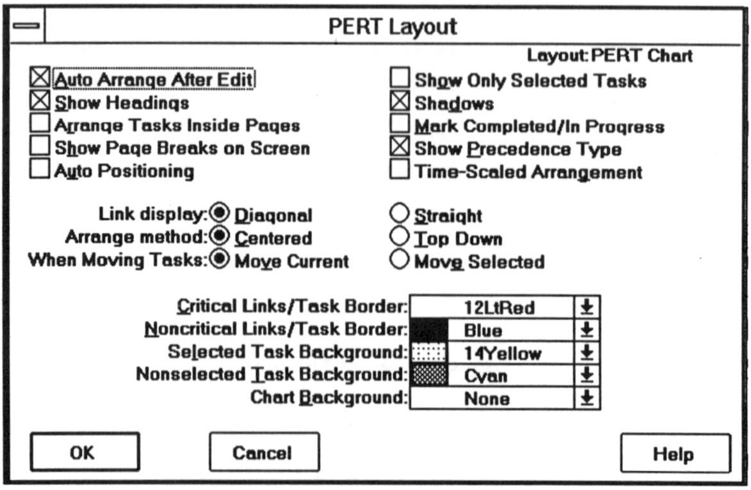

Figure 14.15
The PERT layout dialog box

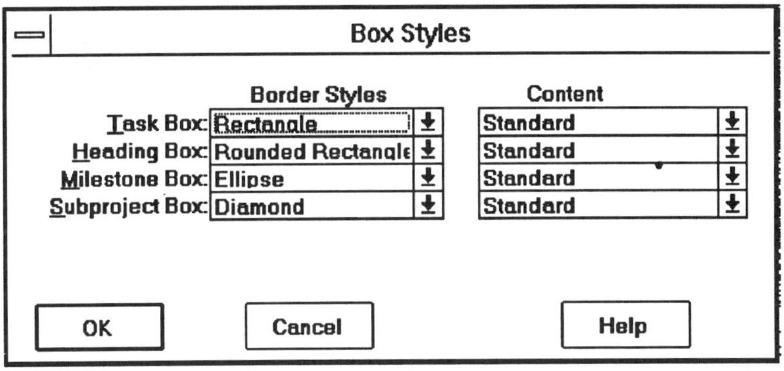

PERT and WBS layout

Figure 14.16
The Box Styles dialog box

click and hold. To restore auto-arrangement of the boxes make sure that Auto Positioning is selected in the dialog box and click on OK. Also notice the choice between diagonal and straight connecting lines and the ability to use a time scale, facilities which were introduced in Version 3.

You can select the appearance of each type of box and its contents by using the Box Styles dialog box, see Figure 14.16, which is accessed via the Layout Menu and allows you to select the shape and content of each type of box. You do not have a completely free choice of what quantities

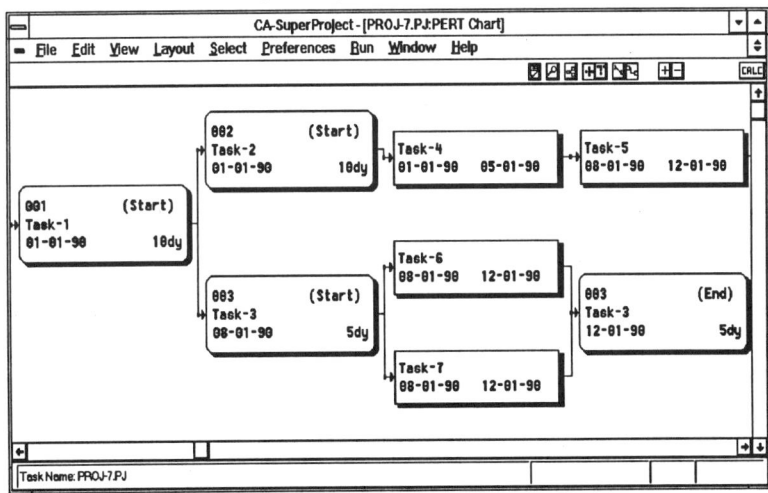

Figure 14.17
A customised PERT chart

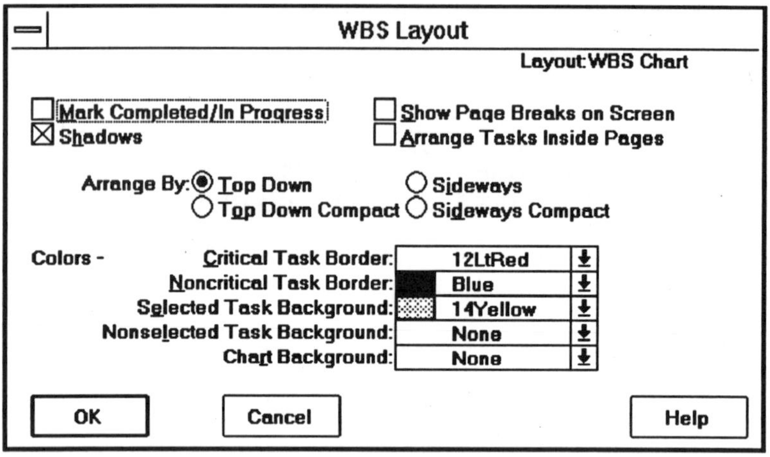

Figure 14.18
WBS Layout dialog box

appear in the PERT box but, using the Contents drop-down menus, you can select from a number of sensible groups - scheduled data, actual data, costs etc.. For example, Figure 14.17 is a PERT chart that shows Start and End dates and durations.

A very similar dialog box controls the WBS chart layout, see Figure 14.18. The only difference is the possibility of selecting one of four orientations and style of chart - top down/sideways and normal/compact. An identical dialog box controls the box styles used in the WBS chart to those in the PERT chart.

Fonts and colours

You can customise the colours used to display different elements of the screen display via the Preferences menu. If you are using Version 3 then you can also select from a range of fonts - see Figure 14.19. What fonts are available will depend on what fonts are installed in your system. If you are using Windows 3.1 then there will at least be Arial, Times New Roman and Courier which should satisfy all your needs. Arial is a sans serif and Times New Roman a

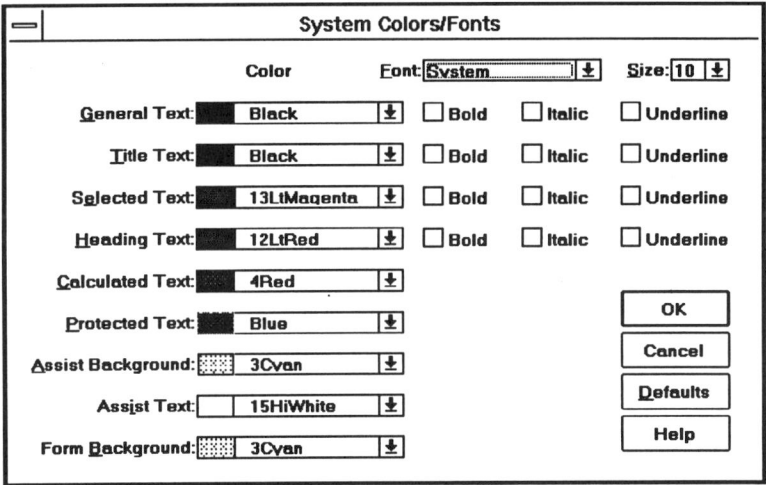

Figure 14.19
Version 3's System Colors/Fonts dialog box

serif font while Courier is a typewriter-style font. The best way of finding out how to use them is to experiment. In a report it is common to use a sans serif font for headings and a serif font for the body data but it is all a matter of personal preference. A much more important function of selecting fonts is being able to set the point size. By reducing the point size it is possible to see more of the view on the screen and reduce the number of pages it takes to print.

Printing reports

So far most of the discussion of presenting the project data has concentrated on the way things look on the screen. The reason for this is that screen views are the basis for all printer output. In the Windows version you will find the commands Print View, Print Reports and Printer Setup in the File menu. In the DOS version corresponding commands are in the Output menu which includes the commands View, Reports and Device Install. The main difference between the way that the two versions work is in setting up and installing printers. In the case of the Windows version it is left to Windows to deal with all output devices. If a printer is installed for Windows then it can be used by any Windows application, including SuperProject. For the moment it will be assumed that the printer is installed and ready to use.

All SuperProject printed output is derived from the screen views that we have been examining in detail for most of this chapter. To print it SuperProject adds titles and legends where necessary and divides the total view into pages. In most cases it is this division into pages that causes most problems.

You can print the current view by selecting the command Print View. This produces the Print View dialog box. This is slightly different in the Windows - Figure 14.20 - and DOS - Figure 14.21 - versions, mainly because the DOS version includes fields to allow the printer to be selected and set up. In the case of the Windows version setting up the printer is a matter for Windows itself. In Version 3 control of fonts and other matters of page layout is contained in a separate dialog box, see Figure 14.22, which appears when you click on the Page Layout button.

The exact form of the Print View dialog box varies according to the current view but its basic details are as shown in the figures. Notice that you can print any of the views including Calendar and Details views. In the case of Details views you

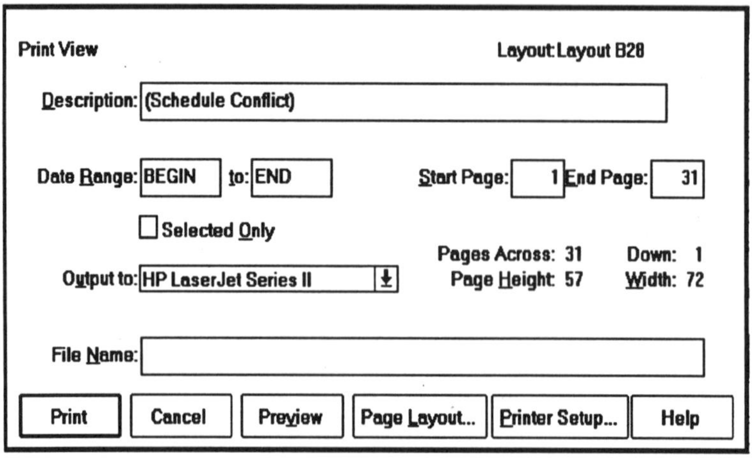

Figure 14.20
The Windows Print dialog box

```
Task Outline                    SuperProject                    PROJ-1.PJ
File  Edit  View  Layout  Select  Output  Preferences  Help
┌─ Output ──────────────────────────────── Layout:Task Outline ─┐
│ Chart Title:                                                  │
│     Options:[ ] Selected Only  [X] Borders   [ ] Spool   [ ] Wall Chart │
│ Date Range:BEGIN    to:END                                    │
│                                                               │
│     Text Size:[12 ]↕  Page Size:[04   ]↕  Font/Style:[Courier Normal  ]↕ │
│     Quality:(_) Draft       ( ) Enhanced                      │
│     Orientation:(_) Portrait    ( ) Landscape   Pages Across: 15    Down:  1 │
│     Page Height: 66  Width: 76                  Start Page:    End Page:    │
│                                                               │
│     Output to:[Installed Laser Graphics  ]↕ Device:Laser Jet  │
│     File Name:                                                │
│                                                               │
│  (Enter=Print) (Esc=Cancel) (F3=Preview) (F7=Copy to Layout)   (F1=Help) │
│                                                               │
└───────────────────────────────────────────────────────────────┘

<Ins> to expand list. <Arrows> to select. <Enter> to accept.      NUM
```

Figure 14.21
The DOS Output dialog box

have the additional option of selecting Repeat to print a summary of each Task or Resource.

You can provide the printout with a title and opt to print borders and repeat the column headings to provide a report that is easy to read on separate sheets of paper. If you are prepared to do some work with sticky tape then selecting Wall Chart will give you a printout minus the repeated headings so that the pages can be stuck together to form a large poster. You can opt to print only selected items and impose a date range for objects to be included in the report.

```
┌──────────────────── Layout Page Setup ────────────────────┐
│                                                           │
│     Font:[Courier      ]↕   Size:[10  ]↕      ┌────────┐  │
│                                               │   OK   │  │
│                       Bold   Italic  Underline└────────┘  │
│   General Font Style:  □      □        □      ┌────────┐  │
│   Heading Font Style:  □      □        □      │ Cancel │  │
│     Title Font Style:  □      □        □      └────────┘  │
│  Selected Font Style:  □      □        □   ┌──────────────┐│
│                                            │Copy to Layouts││
│  Options:  ☒ Page Borders    □ Wall Chart  └──────────────┘│
│                                               ┌─────────┐ │
│                                               │ Header..│ │
│                                               └─────────┘ │
│                                               ┌─────────┐ │
│                                               │ Footer..│ │
│                                               └─────────┘ │
│  Margins: Left[0.25] Right[0.25] Top[0.25] Bottom[0.25]   │
│                                               ┌────────┐  │
│                                               │  Help  │  │
│                                               └────────┘  │
└───────────────────────────────────────────────────────────┘
```

Figure 14.22
Controlling page layout - Version 3

The way in which a report is paginated is controlled by the lower part of the dialog box. The Font and its Size can be selected from the drop down lists in the Layout Page dialog box. Which fonts and sizes are available depend on the type of printer you have installed and selected. According to the font type and size the report will be split up into so many pages as reported by the Pages Across and Pages Down boxes. You can specify the size of the page in terms of text lines and columns and also by controlling the page margins in the Layout Page Setup dialog box in Version 3, see Figure 14.22. In the DOS version you can select the page size directly in the Output dialog box but in the Windows version you have to select the paper type in the Printer Setup dialog box. According to the overall 'shape' of the printout you may also want to select landscape printing. You can do this directly in the case of the DOS version and via the Windows Printer Setup dialog box in the case of the Windows version. If you only want to print part of the report then you can also set a page range to be printed.

In Version 3 you can also define headers and footers to be included at the top and bottom of each page. You can enter the text that you want to appear into the relevant dialog boxes, see Figure 14.23. As well as plain text you can also enter the names of SuperProject data fields that you would like printed on each page.

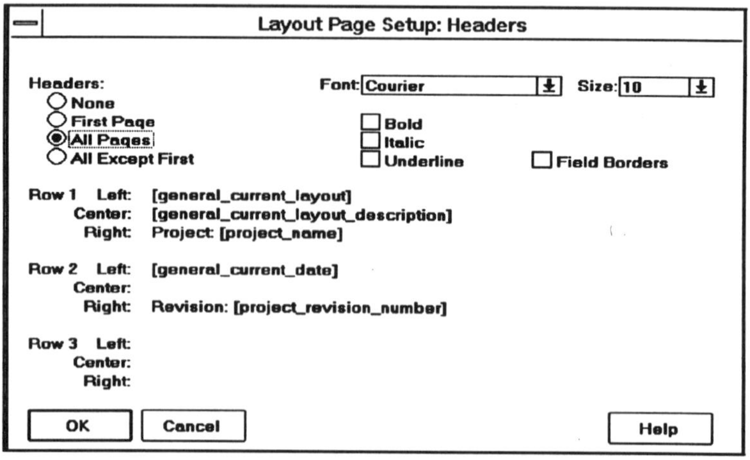

Figure 14.23
Defining a header - Version 3

To find out what your printed report should look like you can click on the Preview button or press F3 in the case of the DOS version. This results in a page by page display of the complete report as it will appear on the printer. How much you can actually see depends on the resolution of the screen display but in all cases it should be enough to see the general details of layout.

As well as being able to print the current view you can also print the data formatted according to any Layouts that you have saved. This is simply a short cut to loading the layout and then using Print (or Output) View but it is a useful one. It allows you to create special 'printer only' layouts and save them to disk for later use. If you select Print Reports then you will be presented with a list of layouts including any that you have saved, see Figure 14.24. Notice that the list includes all layouts from all views and selecting a layout from this list automatically selects the corresponding view. As you cannot save layouts for calendar and details views, these can only be printed using Print View. Once you have selected a layout to print you will see the dialog box that appeared in response to the Print View command. You can use this to set the printing parameters and to preview the output. Notice that if you click on the Copy to Layout button or press F7 in the case of the DOS version, then the printing setup will be saved to the layout and become the default next time you make use of the same layout.

A report example

Armed with all of the facilities described in this and earlier chapters you should find that you can tailor reports to your exact requirement. For example, it is useful to summarise the financial data when a project is complete. In this case the first task is to reduce the number of columns on show to just the financial data of interest using the Column Layout command. Next, Outline Layout is used to select Subtotal Headings. At this point the report can be saved under a suitable name, see Figure 14.25.

```
┌─────────────────────────────────────────────────────────────┐
│ ─                        Print Reports                       │
├─────────────────────────────────────────────────────────────┤
│                                                              │
│ Preference File Name:D:\SPJWIN3\REPORTS.SPJ                  │
│                                                              │
│ Layouts:                                                     │
│   View              Name             Layout Description      │
│  Account Outline   Acct Outline      Account Outline (Default) ▲
│  Account Outline   Layout A01        Account Outline         │
│  Account Outline   Layout A02        Scheduled, Actual, Remaining, B│
│  Account Outline   Layout A03        Scheduled, Actual, Remaining, B│
│  Account Outline   Layout C01        Crosstab: Total Hours and Total│
│  Account Outline   Layout C02        Crosstab: Baseline Cost vs. Tot│
│  Date Outline      Date Outline      Date Outline (Default)  │
│  Date Outline      Layout A01        Date Outline            │
│  Date Outline      Layout A02        Dates and Durations: Sched, Actu│
│  Date Outline      Layout A03        Assignment Allocation and Sched ▼
│                                                              │
│  [ Load ]  [ Cancel ]  [ Browse... ]              [ Help ]   │
└─────────────────────────────────────────────────────────────┘

Figure 14.24
*The Print Reports dialog box*

To print the report all that is necessary is to load the layout and use Output or Print View or Reports and select the layout. In this case it was possible to make the report fit on a single page by selecting landscape orientation and a small point size. Not all printers support landscape orientation and the range of point sizes available varies. This may make it impossible to print the report on a single page using some types of printer. If using Version 3 also remember to turn off the Gantt chart legends using the Footer dialog box. A preview of the resulting report can be seen in Figure 14.26.

This report can be customised further by using a filter to select tasks that have CPI values not equal to 100. This is just a matter of writing a filter to select CPI values equal to 100 and then selecting NOT on the level above. As this is the only selection criterion a dummy criterion has to be

┌─────────────────────────────────────────────────────────────┐
│ ─                        Layout Save                         │
│                                          Layout: Layout B28  │
├─────────────────────────────────────────────────────────────┤
│                                                              │
│    Preference File Name:D:\SPJWIN3\REPORTS.SPJ               │
│                                                              │
│      Layout Name:Final Cost                                  │
│                                                              │
│    Layout Description:Final cost report|                     │
│                                                              │
│         ☐ Compress User-Defined Column Layouts               │
│                                                              │
│  [ Save ]  [ Cancel ]                             [ Help ]   │
└─────────────────────────────────────────────────────────────┘

Figure 14.25
*Naming the new layout*
```

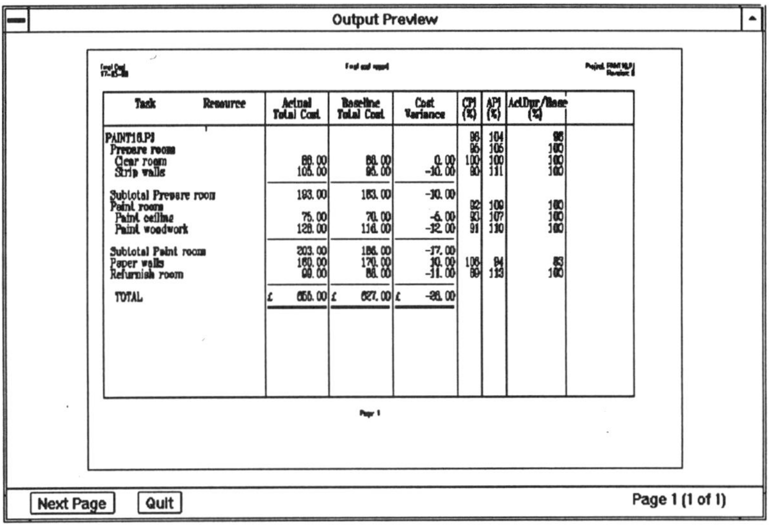

Figure 14.26
A preview of the report

entered at Level 1. You can see the completed filter in Figure 14.27. Notice the use of Task ID to select the entire list of tasks. The NOT ensures that only tasks that satisfy the Level 1 condition and not the Level 2 condition are selected. If you try running the report with this filter in force and remember to select the Selected Only box in the Print dialog box then the report will list only tasks with CPI values not equal to 100. Notice that the subtotals are not calculated when a filter is used.

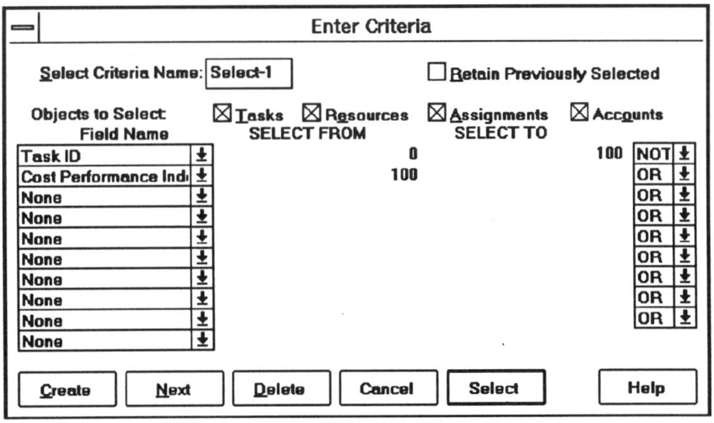

Figure 14.27
A filter for CPI values not equal to 100

Key points

» SuperProject's printed output is derived from screen views. The only difference is that the view is paged according to the size of paper in use.

» You can construct a view by customising the outline, the Gantt chart, the histogram and other aspects of the view and then printing it. Alternatively, you can save the details of the view as a layout and use this at a later date with the Print Reports command.

» The way in which project data is paged depends on the printer installed, the paper size, font size and orientation. By altering these parameters you can obtain a more appropriate fit to the page.

» By omitting borders and repeating titles you can obtain a tiled printout which can be assembled into a single large poster printout.

» You can print calendar and details directly from their corresponding views.

» You can restrict what is printed by applying a filter.

» As well as the basic data you can also obtain subtotals and crosstabulations.

Chapter 15
SuperProject Systems

SuperProject can be used in conjunction with other software packages to build complete systems capable of managing all aspects of a project. The way that this is achieved is by using one of the many forms of data exchange that SuperProject supports. In this chapter we look more closely at the way that SuperProject handles data. Before moving on to consider data exchange in detail it is worth looking at the facilities provided for building large projects by using subprojects and sharing data between projects.

It is worth noting that inter-project connection has been improved in Version 3 mainly as a result of a reorganisation of the menu structure and a rationalisation of facilities. The differences are, however, slight and the basic ideas and operations remain unchanged.

Subprojects

A subproject is, in many ways, nothing more than a logical extension of the hierarchy that we have used to reduce the complexity of projects since Chapter 9. A subproject is a complete project in its own right and stored in a project file on disk. It can be linked into an existing project as if it was a single task. From the point of view of a superproject, i.e. the project that contains the subproject, all that really matters as far as scheduling goes are the subproject's duration, its links with other tasks and any Must dates that have been defined. In other words, a subproject really does behave as if it was a simple task within the superproject. You can create as many levels of subprojects as you like. That is, a subproject may itself be composed of subprojects, which in turn may be composed of subprojects and so on.

The facilities for working with subprojects have been reorganised in Version 3 and are all to be found grouped together in the File,Inter Project Connections option.

You can create a subproject as you would create any other project and then insert it into an another project using the command:

>File,Inter Project Connections,Link to Subproject

or in Version 2:

>Edit,Make Subproject Connection

(This command is only available in Expert mode.) Before you do this you should select the task in the project that the subproject is to replace. What this means is that in most cases you will first introduce a 'dummy' task complete with links to be used as a peg to hang the subproject on.

After the connection has been made you can remove the subproject by giving the command a second time with the subproject selected. In Version 3 a dialog box appears giving you a more flexible approach to deleting or changing the subproject link, see Figure 15.1.

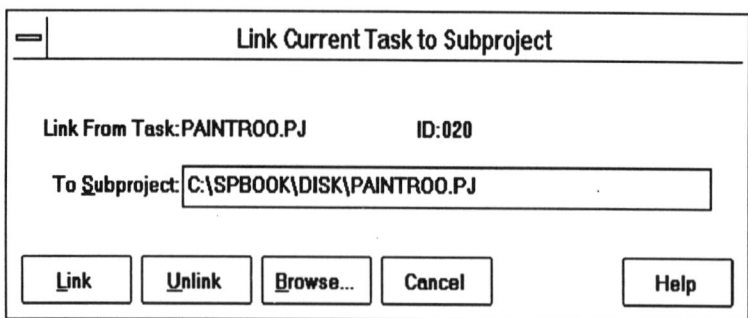

Figure 15.1
The subproject link dialog box

Figure 15.2

Task	Resource	May 04	11	18	25	June 92 01	Est Dur
ROOM.PJ							
Paint room							
Paint ceiling			▄				2dy
	Bill		▄				
Paint woodwork			▄				3dy
	Tom		▄				

Figure 15.2
A room painting subproject

For example, in Figure 15.2 you can see part of the familiar paint project recast as a separate project which deals only with the tasks directly involved with putting paint on the woodwork and ceiling. To make up the whole of the paint a room project this part of the project would be used as a subproject. In Figure 15.3 you can see the rest of the project with a dummy task in the position that the actual painting tasks should occupy. Notice that the dummy task has the links to other tasks that the subproject should have. The next and final step is to insert the subproject. This is just a matter of giving the subproject connection command with the dummy project selected. As you can see in Figure 15.4, the dummy task is replaced by the name of the subproject. Notice that the subproject's Scheduled Start date has been altered to take account of the links in the superproject. If

Task	Resource	May 04	11	18	25	June 92 01	Est Dur	Schd Dur
PAINT13.PJ								10dy
Prepare room								4dy
Clear room							1dy	2dy
	Bill							1dy
	Tom							1dy
Strip walls							2dy	2dy
	Bill							2dy
DUMMY							0dy	0dy
Paper walls							3dy	3dy
	Bill							3dy
Refurnish room							1dy	1dy
	Bill							1dy
	Tom							1dy

Figure 15.3
The paint room superproject ready for the subproject

Task	Resource	lay 04	11	18	25	June 92 01	Est Dur	Schd Dur	Task ID
PAINT13.PJ								13dy	P1
Prepare room								4dy	018
Clear room							1dy	2dy	001
	Bill							1dy	001
	Tom							1dy	001
Strip walls							2dy	2dy	002
	Bill							2dy	002
ROOM.PJ								3dy	019
Paper walls							3dy	3dy	006
	Bill							3dy	006
Refurnish room							1dy	1dy	007
	Bill							1dy	007
	Tom							1dy	007

Figure 15.4
The subproject in place

Must dates had been specified in the subproject then these would have been honoured.

When you want to view the details of a subproject use the command File,Inter Project Connections,Zoom Into Connected Project (or File,Subprojects,Zoom in on Subproject in Version 2). The subproject you zoom into is the one selected before giving the command, and it replaces the superproject in the current display. To change back to the superproject you simply use the command File,Inter Project Connections, Return to Connected Project (or File,Subprojects,Return to SuperProject in Version 2).

Once the subproject is inserted into the superproject you can link it to other tasks in the usual way and set lags etc.. It is used for scheduling just like any standard task, but you cannot edit its data and you cannot see its inner details such as resource allocation unless you zoom into the subproject when you cannot see details of the superproject. When you recalculate the project only the subproject's duration and any Must dates are taken into account. In fact from the superproject's point of view it acts very like a black box.

By default a subproject does not share the resources with its superproject. That is, a resource called Rsrc-1 in a subproject is assumed to be a different resource to Rsrc-1

Subprojects

Task	Resource	ch 05	12	19	26	April 90 02	Est Dur	Schd Dur
SUB1.PJ		▬▬▬						5dy
Task-1		▬▬▬					5dy	5dy
	Rsrc-1	▬▬▬						5dy

Task	Resource	rch 05	12	19	26	April 90 02	Est Dur	Schd Dur
SUPER1.PJ		▬▬▬						5dy
Task-1		▬▬▬					5dy	5dy
	Rsrc-1	▬▬▬						5dy
SUB1.PJ		▬▬▬						5dy

Figure 15.5
A sub and super project that use the 'same' resource

in the superproject. For example, in Figure 15.5 you can see a subproject SUB1 and a superproject SUPER1 which both use Rsrc-1. If you look at the resource view in Figure 15.6 you will see that there is no sign of Rsrc-1's assignment in SUB1. This is because Rsrc-1 is a different resource in each of the projects, and SUB1's Rsrc-1 is handled by SUB1 and SUPER1's Rsrc-1 is handled by SUPER1.

Notice that this implies that levelling will not resolve resource conflicts caused by over-allocation between the sub and super project for the simple reason that they do not have resources in common, despite any similarity in names.

There are three ways around this problem. The first is to ensure that resource conflicts do not occur by manual

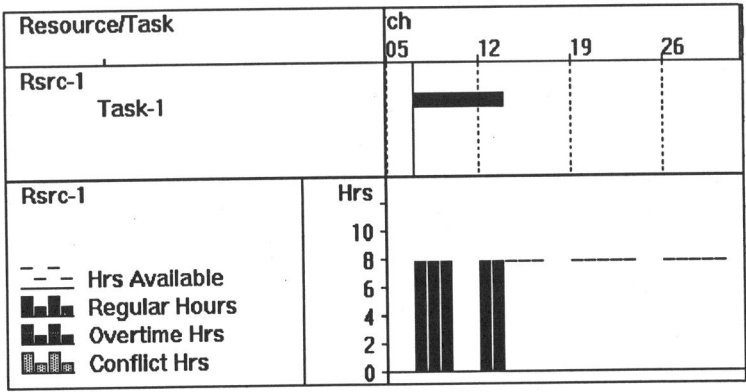

Figure 15.6
The resource view of SUPER1

levelling. The second is to restrict the use of subprojects so that each subproject makes use of a different set of resources - in other words, make resources the key factor in the division of a project into subprojects. The third is to force the projects to share resource details by making them linked projects. Linked projects share resources and they have a wider use than just integrating subprojects with superprojects.

Linked projects

Linked projects share project details, including calendars and resource details. If you link PROJ-2 to PROJ-1 then they share resources and identically named resources in each project will be regarded as the same. For example, if PROJ-2 uses Rsrc-1 then it will appear in PROJ-1's resource view and will be treated as identical to any Rsrc-1 that is used in PROJ-1. Notice that the relationship is two way. That is, resources in PROJ-1 exist in PROJ-2 and vice versa. To link projects all you have to do is use the command:

    File,Inter Project Connections,
        Link Projects with Common Resources

and select the name of the project file to which you want to link. A dialog box appear to give you a chance to modify your choice or make another link, see Figure 15.7.

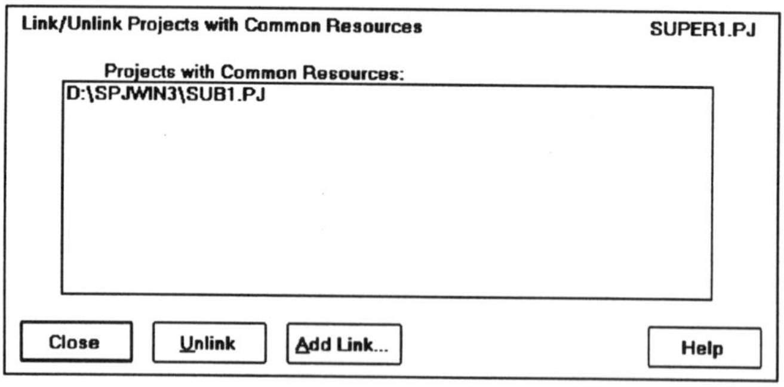

Figure 15.7
The Link Projects dialog box

Project Details view provides a useful summary of the projects to which the current project is linked and in Version 2 it is the only way of making links between projects. To see the project details you can use the command View,Zoom into Details,Project Details - or click on the magnifying glass icon while the project name is selected. You can see a list of projects to which the current project is linked by using the command Layout,View Subwindows, Linked Projects. This produces a list of linked projects which you can edit and add to, as long as you are certain of the project filenames.

If you are using Version 2 then to link the current project with another all you have to do is use the command Edit,Link Project while viewing Project Details and select the name of the project from the list of project files presented. You can unlink a project by using the command Edit,Unlink Project.

Notice that linking is symmetrical and any project that you link to will also contain details of the project linked to it. Version 3 includes a Connected Projects data column which can be used to list the true identity of tasks that are in fact complete subprojects. To display the Connected Projects column use the Column Layout command. A linked set of

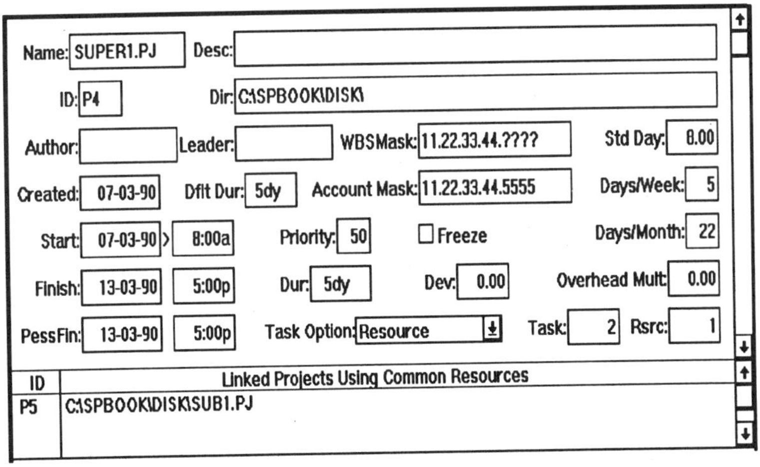

Figure 15.8
Project Details showing linked projects

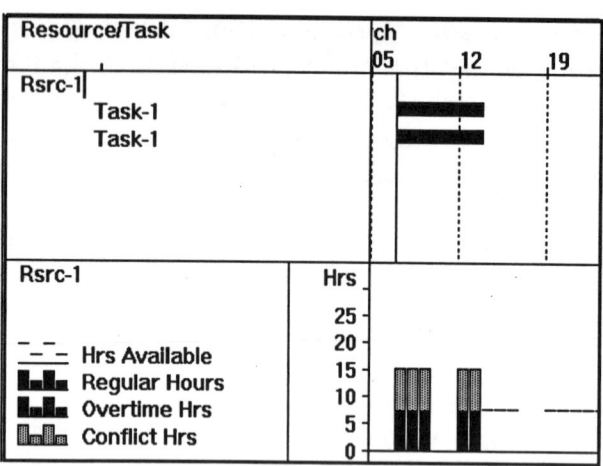

Figure 15.9
The Resource Details view of SUPER1 after linking

projects save, load and recalculate as if they were a single project.

For example, if SUPER1 indicates that it has task links to SUB1 then the Project Details view is as shown in Figure 15.8. Following this SUPER1 and SUB1 share resources and so the Resource Details view in SUPER1 does show the resource conflict caused by the over-allocation of Rsrc-1, see Figure 15.9. Notice the slightly confusing occurrence of Task-1 twice - one is in SUPER1 and the other in SUB1. In this case recalculating the project with levelling enabled does resolve the conflict, see Figure 15.10.

Clearly, if you want sub and super projects to share common resources then they should be linked. If subprojects are

Task	Resource	ch 05	12	19	26	April 90 02		Est Dur	Schd Dur
SUPER1.PJ									10dy
Task-1								5dy	5dy
	Rsrc-1								5dy
SUB1.PJ									5dy

Figure 15.10
Levelling between projects

linked then resource management, and levelling in particular, becomes a project-wide activity. Of course if subprojects don't share resources in reality then don't link the project models together.

Although linking is clearly of use in subprojects its usefulness isn't restricted to this situation. There is no reason why you shouldn't link project models that do not have a sub/super project relationship. Indeed, any set of projects that make use of the same real world resources in the same time period need to be linked to enable allocation conflicts to be detected and resolved.

Updating subprojects

When you recalculate a project that contains subprojects there are two ways of doing it - with or without update. When you press F9 or click on the Calc button a dialog box appears that offers you the choice of recalculating with a full update or not. In Version 2 all recalculations are without update and there is a separate command to perform a subproject update - File,Subprojects,Update Subprojects. The difference between the two types of recalculation lies in how subprojects are treated.

If you recalculate without a full update then only the subproject's duration and any Must dates are taken into account. No levelling will be performed even if the subprojects are linked.

If you recalculate with full update then the subprojects take part in the recalculation as if they were fully expanded into the project model. The subproject files are also modified to reflect the new schedule. In particular, all resource conflicts are revealed and, if levelling is enabled, dealt with. The only problem with full update is that it is slower than a recalculate which doesn't update each of the subprojects.

It looks as if the only time you need to spend the extra time on a full update is when there are resource conflicts between

Task	Resource	y				June 92		Est Dur	Schd Dur	Task ID
		04	11	18	25	01	0			
SUB.PJ		▬▬▬▬▬▬						10dy	P80
Task-1		▬▬▬						5dy	5dy	001
	Rsrc-1	▬▬▬							5dy	001
Task-4				▬▬▬				5dy	5dy	004
	Rsrc-1			▬▬▬					5dy	004

Figure 15.11
A subproject with a potential resource conflict

the subproject and other subprojects or the superproject. However, the situation is more subtle than this would suggest.

For example, the subproject shown in Figure 15.11 has a potential resource conflict which is avoided by the fact that Task-4 has a Must date that moves it to just beyond the end of Task-1. If Task-1's start date moves forward by even one day then Task-1 and Task-4 come into conflict over Rsrc-1 which will be resolved by levelling. As Task-4's start is fixed by a Must date it is Task-1 which will be delayed. If the subproject is used in a simple superproject, as shown in Figure 15.12, then it might seem that recalculation without update would be sufficient because the task-to-subproject linkage ensures that there can be no resource conflicts between the sub and super project. At first everything looks reasonable. As the subproject's duration is 10 days and Task-1 in the superproject is 1 day, the entire project should take 11 days as shown.

Of course the problem with this simple-minded reasoning is that it ignores the fact that a 1-day shift in the start date

Task	Resource	y				June 92		Est Dur	Schd Dur	Task ID
		04	11	18	25	01	0			
SUPER.PJ		▬▬▬▬▬▬							11dy	P79
Task-1		▬						1dy	1dy	001
SUB.PJ		▬▬▬▬▬							10dy	003

Figure 15.12
The effect of the subproject

Updating subprojects 311

Task	Resource	y 04	11	18	25	June 92 01	0	Est Dur	Schd Dur	Task ID
SUPER.PJ									15dy	P79
Task-1								1dy	1dy	001
SUB.PJ									10dy	003

Figure 15.13
After updating the subproject

of Task-1 in the subproject produces a resource conflict in the subproject! When this is resolved it causes the subproject's duration to be lengthened by five whole days. You can see that this is indeed the case if you recalculate with a full update (or use the command File, Subprojects, Update Subprojects in Version 2) and obtain the result shown in Figure 15.13. In this case the subproject's duration is still 10 days but now Task-1 in the subproject cannot start until Task-4 is completed and this has a fixed start date due to the Must date. This is the cause of the delay in starting the subproject.

In general, it is possible for a shift in the starting date of a subproject to alter its duration because of newly generated resource conflicts or because of resource unavailability as indicated by the subproject's calendars. Only a recalculation with subproject update is sure to give you the correct result.

To summarise:

» Subproject update performs a complete recalculation of the entire project, including each subproject. All subproject Must dates, resource calendars, levelling etc. are calculated as usual for each subproject and the entire project.
» If the subprojects are linked to the superproject then resources are shared and levelling will be carried out correctly during a full update.
» Recalculation without a full update only reschedules the superproject using the current durations and Must dates for each subproject.

If you don't want a subproject to change because of the influence of a superproject full update you can freeze it. To do this simply select the Project Details view for the subproject and check the Freeze box.

Retrospective subprojects

It often happens that after building a large project it becomes obvious that a group of tasks would have been better treated as a subproject. You can convert any group of tasks into a subproject by first selecting each task and then using the command File,Inter Project Connections, Build Subproject. (File,Subprojects,Build Subproject in Version 2). This prompts for a filename, extracts the tasks into a project file with the given name and inserts the file as a subproject to replace the selected tasks.

For example, in Figure 15.14 you can see that the set of tasks that make up the actual painting operation have been selected and the Build Subproject command has been used to write them out to disk. When this operation is completed all of the selected tasks will be deleted from the project and their place will be taken by the brand new subproject.

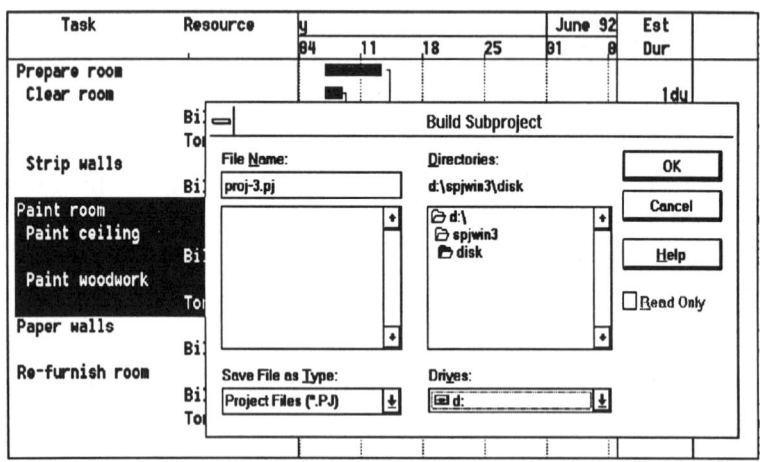

Figure 15.14
Building a subproject

Links to tasks - Version 3 only

A feature introduced in Version 3 is the ability to make FS links to tasks within other projects. This is useful when project models do not have the neat sub/super project relationship with one another, but where separate projects or distinct phases of the same project are keyed together by some task, event or stage.

For example, you may have put together a project model for the design and development of a new product and for its production. Clearly the two models would be related but it may not be as simple as the finish of design/development model signalling the start of the production model. If the two models were put together as a single model then a link would be made between some intermediate stage milestone of the design/development phase and the production phase. Using Version 3's ability to link tasks in different models there is no need to undo the separation into different project models and have to work with a single huge model.

External links in SuperProject are made by a Must date equal to or later than the finish of the predecessor task being imposed on the start of the successor task. This simple linking mechanism is the reason why only direct Finish to Start links can be made externally. However, there are ways around this limitation.

To make a link with an external project you first have to open the project that contains the intended predecessor task and use the command:

File,Inter Project Connections,Link to Task in External Project

As long as you have selected the predecessor task before using the command, the appropriate dialog box will appear, complete with the correct details. You next have to select the name of the successor project that you want to link to and the task within it. You can use the Browse facility to

314 *SuperProject Systems* *Chapter 15*

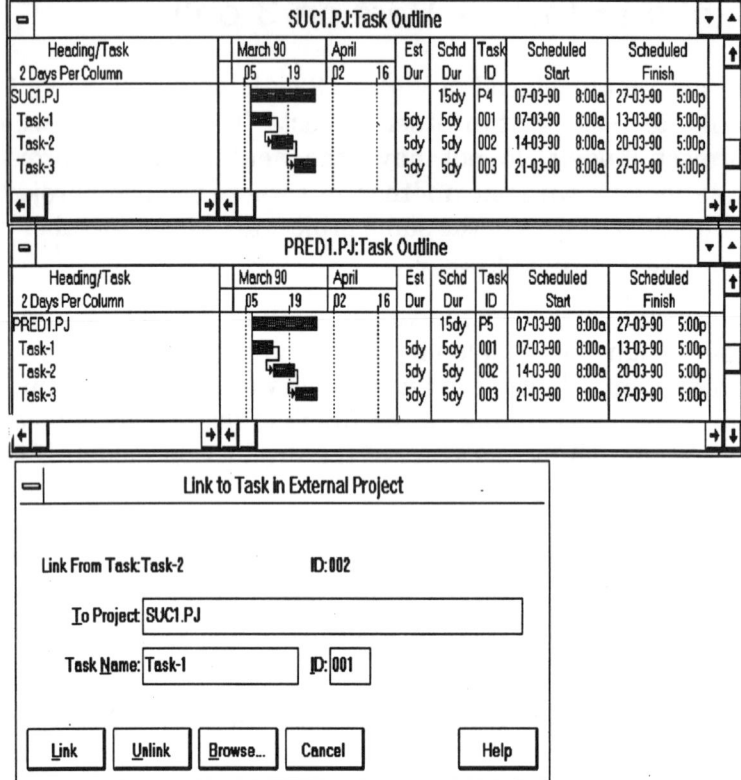

Figure 15.15
Making external links

find the project file but you have to remember the name of the task to link to.

For example, in Figure 15.15 you can see an external link being made between Task-2 in PRED1 and Task-1 in SUC1. When the predecessor project PRED1 is recalculated a Must date is imposed on Task-1 so that its start date is not before Task-2 finishes. The effect of this Must date can be seen as soon as the successor project is recalculated, see Figure 15.16.

You should treat external links with great caution and make sure that you understand exactly how they work if you want to avoid anomalies. Each time the predecessor project is recalculated it inserts appropriate Must dates for

Links to tasks - Version 3 only 315

SUC1.PJ:Task Outline							
Heading/Task 2 Days Per Column	March 90 05 19	April 02 16	Est Dur	Schd Dur	Task ID	Scheduled Start	Scheduled Finish
SUC1.PJ			15dy		P4	21-03-90 8:00a	10-04-90 5:00p
Task-1			5dy	5dy	001	21-03-90> 8:00a	27-03-90 5:00p
Task-2			5dy	5dy	002	28-03-90 8:00a	03-04-90 5:00p
Task-3			5dy	5dy	003	04-04-90 8:00a	10-04-90 5:00p

PRED1.PJ:Task Outline							
Heading/Task 2 Days Per Column	March 90 05 19	April 02 16	Est Dur	Schd Dur	Task ID	Scheduled Start	Scheduled Finish
PRED1.PJ			15dy		P5	07-03-90 8:00a	27-03-90 5:00p
Task-1			5dy	5dy	001	07-03-90 8:00a	13-03-90 5:00p
Task-2			5dy	5dy	002	14-03-90 8:00a	20-03-90 5:00p
Task-3			5dy	5dy	003	21-03-90 8:00a	27-03-90 5:00p

Figure 15.16
After recalculating the external link

the tasks to which it is linked in other project files. When these project files are retrieved from disk and recalculated the Must dates have their usual effect. However, this effect isn't quite the same as a standard FS link to a task in the same project. For example, if you modify the predecessor project so that the Must date is earlier, then the task in the successor project will already have a start date that satisfies the Must date. What this means is that changing predecessor projects so that Must dates are later results in a correct update of the successor project, but modifications that result in earlier Must dates will not automatically reschedule the linked task to start earlier. To achieve this you have to manually alter the task's scheduled starting date to be earlier than the Must date and then recalculate the schedule. Be careful not to accidentally delete the Must date when you edit the Scheduled Start date.

If you would like to see this effect in action simply construct the pair of linked projects as shown in Figure 15.16. If you move the start date of the PRED1 project forward then you will see the correct Must date inserted into SUC1 and the starting date of its Task-1 will move accordingly. However, if you then move the start of PRED1 back to an earlier date you will still see the correct Must date inserted into SUC1, but now the start date for Task-1 will not move back because it already satisfies the Must date!

If you want to make external links other than Finish-Start links you can, by using a milestone (a task of 0 duration) linked to the predecessor task of interest. For example, if you want to make an SS (Start to Start) link to Task-1 you first create a milestone that is SS linked to Task-1 and then make the external link from the milestone. As the milestone is SS linked to Task-1 and has 0 duration, the external FS link is equivalent to an SS link to Task-1. The same trick can be used to create all types of link and to introduce lags.

To summarise:

» To create an external link of a type other than FS or to introduce a lag, create a milestone with the desired type of link to the predecessor task and then make an external link to this milestone.

Again you need to be aware of the limitations of the use of a Must date to implement an external link.

Templates

One of the most useful types of inter-project connection is the simple idea of a project template. A project template is just a normal project file that can be used as the basis for other projects. A template may contain just a set of resources complete with calendars, costing data etc., or it may contain tasks complete with links and assignments. To create a template you can take an existing project, load it, and delete any objects that are project-specific - usually all of the tasks. (Notice that the easiest way to delete all the objects of a particular type is to use a selection filter and then Delete All Selected objects.) If you are creating a template from scratch, notice that you can create resources without task assignment in Resource Outline view and then define their calendars. Make sure that you save the template under a suitable name.

Once you have a template, you can use it by opening it whenever you want to start work on a new project - again remembering to save it under a different name to avoid overwriting the template. Alternatively you can use the File,Include command which will read the contents of any project file into the current project. This adds all of the resources, tasks assignments, etc. in the included file to the current file.

If you are managing a range of similar projects then it is certainly worth defining all available resources in a master template. Notice, however, that any changes you make to the master template will only affect the projects it is used to create after the change. This may be the behaviour you want, but if you need a master template that immediately communicates changes to the projects connected to it then you need to create a set of linked projects.

Network sharing

As SuperProject can be used over a local area network, sharing project data between a number of users seems like a reasonable approach to large scale project management. Working over a network is no more difficult than in a single-user system, as long as you keep in mind the possibility that more than one user may want to update project data and perhaps even at the same time. Clearly, allowing two users to change project data at the same time is dangerous. To stop this from happening SuperProject automatically locks any file that you open. This stops other users from opening and working with the same file. However they can open the file in read only or in browse mode. In browse mode they can modify the file but they cannot save it back to disk using the same name.

Normally the automatic locking mechanisms are quite sufficient, but if you are working with a set of linked files you may not want another user to change a project file that you haven't opened but are using indirectly via links. You can also get into the undesirable position of discovering that another user has opened, and so locked, one of the project files in the set with which you want to work. To stop this from happening, there is an explicit Lock command which can be used to lock any file stored on a network drive. When you are working with a set of project files you might want to lock each file in the set before you open them. There is an Unlock command which can be used to allow other users access to the files once you have finished with them.

Import/Export

The simplest form of data exchange between SuperProject and other applications is the import/export facility. This is crude but it has the advantage that it works in all versions of SuperProject and provides the widest range of data exchange possibilities. Typical uses for exporting data include: for analysis and charting using a spreadsheet, for creating graphs within a presentation package, as task/assignment data in the form of job slips, and financial data to an accounts package. The need to import data is less common but includes: building a unified database of resources, importing holiday data from a staff database, transferring fixed costs from an inventory.

To import or export a project you have to use the command:

File,Inter Project Connections,Export/Import

In Version 2 the command is just

File,Export/Import

The Export/Import command is only available in Expert mode. The details of the import/export operation are determined by the values in the Export/Import dialog box, see Figure 15.17.

Although it is impossible to cover the details of transferring data between every possible type of application, this isn't a serious problem because, once the principles that are used to organise the data are understood, the process is relatively easy.

After choosing between the Import or Export function, the next step is to choose the data with which you want deal. SuperProject keeps all of the project data in the form of seven separate databases. Each database can be thought of as a table of data values which when interpreted together give all the information concerning the project. The seven databases and their structure are:

» Tasks - data concerning each task in the project such as scheduled, actual and baseline start, finish and duration. One row per task.
» Resources - data that defines the resource including its total allocation times, costs etc.. One row per resource.
» Assignments - the details of each resources assignments to tasks. One row per assignment.
» Links - the structure of the project model listed as predecessor/successor pairs. One row per link in the model.
» Holidays - project and resource non-work days. One row per project or resource holiday.
» Work hours - both project and resource regular and overtime work hours for specified date intervals. One row per work period definition.
» Accounts - resource data organised by account code. One row per account code.

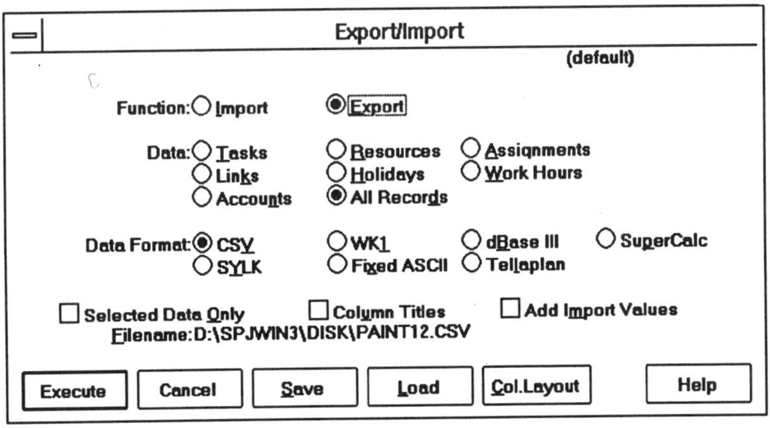

Figure 15.17
The Export/Import dialog box

The detailed listing of what data each database includes can be found at the back of the SuperProject manual. If you are in any doubt about what data is exported/imported then the simplest way of making sure is by performing an experimental export and examining the fieldnames produced, see later.

You can opt for all of the databases to be exported. In this case seven files will be produced with the file names based on adding 1,2.. 7 to the end of the project name. If you export a single database then the project's name will be used with a suitable three letter extension that depends on the type of data format you have selected.

If you export all the data then a fixed column format is used which you cannot change. If you export only a single database then you can select exactly which items of data are exported using the Column Layout. This is achieved in exactly the same way that you would select which fields display and in what order, only now it controls the export format. You can also set a sort order for the rows of the exported database.

For example, in Figure 15.18 you can see that only the resource name and total, regular and overtime hours have been selected for export. Also notice that the exported database will be sorted on Resource Name.

You can also choose to export an initial data line which contains the fieldnames of the data that you have chosen to export. If you only want to export selected objects then you should click on the Selected Only box.

When it comes to data format to export data, the situation is very simple. If the application that is going to read the data is supported directly or claims to read one of the supported formats, then simply use that format. For example, if you are using SuperCalc 5 then select the SuperCalc data format and you will find that suitably named spreadsheets containing the data have been created. These can be opened as standard SuperCalc spreadsheets and will contain the data in the form of a simple table. If

Import/Export **321**

Field Name	Column	Width	Sort
Resource Name	1	21	1
Sched Rsrc Total Hrs	2	12	-
Sched Rsrc Overtime Hrs	3	12	-
Sched Rsrc Regular Hrs	4	12	-
Maximum Units	-	6	-
Sched Rsrc Total Min	-	12	-
Sched Rsrc Total Dys	-	12	-

Figure 15.18
Selecting and sorting exported data

you opt for an application that can read dBase III format then the data will be in the form of one record for each row of the data table.

As well as the specific application formats, two general formats are also supported - CSV and Fixed ASCII. The CSV format can be read into word processors and many spreadsheets and databases. The data is organised as one line per row of the original table and each data field is separated from the next by a comma - hence Comma Separated Values. Text values are also distinguished from numeric values by being enclosed in double quotes.

For example, the resource data defined by the column layout in Figure 15.18 exports the following data from the Paint project in CSV.

"Bill",72.00,10.00,62.00
"Tom",60.00,6.00,54.00

Notice that each resource corresponds to a line, each item of data is separated from its neighbour by a comma and text values are surrounded by double quotes.

A CSV format can often be read straight into a spreadsheet and the data items will be automatically separated into columns using the commas. Another use for a CSV file is in a word processor when the commas can be either used as markers to automatically construct a table or they can be replaced by tabs.

The second general purpose format, Fixed ASCII, is very like CSV but there are no separators between the data items. Instead each data items takes a given number of characters. If the data item needs less then it is padded with blanks. If it needs more then it is truncated and some data is lost. The width used for each exported data type is set as part of the column layout, see Figure 15.18. Make sure that you allocate enough space for each of the data items. Fixed ASCII can be read into nearly all spreadsheets one line per cell. The data can then be split up into separate cells using a Data,Parse command or similar. However, this is much more complicated than using CSV which most spreadsheets also support. The main use for Fixed ASCII is as a simple way of constructing tables in word processors without the need to use tabs.

So far the emphasis has been on exporting data, but there is very little extra to add when it comes to importing data. You can import any one of the databases or all seven. If you choose to import all seven they must have names ending in 1, 2, 3 etc.. The only difficult part about importing data is in making sure that it is in the correct format, i.e. identical to what would be produced as an export of the same data! If you are importing only a single data file then you can use the Column Layout command to select which data items are to be imported, and what the field widths are in the case of importing Fixed ASCII data. SuperProject will ignore any fields in the import file that it normally calculates from more basic data, so the amount of data that you need to define is substantially less than is exported.

The only option that is unique to import is Add Import values. If you select this, the imported values for the actual fields don't overwrite the existing values in the project but add to them. For example, if you import actual total hours with Add Import Values selected the values are added to the existing Actual total hours.

If you are planning to export/import data to another application on a regular basis, then it is a good idea to save the column layouts using the Save button, see Figure 15.17.

Also notice that you can export data by selecting one of the file formats as an output device when you are printing views or reports. In this case the exported data is exactly what would have been printed on a real printer, but modified to suit the destination. For example, in the case of printing to a SuperCalc file all graphics are ignored and each item of data is sent to the file in the form of a table with one item per cell. Notice that this form of export isn't foolproof because occasionally the exported format will contain types of data unrecognisable by the intended application.

One of the biggest problems in using exported data is the treatment of headings. When you export tasks, data headings are included by default and sometimes these get in the way of the more basic task data. The simplest solution is to remember to delete the heading rows from the data table before you make use of it.

Two new additions in Version 3 are conversion utilities for the Microsoft Project and ABT Workbench. These are not part of the standard Export/Import menu but implemented as Realizer programs that can be executed using the Run menu, see later.

DDE

DDE (Dynamic Data Exchange) is a facility provided by Windows, but only Version 3 of SuperProject has the extra commands to make use of it. At its simplest, DDE is just an extension of the Clipboard but in its full form it is very sophisticated. Most users will never need to know all there is to know about DDE but it is important to be aware of its potential.

Most Windows users know that you can use the Windows Clipboard to transfer data between applications. All you have to do is select the data, usually by dragging with the mouse, and then use either the Cut or Copy command to transfer the data to the Clipboard. After changing to the application that is to receive the data, you simply place the cursor at the position where the new data is to be inserted and use the Paste command. In most cases the new data is pasted into the receiving application as if it was typed at the keyboard, but sometimes the behaviour is more complex, and it depends very much on the type of data and the applications involved. For example, in many cases you can copy graphics data to the Clipboard and paste it into a suitable application such as a word processor.

SuperProject will allow you to cut or copy data from a project model which can then be pasted into another application. As the Clipboard is intended to be used as an aid to editing a project model, you may be surprised at exactly what is pasted into the other application. There is usually more data on the Clipboard than you might expect. SuperProject doesn't allow you to transfer data from another application using the Clipboard because this additional information is usually missing. What it will do, however, is to allow you to establish a DDE link using the Clipboard.

If you select some data in an application and copy this to the Clipboard you can paste it into SuperProject, but only as a DDE link. To do this you have to select the area in the project model where the data will be stored and then use the command Edit,Paste Link. The area that you select in the project model has to have some data, dummy data if necessary, already in it and the DDE data overwrites this. Unlike a standard paste operation, the DDE paste link remains active, in the sense that any changes to the data in the original application are passed on to the receiving application. This makes it possible to set up a data table in a spreadsheet and use a DDE link to pass the data to SuperProject in such a way that if the data in the spreadsheet changes so does the data in SuperProject. So,

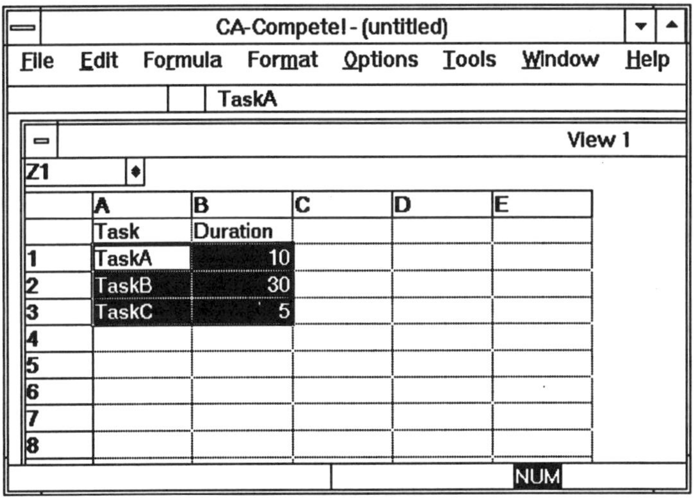

Figure 15.19
DDE data in Compete!

for example, you could use this to take hourly rates or material costs from a spreadsheet.

For example, in Figure 15.19 you can see some data in CA-Compete!, although any Windows spreadsheet would work in the same way, selected and ready for copying to the Clipboard. Once on the Clipboard, the data is ready for pasting into SuperProject. You can see the area selected in Figure 15.20. Notice that the area has to be the same dimensions as the data that you are trying to paste but that only data fields count - i.e. the Gantt chart is not involved in the DDE link. The final step is to use the command Edit,Paste Link to make the DDE link. After this the data in the selected area of SuperProject reflects the contents of the Compete! spreadsheet. Once the link is made it remains active and when you load the project model you will be asked if the application which owns the data should be loaded. If you select no, or if the other application cannot be located, then the data supplied by the link will not be updated.

You can also paste a link into a SuperProject model without selecting a data area in the model. In this case the data is matched up with the fields in the model starting from the

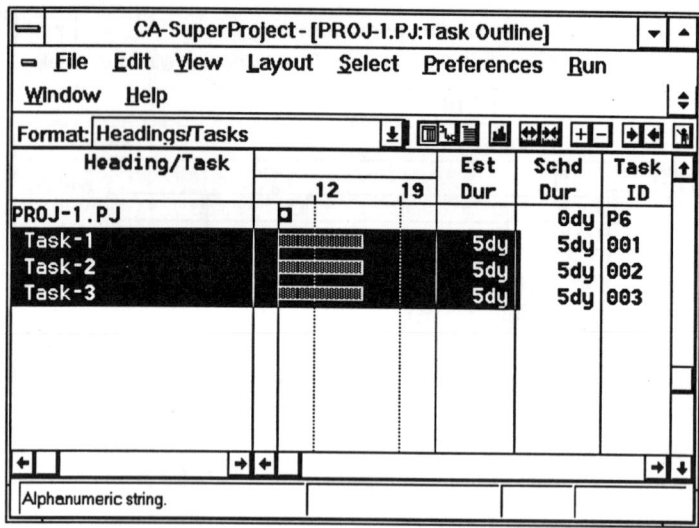

Figure 15.20
The area selected for the DDE data

cursor's current position. In nearly all cases it is simpler to select the area to receive the data.

This use of the Clipboard to form a DDE link is the simplest way of working with DDE and in most cases it is sufficient. However, you can control the nature of the DDE link more accurately. A DDE link can be thought of as a conversation. The end of the conversation that sends the data is the server and the end that receives the data is the client and SuperProject can be both a DDE client and server. If you use the command File, Inter Project Connections, DDE Links with SPJ as Client, the dialog box in Figure 15.21 is produced. This contains details of the DDE link that you have set up. If there is more than one DDE link then you can use the Next and Previous buttons to step through and examine each one. If you are only interested in controlling the links that you have made via the Clipboard the only buttons of interest will be Update, which ensures that the data is the very latest, and Delete, which removes the link. You might also want to change the setting of the Automatic update box which changes the link from hot - i.e. the data

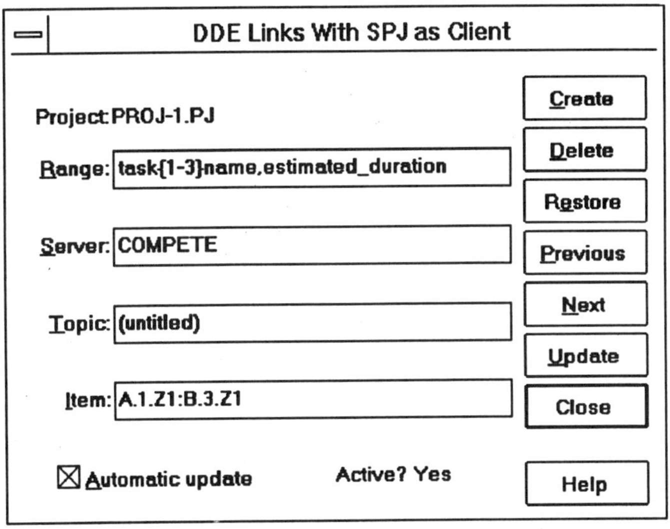

Figure 15.21
The DDE client dialog box

is automatically updated, to cold - i.e. the data is only updated when the Update button is clicked.

If you are interested in creating DDE links without the use of the Clipboard, then the Range, Server, Topic and Item boxes need to be studied. A DDE link needs the data range in the client (in this case SuperProject) to be defined. In the case of SuperProject this is achieved via a shorthand notation which defines the objects and the data fields concerned:

Object{range}fieldlist

This may seem cryptic but it makes more sense if you think of it as defining the rows and columns of a range of one of the outline view data tables. The Object{range} part defines a range of objects - Tasks, Resources, Assignments, Links, Accounts etc.. For example, Task{1-3} specifies the first three tasks in the Task outline view. The fieldlist part of the specification determines which of the data fields are involved. For example, Task{1-3} name,estimated duration specifies the rectangle of data consisting of the first three tasks and the name and estimated duration columns i.e. six items of data. This is the basic principle of defining a data range but there are some special cases. For example, when you refer to an assignment or link, you have to specify the task that the assignment is to or the link is from. That is Assignment{3:2-4} are the second, third and fourth assignments to task 3. Notice the use of the colon between the task and its assignments. You can also specify a list of objects that do not form a continuous range. For example, Task{1,4-5,8} specifies task 1, 4 through 5 and 8. Notice that task numbers refer to task Id numbers and have nothing to do with task names. It is also possible to repeat the specification to create quite complicated regions. For example:

Task{1-3}name;Link{1:1-9999}link_type

specifies the name field for the first three tasks and the link type of all the links to the first task. You can find a full list of fieldnames that can be be used in DDE Links at the back of the SuperProject manual. Also notice that these are the same fieldnames used in user-defined formulas.

Once you have defined the area of SuperProject to be involved in the DDE link, you have to define the application and the data within it to be used as the server. This is just a matter of specifying the server's name - Compete in our example, and the Topic. The Topic is generally the name of the data file involved in the DDE link i.e. the name of the spreadsheet file that contains the data. The final specification is the data range within the file that is to be linked. How this is specified varies according to the server application being used. In the case of Compete!, which is a 3D spreadsheet, the 2D range and the page have to be specified. In the example this is A.1.Z1:B.3.Z1 which means the rectangle of data contained in A1 to B3 on page Z1. Of course the two data areas have to match up for size and type of data if this is appropriate.

You can create DDE links with SuperProject as the server in roughly the same way. In this case the command that you

```
┌─────────────────────────────────────────────────┐
│ ═ │        DDE Links With SPJ as Server          │
├─────────────────────────────────────────────────┤
│                                      ┌────────┐ │
│  Project: PROJ-7.PJ                  │ Create │ │
│                                      ├────────┤ │
│    Name: SPJDDE_1        ↓           │ Delete │ │
│                                      ├────────┤ │
│                                      │Restore │ │
│   Range: task{1-3}name,estimated_duration       │
│                                      │ Close  │ │
│                                      ├────────┤ │
│                                      │        │ │
│                                      │  Help  │ │
│                                      └────────┘ │
│   Users:   1                                    │
└─────────────────────────────────────────────────┘
```

Figure 15.22
The DDE Server dialog box

have to use is File, Inter Project Connections, DDE links with SPJ as Server. This produces the dialog box that you can see in Figure 15.22 in which all you have to specify is a name for the DDE link and the data range in the project model that you want to be involved in the link. The data range is defined in exactly the same way as in the client dialog box. Notice that you don't have to specify the application to which the data will be supplied or its data range. The reason is that the DDE link from a server is put on offer to other Windows applications which can connect to it or not as they please. Of course you have to know how to make a DDE client connection in the other application to make use of SuperProject's offer, and how this is achieved varies greatly according to the application. In the case of Compete! and many other Windows spreadsheets you have to make use of a formula which makes a DDE connection to a single item of data. For example:

=EXTERN("SPJWIN","D:\SPJWIN3\PROJ-7.PJ","SPJDDE_1",1,1)

makes the connection to the item of data in row 1 column 1 of the server's data range. You can see that the first entry in the formula is the name of the server, then the topic, then

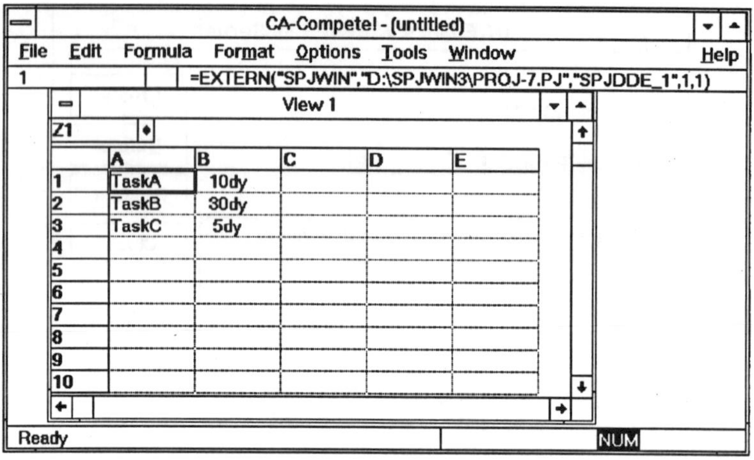

Figure 15.23
Compete! as a DDE client of SuperProject

the DDE name and finally the data item. You can see Compete! acting as a client in Figure 15.23.

You might be relieved to learn that you can use Copy and Paste Link to establish a server DDE link without having to fill in the Server dialog box. All you have to do is select the data in SuperProject and copy it to the Clipboard. When you have swapped to the other application, selecting the data range and giving the command Paste Link usually works.

You can see that it is possible to set up complicated systems of data exchange between SuperProject and other applications which are live in the sense that the data is automatically updated. In practice you should treat such systems with caution because they nearly always take longer than you would have expected. Unless you are prepared to set aside time to debug a DDE system, don't go beyond the use of the Clipboard to establish DDE links.

DDE commands and Realizer

As well as being a way of exchanging data, DDE allows one application to send a command to another application. In most cases this isn't a particularly useful feature because the range of commands that can be issued over a DDE link is limited. In the case of SuperProject the situation is very different because there is a comprehensive range of DDE commands. This makes it possible for another application to use SuperProject's facilities as extensively as you can using the keyboard. This makes it possible to write automatic procedures using any programming language that supports DDE command execution that can control SuperProject's behaviour. This can be used to automate the production of reports, the entry of special data, and to generally enhance SuperProject's capabilities.

The only problem with this idea is that it involves using a programming language of some sort. You could opt to use the macro language of an application such as Word or Excel, but there are huge advantages to using a standard high-level language. Computer Associates provide special Dynamic Link Libraries (DLLs) that can be used in conjunction with C, Visual Basic and the Realizer language.

A version of Realizer, Realizer Lite, is also included with SuperProject Version 3 and this is sufficient for you to start writing DDE based procedures. There are also a number of sample Realizer programs which automate SuperProject procedures - the most impressive being the Project Manager's Assistant, the use of which was described in Chapter 1. If you know how to program in Realizer, which is a Basic-like language, or in one of the other high-level languages, then making use of SuperProject commands within programs is a small addition to your knowledge. A full list of SuperProject commands is included at the end of the SuperProject manual. For example, the command:

> err= SPJViewPERTChart()

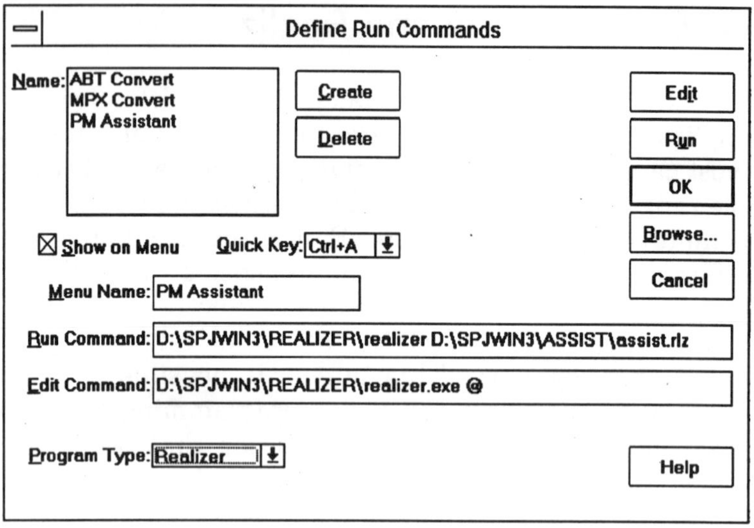

Figure 15.24
The Run dialog box

will change SuperProject into PERT Outline view. There is a Realizer function for every SuperProject menu command plus a few additional ones. (Notice that the same set of commands can be used via a DDE link, and from any language that can make use of the DLL libraries supplied.)

To facilitate running other applications, and Realizer procedures in particular, the command Run has been added to the menu. This produces the Run dialog box that can be seen in Figure 15.24. The program details displayed are for the Project Manager's Assistant. If you need to install this program you will need to enter the actual disk and directory on which the program is stored on your machine.

You can assign particular keypresses to run other programs or applications and define which application is needed to run or edit a program. So if you have written a Realizer program you can add it to the list of programs in the Run dialog box and so be able to run it from SuperProject without

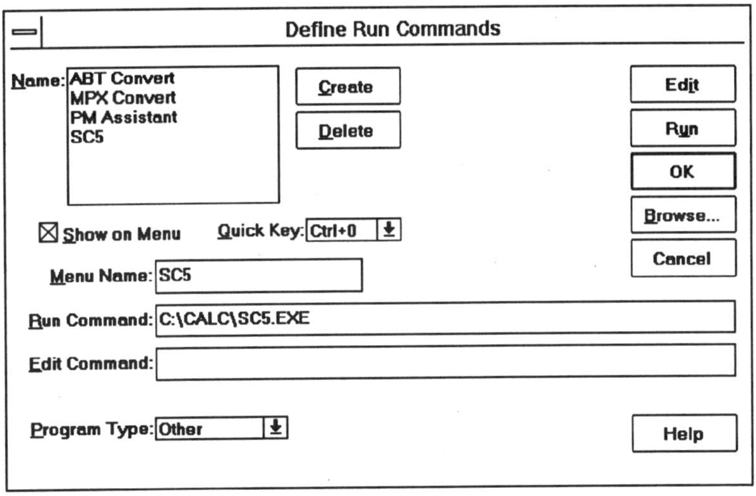

Figure 15.25
Running SuperCalc from SuperProject

having to explicitly load Realizer, then the program file and run it.

Notice that this ability to run another program from within SuperProject is completely general. For example, in Figure 15.25 you can see a Run dialog box entry that enables SuperCalc 5 to be executed either from the Run menu or by using the Quick Key combination shown.

If you don't know how to program in Realizer then a prerequisite for constructing such automatic procedures is to learn how to! This isn't difficult, but it is outside the scope of this book.

Key points

» Subprojects can be used to simplify large projects by breaking them down into smaller units.

» Projects can also be linked so that they share resource definitions.

» You can create a subproject from a group of tasks within an existing project.

» Template projects make the construction of a set of similar projects easier and ensure consistency.

» When working with shared project files on a network it is important to lock any group of files that you are using.

» The export/import facilities of SuperProject can be used to transfer data to and from other applications in the form of data files.

» DDE links can be used to link data in one application to another. SuperProject Version 3 can act as a DDE server and client.

» DDE can also be used by another application to send SuperProject commands. This allows almost any programming language to be used to extend and automate the way that SuperProject works.

» A copy of Realizer Lite, a Basic-like language, is included with SuperProject and this can be used to create programs which make use of DDE commands and data exchange to work with SuperProject. The Project Manager's Assistant is an example of such a program.

Index

A
Accrual, 257
Accum, 286
activating conditions, 159
Actual Duration, 216
Actual Duration/Baseline Duration %, 251
Actual Performance Index Percent, 255
Add Import Values, 322
Add-Assignment, 22
Advanced mode, 42
Advanced Planning, 43
Advanced Planning Symbols, 80
ALAP, 111
All Cost/Rsrc, 85, 232
Alloc/Day, 133
Allow Staggered Assignments, 179
API, 255
Arrange Chart, 98
Arrange Tasks Inside Pages, 290
As Late As Possible, 111
As Soon As Possible, 111
ASAP, 111
ASCII, 321
assignment delay, 198
Assignment Only, 83, 88
Assignment pop-up editor, 141
assignment status, 181
Assignments/Priority Over, 190
Assist mode, 16
Auto Actuals, 217
Auto Arrange After Edit, 290
Auto Positioning, 290

B
Baseline,Compare, 207
BCWP, 246
BCWS, 246
Beginner mode, 18, 77
Benchmark Fixed Milestones, 283
Box Styles, 291
Browse, 313
Budgeted Cost of Work Performed, 246
Budgeted Cost of Work Scheduled, 246
Build Current Chart, 86
Build Subproject, 312

C
CALC, 44, 309
Calculate, 44
Calculated Estimate at Completion, 256
Calculation Options, 175, 265
calendars, 35
circular dependency, 105
Clipboard, 323
collapse hierarchy, 100
colours, 292
Column Layout, 155, 269, 297
Column Layout dialog box, 278
complexity control, 61
conditions, 158
confidence interval, 201
conflict hours, 31
Connected Projects column, 307
constraints, 145
copy, 74, 324, 330
copy and paste, 74
Copy to Layout, 297
copying conditions, 159
Cost Variance, 253
Cost Variance Index Percent, 253
Cost Variance Percent, 253
Cost/Rsrc by Resource, 85, 232
CPI, 253
create links, 96
create task, 95
creating account codes, 236
creating conditions, 158
critical path, 12, 174
critical task, 174
Crosstabs, 281
CSV, 321
Ctrl-A, 98
Ctrl-B, 86
Ctrl-C, 156
Ctrl-E, 82
Ctrl-N, 41, 157
Ctrl-P, 157
Ctrl-R, 82
Ctrl-S, 15
Ctrl-T, 80, 98
current date, 14
cut, 74
CV%, 253

D

date constraints, 113
date display, 37
Date Outline view, 88
dBase III, 321
DDE, 323
DDE client, 326
DDE server, 329
decomposition, 63
default layout, 155
delay, 177
delaying assignment, 198
deleting duration, 138
deleting conditions, 159
deleting links, 11
deleting objects, 159
deleting resources, 23
deleting tasks, 6
Details views, 47
direct entry - resource hours, 138
dragging, 9
dummy task, 108
duration, 6
dynamic costing, 227

E

early finish, 181
early start, 181
Earned Value Analysis, 241, 245
Edit menu, 10, 39, 41
Edit, Go To Column, 156
Edit,Copy, 74
Edit,Cut, 74
Edit,Paste, 324
Edit,Position, 71,100
Edit,Project Formulas, 271
efficiency factor, 28
Effort driven, 128
Elapsed time task, 110
Enter Criterion, 157
entering costing data, 229
Erase All Holidays, 59
expand hierarchy, 100
Expert mode, 19, 78, 103, 111
Expert Modes, 43
Export/Import, 318
external links, 313

F

F1, 16
F2, 11, 96
F3, 6, 95, 236, 297
F4, 10
F5, 6, 23
F6, 22, 32
F7, 157, 297
F9, 44, 309
Feedback Current Date, 213
FF, 104
file locking, 317
File menu, 293
File, Inter Project Connections, 302
File,Include, 317
File,Save, 15
filter, 160, 281, 299, 316
Find, 160
Find date, 58
Finish-to-Finish, 104
Finish-to-Start, 103
Finish-Start dependency link, 8
Fixed Cost, 228
float, 174
Font, 296
fonts, 292
footers, 296
free float, 174
Freeze, 312
FS, 104

G

Gantt chart, 6, 81, 104, 270, 283
Gantt Window Commands, 81, 232
Gantt, Henry L, 6
General Preferences, 227
Graphs button, 286

H

headers, 296
Help, 16
Hide Lower Level, 70, 144
hierarchy, 143, 236
Histogram Symbols, 230
holidays, 35
HP LaserJet, 276

I
identifying tasks, 146
inserting tasks, 6
inter-project connection, 301
interrupted tasks, 222
Inventory, 263
Inventory Level, 286

J
Just-In-Time, 112

L
Labor resource, 22, 259
lag, 108
landscape orientation, 296, 298
late finish, 181
late start, 181
layout files, 97
Layout, 58, 78, 155
Layout Page dialog box, 296
Layout View Options, 82
Layout, Bar Symbols, 206, 270, 283
Layout, Gantt Layout, 283
Layout, Histogram Symbols, 230, 286
Layout, Load, 79, 175, 283
Layout, Page Setup, 296
Layout, PERT Layout, 290
Layout, Save, 155, 277
Layout, View Subwindows, 47, 232
levelling, 31, 165, 199
Levelling Full, 265
levelling materials, 265
likely total duration, 202
link, 9, 324
Link dialog box, 10
Link Projects with Common Resources, 306
Link Tasks, 10
Link to Subproject, 302
Link to Task in External Project, 313
link types, 103
linking projects, 306
local area network, 317
Lock, 318
logical constraint, 145, 266

M
Material Allocation, 260
Material Resources, 260
Material Units Used, 286
milestones, 74, 113
modelling, 13, 123
move columns, 155
moving tasks, 71
Must Finish, 114
Must Start, 113

N
naming conditions, 158
naming projects, 15
negative lags, 109
network diagram, 91
networking, 317
Next Selected object, 157
node, 91
Note Text, 163

O
one-off holidays, 38
online help, 16
optimistic estimate, 200
Other resource, 259
outline, 143
Outline Layout, 161, 281
Output menu (DOS), 293
Output, Device Install, 293
Output, Reports, 293
Output, View, 293
over-commitment, 165
Overhead Cost, 228
overtime, 42, 186, 228

P
page range, 296
Pages Across, 296
Pages Down, 296
partial allocation, 132, 185
paste, 74, 324
Paste Link, 330
patterns of working, 35
Percentage Complete, 216, 246
PERT chart, 91, 290
PERT Layout dialog box, 290

pessimistic estimate, 200
pop-up editor, 139, 269
PostScript, 276
predecessor task, 105
Preferences, 19, 37, 43
preferences file, 81
Preferences,Calculations, 166
Preferences,Expert Modes, 103, 207
Preferences,General Options, 201, 260
Preview, 297
Previous object, 157
Print Reports, 293
Print View, 293
Print View dialog box, 294
Printer Setup, 293, 296
printers, 276
printing a range, 296
priority, 190
probability, 200
programming languages, 331
project calendar, 35
project costs, 227
Project Details, 47, 205, 307
project holidays, 36
Project Manager's Assistant, 17, 333
project model, 13
Project Workday, 51

R
Realizer, 331
Regular Cost, 228
Remaining/Baseline Duration %, 251
Repeat, 295
Reset Delay Before Calculation, 199
Resource pop-up editor, 141
resource, 21
resource Auto Actuals, 220
resource calendars, 35, 41
resource conflict, 265, 310
resource dialog box, 22
resource driven task, 125
resource levelling, 165
resource over-commitment, 165
resources, 14
Resources Details, 48
Resources Only, 87
Resource Outline view, 29, 77, 83
Return to Connected Project, 304
Return to SuperProject, 304
Rollup, 279

S
Save as Default, 39
saving projects, 15
Sched Rsrc Total Hrs, 137
Scheduled Costs, 228
scheduled duration, 6, 139
Scheduled Performance Index, 251
scroll, 24
Select Flag, 161
Select object, 157
Select, Delete All Selected, 159
Select,Sort Layout, 156
Selected Only, 299
selection criteria, 157
Shift-Down, 155
Shift-Up, 155
Short Names Box, 99
Show Breaks on Screen, 290
Show Cost Fields, 227
Show Material Fields, 260
Show Next Level, 144
Show Only Selected, 193
Show Probability, 201
Show Workday, 286
sizing histogram window, 85
Smoothing, 183
Span, 131
split bar, 85
Split Resource Assignments, 178
splitting assignments, 178
SS, 104
staggering, 179
standard day, 24
standard layouts, 276
start date, 14, 205
Start Delay column, 198
Start-to-Start link, 104
status column, 181
subproject, 301
Subtotal Headings, 280
Subtotal Lowest Level, 280
successor task, 105
SuperCalc, 320
superproject, 301
Symbols, 284
SYSPREF.SPJ, 81

T
task, 5
task dependencies, 145
task descriptions, 162
Task Effort pop-up editor, 139

Task ID number, 10
task notes, 163
Task Outline Layout, 278
Task Outline view, 81
Task Type, 114
tasks, 21
Tasks/Headings/Assignments, 83
template, 316
text editing window, 163
Tiny Box Style, 97
To Next Layout, 80
top down decomposition, 63
top down hierarchy, 67
Total Cost, 229
Tracking Actuals, 209

U
unit of duration, 7
Units Assigned, 26, 261
Unlink, 11
Unlink Project, 307
Unlock, 318
Unselect, 159
User Defined Formulas, 271
user-defined fields, 269

V
Variable Cost, 228
Variance at Completion, 256
View menu, 30, 36, 77
View Options, 87
View,Subwindows, 47
View,Subwindows,Linked Projects, 307
View,Subwindows,Assignments, 58

W
Wall Chart, 295
WBS chart, 91, 241, 290
WBS codes, 241
weekends, 38
Work Breakdown Structure, 91, 241, 290
Work Periods, 187
workday driven task, 127
WYSIWYG, 275

Z
Zoom into Connected Project, 304
Zoom into Details, 47

!
!, 44

Other books of interest

The 386/486 PC: A Power User's Guide
by Harry Fairhead
In order to make the most of a sophisticated applications package such as CA-SuperProject you need a powerful computer system. At the moment this means one based on 80386/486 processor and you will find information specific to this range of machines in Harry Fairhead's comprehensive guide. This book explains every aspect of the 386/486 PC including extended and expanded memory, LIM, hard disk seek rate, wait states, caching, memory interleave, shadow RAM and other technical topics. It also provides advice about configuring and optimising your system and includes information on Windows 3.1 and OS/2.
ISBN 1-871962-22-6

MS-DOS 5: A Power User's Guide
by Harry Fairhead
Even if you are a seasoned computer user, there are many hidden corners of the MS-DOS operating system to explore. This is especially true of Version 5 which has many more features than any previous version. It also represents a departure for Microsoft in that it is available as an upgrade which you can buy and install yourself. This also means that you have to configure and optimise it yourself. The early part of the book concentrates on the basics of commands, files and directories. There follows a section devoted to batch files, explaining their technicalities and what they can be used for. The final chapters cover configuration, customisation and optimisation.
ISBN 1-871962-13-7

The Expert Guide to SuperCalc
by Janet Swift
SuperCalc is Computer Associates' highly successful spreadsheet program. Once you have mastered the basics of its use (covered in Janet Swift's first-level book SuperCalc Professional, ISBN 1-871962-18-8) the range of tasks you can do with it is enormous. Most users only ever take advantage of a fraction of their spreadsheet's potential and this book aims to introduce users to a wider range of possibilities. There are methods and techniques discussed in this book that are explained nowhere else. So if you want to make the transition from spreadsheet user to spreadsheet expert then its help will be invaluable.
ISBN 1-871962-10-2

Forthcoming titles

Data: A Power User's Guide
by Harry Fairhead
Data is the most important element of your computer system. If you lose it your whole enterprise is at risk, yet many users never give it a second thought. This book covers all the aspects you need to consider - types of storage device, the selection of backup media, protection from virus attack and access security. In short, everything you need to know to keep your data safe. It also covers disk optimisation and, in the event of the unthinkable - a disk crash - methods of data recovery. If you value the data that you store on your PC, or just want to make the best of your hard disk and other storage devices, then here is the information you need.
ISBN 1-871962-21-8

Financial Functions using a spreadsheet
by Mike James and Janet Swift
All spreadsheets have a comprehensive range of financial functions, many of which are never investigated simply because the calculations they perform are described in the fewest possible words in the manual - accurate but terse is perhaps the best comment to make. This book makes up for this shortcoming by presenting in simple terms and with plenty of illustrative examples exactly what each function can do - on its own and in combination.
ISBN 1-871962-01-3

I/O Press also has plans to publish titles covering CA-SuperCalc for Windows, Networking PCs in the Windows environment and writing applications using Realizer.

For more information or a catalogue contact::

I/O Press

Oak Tree House, Leyburn, North Yorkshire DL8 5SE
Tel: (0969) 24402
Fax: (0969) 24375